# *Psychoanalysis*

## SCIENCE AND PROFESSION

### MAXWELL GITELSON

INTERNATIONAL UNIVERSITIES PRESS, INC.

NEW YORK

Library of Congress Cataloging in Publication Data

Gitelson, Maxwell, 1902–1965.
　Psychoanalysis: science and profession.

　Bibliography: p.
　1. Psychoanalysis.　I.　Title.
[DNLM: 1. Psychoanalysis. WM 460 G536p 1973]
RC504.G58　　616.8'917　　72-8789
ISBN 0-8236-5255-6

To Derek

# Contents

# Contents

# Acknowledgements

THE PAPERS contained herein are gathered from scattered publications. Editorial notes have been added to give the reader some idea of the circumstances surrounding the writing of the articles, most of which have been subjected to moderate revision. We wish to express our thanks to the various publications for granting permission to publish the articles.

"The Critical Moment in Psychotherapy" is reprinted with permission from the *Bulletin of the Menninger Clinic*, Volume 6, pp. 183–189, copyright 1942 by the Menninger Foundation; "A Critique of Current Concepts in Psychosomatic Medicine" is also reprinted with permission from the *Bulletin of the Menninger Clinic*, Volume 23, pp. 165–170, copyright 1959 by the Menninger Foundation. "Intellectuality in the Defense Transference" originally appeared in *Psychiatry* (1944), Volume 7, pp. 73–86 and is reprinted by special permission of the William Alanson White Psychiatric Foundation, Inc., which holds the copyright.

The *International Journal of Psycho-Analysis* has given permission to reprint the following articles: "The Emotional Position of the Analyst in the Psychoanalytic Situation" (1952), from Volume 33, pp. 1–10; "Re-evaluation of the Role of the Oedipus

*Acknowledgements*

Complex" (1952), from Volume 33, pp. 351-354; "Therapeutic Problems in the Analysis of the 'Normal' Candidate" (1954), from Volume 35, pp. 174-183; "On Ego Distortion" (1958), from Volume 39, pp. 245-257; "The Curative Factors in Psychoanalysis" (1962), from Volume 43, pp. 194-205; and "On the Present Scientific and Social Position of Psycho-Analysis" (1963), from Volume 44, pp. 521-527.

"Problems of Psychoanalytic Training" first appeared in *The Psychoanalytic Quarterly* (1948), Volume 17, pp. 198-211. "Clinical Experience with Play Therapy" (1938), "Direct Psychotherapy in Adolescence" (1942), and "Character Synthesis" (1948) are in the copyright of the American Orthopsychiatric Association and are reproduced by permission.

"On the Problem of Character Neurosis" is reprinted with the kind permission of the *Journal of the Hillside Hospital* (1963), Volume 12, pp. 3-17. "Psychoanalyst U.S.A., 1955" is reprinted from the *American Journal of Psychiatry* (1956), Volume 112, pp. 700-705, copyright 1956, The American Psychiatric Association. "The Role of Anxiety in Somatic Disease" originally appeared in the *Annals of Internal Medicine* (1948), Volume 48, pp. 289-297. "On the Identity Crisis in American Psychoanalysis" was first published by *The Journal of the American Psychoanalytic Association* (1964), Volume 12, pp. 451-476. *Geriatrics* has graciously allowed permission to reprint "The Emotional Problems of Elderly People," which they published in 1948, Volume 3, pp. 135-150.

# Introduction

IN PSYCHOANALYSIS, as in other scientific disciplines, the simultaneous occurrence of theoretical excellence and clinical proficiency in the same person is not common.

With Maxwell Gitelson, theory and practice of psychoanalysis found a fortunate synthesis. This was certainly related to and perhaps entirely based on a propitious combination of certain personality traits. He possessed sensitive intuition and a capacity for empathy capable of accurately perceiving the complexities of the emotional fabric of his fellow man. He was a true "Menschenfreund," a sincere lover of mankind. These characteristics were augmented by a native intelligence of a high order, and a curious and searching intellect. He found pleasure and joy in the discovery, understanding, and explaining of psychic phenomena. The blending of these features provided the matrix for his development into a superb clinician and thoughful theoretician of psychoanalysis. They are reflected in the essays collected in this volume. Each of these is the result of careful thought and meticulous intellectual labor. All have been produced by a studious and creative mind.

## Introduction

The material gathered by the editors extends from early efforts at orientation in the psychology and treatment of children and adolescents to the elaborate and sophisticated theoretical productions of the later years. Some of the ideas contained here have stood the test of time, others are still being debated in psychoanalytic circles around the world.

A few samples, selected at random from the rich substance of this book, may inform the reader who is not yet familiar with Gitelson's work of its enduring merit and pertinence.

A significant early paper contains an investigation of the process of character synthesis during adolescence and of the manner in which the therapist can aid this process. Gitelson believed that synthesis, not analysis, was the primary aim of the therapist's efforts in his work with adolescents.

He devoted much thought to the emotional interaction between the analyst and his patient, i.e., to the problems and uses of the countertransference. This concern is reflected in several papers, notably "Intellectuality in the Defense Transference" (1944), "The Emotional Position of the Analyst" (1952), and "The Curative Factors in Psychoanalysis" (1962). The first of these valuable contributions still shows the influence of the brilliant but erratic and sometimes histrionic Lionel Blitzsten, but the later works are the product of independent thought and maturing clinical experience. "The Emotional Position of the Analyst" examines, among other issues, the relationship of the analyst's interventions in the treatment situation to the countertransference phenomenon: "Whenever the analyst feels impelled to do something 'active,' it would seem advisable for him to examine his own motives carefully." In the essay "The Curative Factors in Psychoanalysis," the interesting suggestion is made that the "techniques which establish the psychoanalytic situation induce an infantile dyadic condition having the qualities of transition from narcissism to object love."

In 1958 Gitelson contributed an original description of a certain type of defensive characterological structure which he termed ego distortion. In ego distortion, according to his challenging formulation, "from a functional standpoint we behold, not 'ego defect' or 'ego weakness,' but rather adaptive capacity which may be looked upon as strength."

The "Re-evaluation of the Role of the Oedipus Complex" (1952) illustrates Gitelson's efforts to bridge the theoretical and practical differences between various analytic schools of thought. He concludes that "the Oedipus complex may be absent or at best vestigial, that pathological development may be established by earlier constellations of factors and that there are more primitive libidinal positions which may be of central importance." That "the Oedipus complex thus has apical importance not so much as the nucleus of the neuroses but as the nucleus of normal character structure and as the basis of mature life." His conclusions anticipated and gave direction to much of the subsequent work and developments in psychoanalytic research and practice.

Other papers, most notably the last in this book, bear witness to Gitelson's steady struggle against the current tendencies to abandon the basic tenets of psychoanalysis. Putting his analytic scholarship and his erudition to best use, he argues effectively, and with commendable restraint, against all efforts to dilute or adulterate the body of psychoanalytic knowledge and resists the admonitions to "adapt" psychoanalysis to the changing social moods and transient trends in psychiatry and psychotherapy fashionable in his day— and ours.

We behold in these pages the rich harvest of a lifetime of scientific, educational, and therapeutic effort in the service of psychoanalysis.

PAUL KRAMER

# Clinical Experience with Play Therapy

## (1938)

---

THE CLASSICAL techniques of child guidance frequently fail. When our efforts to modify parental attitudes, to change pernicious factors in the environment, and to correct educational discrepancies have been exhausted, we must still deal with such problems as the following:

A boy was first examined at age four years, 11 months after the parents had been advised in another clinic to place him in the Training School at Vineland. He was found to be of average intelligence but presented a peculiarly diffuse stream of ideas, made irrelevant responses, seemed not to be in close rapport. He was very hostile to his parents and grandmother and was withdrawn from other children. Serious feeding problems were presented. Later, we found that he was given to much daydreaming and exhibited a compulsive interest in war and soldiers which consumed much of his waking time.

---

*Editorial note:* This is the very first description of a technique that has come to be taken for granted. It was also the first such experiment undertaken at the Chicago Institute for Juvenile Research.

Psychiatric consultation with both parents and the grandmother, who lived in the home, continued over a period of two and a half years. We had good intellectual cooperation from the mother. Ultimately, a private school placement was tried, and the teachers at the school were conferred with. Various changes were made in the home: the child was no longer permitted to sleep in the parents' bedroom. A few psychiatric interviews with the child himself were attempted. All of these efforts produced little effect.

This case, after 69 playroom interviews over a period of 16 months, is now in the closed group of our series. During the period of treatment the boy had developed affectionate attitudes toward the therapist and other adults. He was on general friendly terms with children. He had the courage to strike out for himself when necessary. He was adjusting at school. His daydreaming, his diffuse verbalization, and his preoccupied play with toy soldiers had greatly diminished.

Such cases as this continue to challenge us despite the fact that we have long since given up the naïve expectations which characterized our work in the early days of the mental hygiene movement. We still cast about for methods of treatment which might better satisfy the urgent demands for help which continue to confront us. Out of such experience came our decision two years ago to test in our clinic the potentialities of the so-called "play therapy" which for some time had been under discussion in child psychiatry. Individual therapists among us had, of course, made use of a few incidental toys in the often fruitless attempts at verbal interviews with younger children; but none of us had

had any formal experience with, or training in, play techniques.

I should like to emphasize that we have not conducted anything in the nature of a controlled experiment. We had available a number of cases of the type just described. Everything else had been tried with them. We seemed to have nothing to lose. We decided to see quite pragmatically what play therapy had to offer.

The therapists using the method were made up of a mixed group, at first comprising a female psychiatrist, two experienced clinical recreational workers and an experienced psychiatric social worker. Later on, a number of cases were treated by male psychiatric fellows in training. During the first half of the period of our experience, I acted as consultant to the therapists; in the latter half of this period, Miss Helen Ross, a trained child analyst, has been the consultant.

In these two years approximately 60 cases have been treated. For reasons external to the purpose of this paper, only 40 cases are being reviewed here. The intention is to describe our general experience and give some examples of that experience.

There was no purposeful selection of cases as to sex, age, or intelligence. We find our material to be equally divided between girls and boys—20 cases of each. At the beginning of play treatment, 34 of the cases fell between the ages of four and 10; four were over 10 and two under four years of age. The youngest child is three years, nine months old, the eldest 13 years, two months. Seeming to follow the usual tendency to think more favorably of the high IQs as therapeutic risks, we find 16 of the cases classified as of superior intelligence, seven are high average, 10 are average; six are in the dull group; and one is a borderline mental defective. There is reason to believe that this last case will ultimately prove to be better endowed than the original rating would indicate.

TABLE 1

PRESENT GENERAL STATUS OF CASES

| | Much Improved | Significantly | Unimproved | Totals |
|---|---|---|---|---|
| Open | 7 | 8 | 10 | 25 |
| Closed | 6 | 3 | 6 | 15 |
| Totals | 13 | 11 | 16 | 40 |

In the above classification of our results, "improved" refers to the status of the manifest behavior problem as reported by the parents, the guardians, or the teachers. "Much improved" signifies definite general improvement in symptoms, relationships, and apparent subjective states. "Significantly improved" indicates cases in which the major symptom has cleared up or is much improved while other problems remain, or in which the child's adjustment in one important difficult relationship has improved while in others there may be no change. At any rate we have a group of 24 cases which definitely show a greater or lesser degree of external improvement.

Following is an example of a much improved case: An eight-year-old girl of average intelligence and with correct grade placement was referred by the school because of poor application to studies. She suffered from flushing of the face and complained of a sense of stricture in the throat in moments of stress, such as recitations. She was easily moved to tears. The mother reported her to be forgetful and dawdling, and to have been excessively timid since infancy. She associated only with younger companions.

There were 14 playroom sessions over a period of three months at approximately weekly intervals. Three months after the case was closed, the school reported that the child no longer stood out as a problem; timidity was decreased; she volunteered participation in school events, she did not flush so much or seem so troubled during recitations. The mother reported that the child had begun to play with older children and was asserting herself with them.

The following case illustrates what is meant by "significantly improved." A girl, eight years and nine months of age, rated as dull on the Stanford-Binet, was referred because of extreme shyness and withdrawal from social contact. She was described as seeming either to refuse or to be unable to talk in the presence of adults. This problem was lifelong. She would not recite at school. Altogether she presented an extreme degree of social inhibition. Her treatment this far covers a total period of 18 months. For external reasons there have been three interruptions of two, six, and three months, respectively. A total of 25 interviews have been held. At present, her school work has improved and the patient recites voluntarily. She has begun to talk to adults. She is described by different outside observers as being more "alive." In interesting contrast to this she has uttered very few words to the therapists. The most directly personal expression that has occurred in the play hours thus far is her repeated writing of her name on the blackboard in one of the recent hours.

Among the 16 cases belonging to the "unimproved" group, there are 10 which give evidence of what we have designated "internal progress," whereas on the other hand, only two of the improved cases failed to present evidence of such internal progress. To understand what we mean by this, it is necessary to offer some examples of the initial reactions of children to the playroom situation and to the therapist. For it is the character of the modification of these initial reactions which determined for us whether or not internal progress had occurred.

The most frequent type of initial reaction was one of apparent friendliness toward the therapist with immediate initiation of an acting-out process concerned with the presenting problem. In short, in these cases no massive resistance to the treatment situation was presented. The following case is illustrative:

A boy, age seven years, six months, IQ 100, was referred because he had locked himself in the bathroom and threatened suicide after he had been discovered in the theft of 10 dollars from an older brother. He had cried out behind the locked door, "I don't believe in God. I don't like God. Where is a knife? I don't want to live." His father, who had deserted the family some time before—after much domestic difficulty—was described as arrogant toward his wife and indifferent toward his children. The patient had a provocative, sadomasochistic attitude toward the mother.

The boy was sullen and unresponsive in a psychiatric interview. Immediately upon entering the playroom, however, he approached one of the "grown-up" male dolls and said, "This is the father. He kills bad people. He works." Then the patient initiated warfare between two groups of soldiers, respectively "good" and "bad." He killed all the bad soldiers except one, and that one then killed all the good soldiers. This theme was recurrent for a time. He then shifted his play to the following: A girl was going to have a party. A bad man was looking in through the bathroom window. The girl was taking a bath. Some men came to call on the girl, and they all went into the bathroom. The patient then exclaimed, "But they can't be in the bathroom!" He put the dolls down and suddenly lost interest in the play. It is not the purpose of this presentation to make any analysis of such material as this. It can be said however, that this boy obviously plunged immediately into a representation, though quite highly condensed, of the profound conflict he had in respect to very important family relationships.

This type of initial reaction occurred in 12 of our 40 cases. Occasionally it was accompanied by the child's recognition of the "special character" of the playroom situation. In such instances the therapist had the impression that the child already sensed the therapeutic implications, though no discussion of them might have been entered into. For instance, one child taken on for playroom treatment by a social worker after there had been a preliminary series of interviews with a male psychiatrist, commented during the first play hour, "Dr. S. is nice too." The comment occurred in a context which indicated that the patient understood that the worker was a therapist and occupied some help-giving relationship to her. This sort of reaction is the closest to explicit sickness insight that has been seen at the beginning of a case.

The other types of initial reactions occurred with less frequency, but their incidence was about equally distributed among our cases. It can be stated that they are defensive reactions adopted in an anxiety-activating situation and may be described as follows:

1. Fear and guilt attitudes. The child may appear quite self-conscious, or there is evident expectation of prohibitions and punishments.
2. Attitudes of reserve. The therapist is treated as nonexistent. The child may play but does not talk.
3. Apathy; seeming lack of impetus; stereotyped fussing with toys.
4. Rebellious denial of problems. Refusal to enter the playroom.
5. "Testing out" of the therapist by provocations and demands.
6. Competitiveness with and domination of the therapist.
7. Restless exploration of the playroom, and apparent information-seeking questions directed to the therapist. In these cases the breathlessness of the questioning and the obviousness with which the child fails to wait for any answers are indicative of the anxiety.
8. Hypermotility; glib talk; distractible, random play; boisterous aggressiveness. Despite the friendly facade, one senses an emotional barrier in these children.

It is interesting to note that the five cases in which the last type of initial reaction was present belong to a group of behavior problems which may be categorized as the hyperkinetic-hostile-aggressive type. They exhibit, in general, precocious sexual activity, cruelty, destructiveness, restlessness, and extremely provocative behavior. Four of these five children belong to our "unimproved group," and the other only shows some improvement. This is an instance of the correlation between the habitual type of defense exhibited by the patient in the external life situation and the defense technique adopted in the treatment situation.

A final word as to the above classifications: None of these reactions occur in pure culture, though one or the other of them tends to preponderate in each case.

We considered internal progress to have occurred when the defensive techniques described above tended to disappear and to be replaced by tendencies toward:

1. Explicit or implicit evidence of a positive transference as manifested by a "warmer" attitude toward the therapist, by help-seeking gestures, by expressions of confidence, by the inclusion of the therapist in the play, and, finally, by personal interest in the therapist.

2. Diminution of anxiety as indicated by an increased daring to indulge in aggressive play and the disappearance of obvious fear in relation to certain types of toys or activities—e.g., play with sand or water.

3. Explicit or implicit evidences of "sickness insight" as manifested by connecting the treatment situation with the presenting problem or by discussion of the problems.

4. Decreased pure fantasy and symbolism with concomitant increase of explicit verbal communica-

tions concerning the emotions and attitudes, particularly revelations of hostilities and aggressions.

5. The appearance of creative and constructive fantasy or play after a preceding period of diffuse and disorganized behavior or stereotyped play.

6. Progressive development in the acting out of the problem oriented toward some intrapsychic solution. Explicit verbalization may or may not occur.

These evidences of internal progress might be ranked according to their respective independent significance, but it seemed to us more practical to consider their importance in relation to what may have been the child's initial reaction to the treatment situation. For instance, an extremely inhibited aloof child has made significant internal progress if there has been a noticeable increase in confidence in the therapist as a helper and friend, while a demanding aggressive child is progressing if these manifestations subside and he becomes involved in play referring to the conflict situation at home.

In attempting to understand the possible reasons for the external improvement and for the occurrence of what we have called internal progress, a consideration of the techniques employed must be entered upon.

First of all, the playroom: 13 by 21 feet, sandbox, blackboard, small and large tables, small and large chairs, a sink close to the floor, a chest for tools and lumber, a geographical globe, a vise attached to the large table, three shelves for toys, and a one-way observation screen. The last is now boarded up; the youngsters soon became quite aware of it and initiated its destruction. As for toys, our error has been to overstock, and this has introduced the problem of distractibility as a defense.[1] Finally, finger paints and other plastic materials.

Schedules have been quite variable. Two children have been seen as frequently as three times a week. One of these is in our closed group after 10 interviews, "much improved," and the other is still in treatment after more than 60 interviews, condition also "much improved." Eleven of our cases were seen at intervals of once a week. Six have been seen at intervals of twice a week. Twenty-one have been seen more or less irregularly from one to three times a week. Some of these have had quite long interruptions, yet in four such cases in which the transference was strongly established, the interruptions did not seem to handicap the total progress of the treatment.[2] The treatment periods were of constant length for a given child, but varied in length among the several therapists between 45 minutes and an hour.

The cases which were seen at quite frequent intervals, such as the two mentioned, were usually those in which we felt that because of the urgency of the problem we should work for the establishment of a positive transference as soon as possible. This, for example, was the point involved in two cases of compulsive truancy from home, in which crises indicating the need for placement occurred, and in which the success of the placement was problematic while the child was in the original emotional situation.

[1] Another problem which this leads to is the difficulty of managing the demands of deprived children who cannot understand why some of this abundance should not be theirs.

[2] This should not lead to the assumption that interruptions are of no significance. They do introduce a complication which should be avoided.

As to preparation of the child for treatment, 15 received no explanatory statement from the therapist; they were simply asked to còme in to the treatment room and invited to play. Thirteen received a general statement to the effect that the therapist knew the child was in some way unhappy, that children sometimes had difficulty in talking about their troubles, and that therapist and patient would just try to get acquainted in the playroom so that after a while the child might find he could talk over his troubles. Ten children were specifically informed that the therapist was interested in helping them with the problems they presented and were given permission to use the playroom as a part of the treatment. Two children were given *carte blanche,* but this liberty was not accepted. Both of them presented an inhibited type of initial reaction. Of course there were a small number of children toward whom coercive and deceptive measures had been adopted by the parents in getting them to treatment, but the problems thus created were managed by the therapist as a part of the general problem.

It is impossible to draw any general conclusions on the basis of 40 cases, but the material does give the impression that there was no significant qualitative relationship between the type of initial response and the type of preparation the child received. For example, the 12 children who entered into the play activity without marked preliminary defense attitudes were quite proportionately distributed among the cases which received the various types of preparation. The kind of initial reaction within the treatment situation seems to be more related to the reaction pattern outside. However, there may have been an acceleration of the tempo of the developments in the case when the problem was specifically alluded to in the preparation of the child.

Reference must also be made to specifically difficult cases which had to be dealt with in initiating the play treatment. Among our improved cases, both open and closed, there were a number of children who were unwilling to come to the clinic, although not all of them exhibited this attitude openly in the playroom. The preparation of such children for treatment must of necessity include the early management of the massive defense erected against it. The following are examples:

One child was deeply humiliated because her mother had told her that she was to receive treatment because there was "something wrong" with her. The child's resentment against the mother was displaced with considerable violence to the therapist, and the treatment seemed for a time endangered. The persistent, kindly tolerance of the therapist was attended, after 12 hours, by the subsidence of the massive resistance.

An eight-year-old boy had never gone to school because he had refused to leave his mother's side since his fifth year, when the next sibling was born. This patient was permitted to bring his mother into the treatment room during the first hour. During the six succeeding hours, the county nurse who brought him to the clinic, or his older sister, remained with him in the treatment room during the first part of each period. His tolerance of the separation increased progressively. He is finally going to the playroom with the therapist alone.

A boy whose reading disability had not been helped by more than a year of tutoring and who had many other problems was one of the cases described as reacting with "rebellious denial of problems and refusal to enter the playroom." The therapist conveyed to the boy that she felt he had difficulties and that she was interested in them, and in a persistent but gentle manner, indicated she expected him to come with her. This insistence was necessary during the first two visits. The boy subsequently has gone on to much improvement.

In another case the therapist confessed to a child who had all sorts of good rationalizations for not spending time at the clinic, "I know it must seem crazy to think that you can help anybody by playing with them," and succeeded in holding on to the child by a direct plea to her ego.

But other cases have escaped from the treatment usually because no means was hit upon to handle the anxiety. It is these which must be thought of most seriously. A nine-year-old girl left treatment, condition unimproved, after 9 playroom hours. She was one of the hyperkinetic-hostile-aggressive children. In the playroom she oscillated between clinging and demanding attitudes. No interpretations were made, nor did the therapist's kindly tolerance suffice to allay her anxiety. A very passive boy, the oldest of our cases, presented an extreme degree of apathy in the playroom and similarly failed to respond to the mere implications of an acceptant, tolerant attitude on the part of the therapist.

The experience in these two cases was repeated in several other instances. It would seem to me that there are cases in which the permissiveness and indulgence of the treatment situation serve as a seduction, with consequent unmanageable accentuations of the guilt and anxiety. This may be a contraindication to attempting play therapy with such cases.

No general statement about psychotherapy can be fully valid, inasmuch as the individual therapist must be so much his own master. Especially is a discussion of interpretive technique likely to be sterile when interpretations occur in a living medium which cannot be adequately transcribed. Nonetheless I shall try to give some idea of what was attempted.

Interpretations were minimal. This must be emphasized. Those which were offered referred principally to the affect which the child seemed to be experiencing. At first we were inclined to give rather direct descriptions of the transference or of the general emotional situation, such as, "You seem to be angry with me." "You seem to be afraid of me," or "You seem to be worried about whether your mother likes you or not." We soon discovered that even a good relationship with the child did not sufficiently mitigate the accusatory implications of such comments. Either they were tossed aside by the patient, or, if the anxiety they produced was greater still, there would be a halting in the progression of the play for longer or shorter intervals and some type of defensive activity would be entered upon. It has become our common procedure to generalize interpretations in some manner such as is illustrated in the following cases:

A six-and-a-half-year-old boy was dealing with his own insecurity at a point in the treatment when the known fact of the adoptive status of his younger sister was in the foreground. The therapist commented, "All children worry about whether they are adopted some time or other." This comment indicated to the child that the therapist had recognized that the patient was concerned about his own relationship to his parents and that it was quite natural he should have various emotional reactions to it, even resentment.

An eight-and-a-half-year-old girl who had had a very traumatic relationship with a stepmother since early childhood, and who had been asking the therapist, a recreational worker, to be allowed to see a "doctor" instead, was told, "Some little girls think that only a man can help them." She continued with the woman worker.

Such interpretations, if they were pertinent and assimilable, had the advantage of allowing the patient to respond without too much anxiety; on the other hand, if they were beside the point at the moment, or were too threatening, there was less likelihood of unmanageable anxiety developing. In the first of the above instances the child turned to another connected aspect of his problem until some time later when the relationship with his adoptive sister had improved. At that time he made the single comment, "I don't worry about adoption any more."

The purpose of generalized interpretations such as this has, however, not always been served. One very inhibited boy of superior intelligence to whom the therapist had suggested that, "Sometimes children do feel angry toward their mothers," retorted, "Have you known anybody like that?" It appeared that he felt the therapist was deceiving him and beating about the bush. In such an instance, in order to avoid apparent deception, it seemed better to say something like the following. "I sometimes wonder if you might feel angry at your mother. Lots of children do at times."

In other instances it has been possible to paraphrase in more explicit terms what the patient seemed to be alluding to in a ruminative way. For example: A seven-year-old girl presented a great many questions about what went on in the clinic, who worked there, who came there, etc. These questions and the apparent anxiety subsided when the therapist commented, "You seem to be wondering who else I see and what else I do besides this."

At this point it should be emphasized that no interpretations of deep, unconscious mental content have been given to any of the patients. Some quite direct interpretations of conscious conflicts have been effectively given. We have judged them to be effective for two reasons; first, because the child took them up in the play or in the verbal productions and further elaborated and defined them without obvious anxiety; second, because the existing anxiety seemed to subside and the play process to proceed in the line of the problem with which the child at the moment seemed to be dealing. For example: An eight-year-old boy, classified as a borderline mental defective, had been under treatment for 48 hours because of chronic truancy from home. Recently he had been informed of his mother's desertion. In the treatment hour under discussion he was engaged with this aspect of his insecurity. The therapist commented, "You seem to be afraid that you cannot be sure of me any more than you are of your mother." The child turned to the therapist and responded, "I wish I could be sure of you." Subsequently he busied himself with interrogations intended to establish a comparison between the therapist and his mother, with the evidence in favor of the former.

Such direct interpretations as this have been possible when the positive transference was definitely assured. I have the impression that they were best applied to situations in which the immediate conflict was connected with a definite external trauma, such as the one illustrated, of which the therapist was aware. Of course, direct reassurance and open sympathy were given when necessary. Usually this has been when the therapist was frankly at a loss. It seemed best under such circumstances to let the child know that his difficulties were appreciated even though temporarily they might not be understood.

It must be kept in mind, however, that a merely sympathetic permissive attitude is not finally sufficient in this type of attempt at therapy, any more than it is in any other therapeutic setup. While it may be effective in decreasing the tension and anxiety which is necessary to allow the establishment of a working transference—that is, a positive transference which will set the therapeutic process in motion—it cannot continue to be effective against the specific tension and anxieties which come to the surface as the treatment proceeds. Unless these are specifically apprehended and appropriately dealt with, the results may not be desirable.

We could perhaps summarize the aim of all comments made by therapists as follows:

1. To decrease the feeling of being exceptional or irretrievably bad.

2. To introduce an attitude of self-tolerance with regard to the anxiety arising out of the hostile, aggressive tendencies, and to attempt to make some of these tendencies appear to have a natural sanction out of the situation in which they arose.

3. To convey to the patient the fact that the intensity of his difficulties were appreciated, though they might not at the moment be understood.

4. To supply some lacking information when the anxiety came from obvious ignorance.

5. To clarify, where possible, conflictual relationships in the immediate life situation.

6. To point the way to compromises with realities that were inevitable.

7. Finally, in some cases, as made possible for the therapists through consultation with the consultant, to attempt to deal with specific conflicts which had come to the surface.

I come now to an attempt at an evaluation of our results. Fifteen of the 24 improved cases received other types of treatment collateral to the play therapy. Only 5 of the 16 unimproved cases received such collateral treatment. Stated differently, of the 20 cases which received collateral treatment, 15 (75%) are classified as improved. Of the 20 cases which received play therapy alone, only 9 (45%) showed improvement. Collateral treatment included foster home or institutional placement, social worker's or psychiatrist's treatment of the mother, concomitant treatment of the siblings involved in the problem of the given patient, and so forth. In some cases in which the problems extended into the school, the cooperation of the school was obtained in relieving educational or disciplinary pressures.

It would seem that such external factors would vitiate any conclusions as to the specific validity of the play therapy. But the following data must also be considered:

TABLE 2

PRESENT TREATMENT RESULTS IN PREVIOUSLY TREATED CASES

| | | Improved | | Unimproved |
| | | Play Therapy only | Play Therapy with Collateral Treatment | |
|---|---|---|---|---|
| Manipulative and Corrective | 12 | 3 | 7 | 2 |
| Psychiatric Interviews | 7 | 2 | 3 | 2 |
| Totals | 19 | 5 | 10 | 4 |

The four unimproved cases are among the most difficult of our group, including two children classifiable in David Levy's terms as cases of "primary affect hunger," an inhibited enuretic boy, and a boy whose problem was nucleated by strong passive homosexual tendencies.

The results indicated above do not permit of final general conclusions both because of the small number of cases and because of the fact that we do not have a sufficiently detailed analysis of the reasons for the failure of the previous treatment. Nevertheless, the seriousness of the problems presented by some of the improved cases which received only play therapy must be kept in mind. The following case is illustrative:

A seven-year-old boy with marked reading disability, enuresis, thumb sucking, and a lisping, infantile speech. He was extremely timid and dependent. A medical history of hay fever and asthma was presented. At irregular intervals over a period of five and a half months, 15 playroom sessions have been held.

The boy has without tutoring begun to make strides in his reading and arithmetic at school. The teacher said to the parents, "What are you doing to Jack?" in reference to the change which has been observed in him. At Christmas time the patient requested a set of boxing gloves and is now using them. The father, an intelligent, competent man, who was originally very much worried about the boy, comments on the patient's increasing vigorousness and suggests discontinuation of treatment—it having served its purpose.

Furthermore, we are impressed with the fact that a number of our unimproved closed cases are thus classified because we were unable to manage the external situation or the attitudes of the mothers, both because of their extremity and our mistakes. But the children themselves displayed convincing evidence of what we have called internal progress. In other cases where we were successful in overcoming such difficulties, especially the mother's jealousy or her sense of being dispossessed,[3] we have been able to continue the treatment and to see favorable results.

Finally, we must consider the superficial but practical factor that in a number of instances of children now successfully placed in an institution or foster home, the clinic's intensive and hopeful efforts fortified the doubtful attitudes of those who had to deal with the problems outside.

The economic evaluation of the various aspects of the total therapy of our cases cannot be dealt with

[3] The management of parental attitudes was a very important problem which lack of time does not permit us to discuss here.

here. It is my impression that the influence of the play interviews and of collateral treatment was interdependent and that neither one aspect of the therapy nor another would have been separately effective.

It does seem that under the conditions of the work in our clinic and with our personnel, play therapy is a significant new factor in treatment.[4] As such, it appears to be a valid part of the general procedure of a child guidance clinic. However, we cannot look upon it as an isolated therapeutic entity. Even in those instances in which no active collateral treatment is undertaken, a preliminary, broad, general survey is required. In those cases in which collateral treatment is necessary, the complicated relationships that are originally present between the child and his milieu and the new ones that develop under treatment require the most careful consultative efforts of the play therapist and the others who are engaged on the case.

Finally, considering the play technique itself, we must emphasize that it is not the mere turning loose of a child in a room stocked with toys, attended by any kindly adult. We cannot stake our hopes on transference and catharsis alone, though it is true that in quite a number of our cases this may be the chief cause of the improvement we see. We must remember that in the permissive and secure atmosphere of the treatment room, a dynamic process is set in motion to a greater or lesser extent in all cases. This occurs even when the child is seen at intervals of a week or longer. There are no rules of thumb. The therapist cannot be too sensi-

---

[4] It must be mentioned that some of our improvements may have been in the nature of "flights into health." One case in particular, reported as "much improved" but without "internal progress," showed this.

tive to the developments in this process. Our open cases in all states of improvement and lack of improvement continue to confront us with many problems of understanding and management. We feel, therefore, that for the present this work must be pragmatic, and the results considered tentative until a more complete analysis of a much larger number of cases is possible. Because of this it seems imperative that the clinical experiment we call "play therapy" be limited to individuals of established personal aptitude or verified special training and experience. It is strongly advisable that even when such personnel is available serious consideration should be given to the necessity for qualified consultation and supervision.

# The Critical Moment
# in Psychotherapy

## (1942)

---

I N THE FIELD of organic medicine our approach to the patient is, from the beginning, rational. Long before any of us has gained access to a bedside he has been thoroughly grounded in the anatomy, physiology, and pathology of somatic illness. This is antecedent to all clinical techniques. What we do or refrain from doing is determined by our understanding of the implications of the syndrome which confronts us.

I propose to demonstrate, by describing a single clinical experience, that the same holds true in the field of psychological medicine. I propose to show that there is no room in psychiatry for an empiricism which takes symptoms at their face value and deals with them according to a rule-of-thumb therapy.

### CASE HISTORY

Some time ago a young professional man appeared in my office, greatly distressed by the fact that his wife had been diagnosed as having a schizophrenic psy-

---

*Editorial note:* Written before psychiatry and psychoanalysis had made their full impact on the United States, this presentation elucidates the ingredients of an interpretation.

chosis. Shock treatment had been advised; what should he do?

He gave the following history: He was an emigré. He and his wife had met as students and had been married five years. Together they had worked toward the same professional career. At the time of their arrival in this country he had completed his training and had been able to obtain employment in his field. His income, however, had been inadequate to support them both, and it had been necessary that the patient, too, seek employment. She had intended to complete her own training in this country, and consequently had looked for work in a minor capacity in her chosen profession. Unfortunately, the best she had been able to do was obtain a position as a charwoman in an institution where her specialty was taught. She had accepted this work hoping that ultimately she would be given an assignment commensurate with her actual talent. On this basis she seems to have made a good adjustment. Then, after some months, she was transferred to work in the same menial capacity in the dormitory of the institution.

For some time thereafter no disturbance was noted. About three weeks before I saw her, however, the patient began to complain to her husband about ill treatment. The residents of the dormitory were making specious remarks about her. She "heard" that they were accusing her of thefts. They were "whispering" about that she had some nefarious purpose in working as a housekeeper. They were making insulting remarks which depreciated her. Two or three days before my interview with the husband, she had become quite upset, reporting that she had heard two of the residents of the dormitory talking about paying someone to rape her and kill her. She also reported that these persons had induced the cook to poison her food in order to be rid of her.

The husband stated that the patient had previously been an earnest, energetic, cheerful person. She had never been seriously ill. He himself had tended to depressiveness and anxiety, and his wife, from the beginning of their acquaintanceship, had been his mainstay.

What are the essential facts? First and most important, we hear that the patient's husband, formerly dependent on her, is now successfully launched on a career to which she also has aspired; second, we are struck by the contrast of her own lowly employment; finally, we observe a disturbance characterized by fantastic notions of hostility directed to her by persons of whom she was the actual equal but whose conventional status was superior.

What must we understand from these facts before we have ever seen the patient herself? It must be obvious that she had sustained a severe blow to her self-esteem. On the basis of what is known of human interpersonal relationships, we must see that this must have involved self-comparisons not only with the residents of the dormitory but with the husband, whose equal or superior she had been. We must surmise her bitterness and suspect the intensity of the hostility she must have felt for all those, including her husband, who were more fortunate than herself. Finally we must appreciate how untenable such a hostile position could be for a decent, faithful wife, and how the fantastic delusions could be her way of turning on herself the unacceptable feelings toward others which circumstances had generated in her. In these understandings were found the specific indications for my activity as a psychotherapist.

First of all this meant a bolstering of her lost self-esteem. Consequently, though she was administratively a clinic patient, I arranged to see her in my private office in the hospital. When she was announced by the room clerk, I did not wait for her to come to me. I went directly to her in the lobby, greeted her as a social equal, and conducted her personally to my office.

I saw a pale, thin young woman, poorly but neatly dressed. A smile played fitfully over her face throughout the interview. She appeared distant and unaffected. I opened the way for her with a question to this effect: "Your husband has told me that you are unhappy and in trouble. Can you tell me about it?" I listened with quiet attentiveness, and only occasionally did I ask a question which aimed at elaborating what appeared to her to be the facts of the case. These were essentially as stated by her husband. She did not consider them fantastic, and I did not enter into any discussion of them. When she had finished, I said to her, quietly but positively, that I did not believe that these were her troubles. I said that it looked to me as if she must really be upset by what she was having to do in the interest of her career. I said that it looked to me as if this had been harder to bear because of the others, to whom she felt at the same time equal and inferior. Finally, I told her that I would like her to know that I myself had worked at lowly jobs in the interest of my career. And I described some of their details to her. I concluded a 30 minute interview with the suggestion that she herself phone me the next day for an appointment. And I conducted her back to the lobby of the hospital.

The following day I again met her in the lobby. The picture was entirely changed. The affectless smile was gone, and she was manifestly depressed. She informed me that after the first interview things had suddenly taken on a different shape. The fantastic character of her story had dawned on her. She had been able to reconstruct the situation which seemed to her to have produced the acute elaboration of her illness.

She told me that two weeks previous to the onset of the acute symptoms, one of the instructors at the institution where she was employed had asked her to translate a certain foreign article for him. She had agreed to meet him in the library, and they had arranged that he should call her from the housekeeping quarters for this purpose. His subsequent failure to keep the appointment had impressed her as meaning that he would have been glad enough to get her help but would have been ashamed to be seen with her. The day before that her husband had been promised an improved professional connection by the benefactor who had brought them from Europe. This person had at the same time told the patient that for the time being she must continue to work where she was. These episodes had been preceded by several months of depression which she had been unable to reveal to her husband because of his egoistic concern with his own prospects and his emotional dependence on her.

It must be clear that by treating her tacitly as an equal and by taking her into a degree of confidence about myself I had made it possible for the patient to face more directly the fundamental emotions from which she had fled into psychosis. By thus giving her a basis for a tenable self-comparison I had demonstrated to her that her position was not so hopeless or so depreciated. Furthermore, it can be seen that my early understanding of the dynamic relationship of the elements of the situation had made it possible for me to go directly to the heart of the matter and thus to establish a *real* contact with her. We can now appreciate that the apparent paranoid schizophrenia represented an effort to throw off unbearable desolation and unacceptable hostile resentment by the method of projection. The upshot was the uncovering of a reactive depression which had been the primary consequence of the pathogenic insults.

At the end of the second interview, I advised that she must give up all thought of work for a time and that I would see what could be done meantime in the way of getting a more suitable placement for her. This I proceeded to do. In the third interview, two days later, I was able to bring into quite open discussion her angry resentment against the residents of the dormitory and against the instructor who had snubbed her, connecting this with her envy of them. These feelings were at this time more readily accessible and more easily acceptable to this emotionally sensitive patient.

The fourth interview, again two days later, saw the depression lifted. Ventilation of her hostile feelings and my natural acceptance of them had relieved the need for self-criticism and self-punishment. She spontaneously now talked with much tender emotion of the terrible things that Nazi nurses had done to young men who had been returned from concentration camps to urban hospitals. One of these had become psychotic as she herself had been. When I asked her what she thought was the point of the occurrence of such painful memories now she responded immediately, without apparent insight, as follows: "Yesterday my husband got his new position." She then expressed herself as happy about this, though it was a disappointment, too, because it meant that she could not leave the city, which she would have liked to do in order to escape from the stigma of her illness. She then went on to describe a dream she had had the night before.

*Dream:* First she is a student. Then she has attained her ambition and is at work in her profession. But the head of the doctor who first examined her keeps bobbing up before her, telling her she is crazy and should not be successful.

I now suggested that there might be reasons for her disappointment about her husband's new job other than the one she had given. I recalled that she had said that she was disappointed but happy too. I asked her if she was under the impression that human beings could be perfect. She responded negatively. I commented then that it would be natural for imperfect human beings, despite a sense of moral obligation to others, to have feelings which had regard only for their own interests and wishes. Perhaps her disappointment was not merely with the fact of having to remain in the city? Perhaps it had something to do with seeing her husband arrive at a goal which was for her still far away? Decent people do not give free play to the feelings attached to their personal disappointments. That was why she was happy about her husband's new work. But that, also, was why she had become ill. That was why in the dream she seemed to be saying to herself: "I do not deserve to be a student or to attain my ambition because I am disappointed to see my husband get something which I want for myself."

The patient accepted this with silent acquiescence. I did not discuss with her the deeper implications of the emergence of her bitter memories about the Nazis. We ourselves can see clearly enough that these memories, unlike the self-punishing dream, were a more direct expression of her envious anger against her husband. We recognize that the pity and sorrow served to deny to the patient the awareness of the more primitive and most unacceptable aspects of her hostility. But in a limited psychotherapy such as this, I purposely refrained from breeching such a defense. Instead, I capitalized on its existence to make it possible for her to tolerate the socially acceptable degree of resentment which had also been rejected.

At the end of this interview I told the patient that the situation seemed to be moving toward a final successful conclusion. It was my purpose with this remark to decrease the possibility of fixation in the transference and a possible regression. Again, because my therapeutic goal was limited to the patient's social rehabilitation, I chose to avoid the initiation of a process which would inevitably result in the evolution of deeper affects. Consequently, I talked with her in terms of the fact that she would have to continue to work and struggle and that some compromises might be necessary as was the case with all of us. I hoped thereby to support her hold on reality by decreasing her sense of difference and isolation.

During the next three and a half months, I saw the patient five times at increasingly longer intervals, although she knew that I was always available to her. We continued to discuss various aspects of her competitiveness with her husband which were covered up by attitudes of protective wifeliness. She suffered a number of minor depressive reactions, but continued to gain ground physically and emotionally. When I saw her for the last time she was again an active, cheerful young woman. For the first time in her relationship with her husband, she reported, she had been able to allow herself to be justifiably angry and had felt better for it. I approved of the validity of her feelings.

## FOLLOW-UP

A report 10 months later by an interested social agency reads in part as follows: "through her own efforts Mrs. X. secured a factory job . . . and made another attempt to obtain a placement in a professional school but failed . . . She gave the worker this information with a surprising amount of ease. . . . The general tone was one of 'better luck next time.' She was more relaxed than the worker had ever seen her."

A final follow-up report, obtained 15 months after the first interview and 11 months after the last one, indicates the patient is continuing in good physical and mental health. She has been able to take several difficult situations in her stride and is at the present time considering a necessary change in her plans which involves the choice of a more modest career.

## CONCLUSION

The critical moment in psychotherapy is determined by a complex of several factors. The physician contributes to it his immediate sensitive awareness of the basic realities of the patient's problem, regardless of the phenomenological elaboration the problem has undergone. This means that intuition must stem from an explicit knowledge of the laws of interpersonal experience and behavior. As in somatic medicine, thus also in psychological medicine, we must accept the limitations of our information and powers. Within these limits, however, we are fully responsible, in both fields of our endeavor, for that knowledge and understanding which makes it possible to act definitively where such action is called for by the facts. It is not a mere matter of persuasion, or suggestion, or re-education, or domination, or shock treatment, as the case may be. Our techniques must be precisely psychological, specific in terms of the specific instance of human trouble we are called upon to treat. In each instance we must hope to act with precision and timeliness.

If this is possible and the physician can quickly penetrate the overt symptoms to a realization of what they truly imply, then the latent "sense" can be dealt with more or less explicitly and the likelihood of a dynamic contact with the intact ego of the patient is vastly increased. This does not mean that the fortunate case which I have presented is an example of what we can always expect. No one will think that I am talking of panaceas. It does mean, however, that existing knowledge provides me with the basis for more effectively reaching and mobilizing the patient's own powers for movement toward emotional health.

The patient's part in the critical moment is his readiness to be thus mobilized. This comes, first, from his actual fear of the rampant impulses that psychosis liberates, and then, from his yearning for the renewal of a real contact which is more bearable than that with the original traumatic reality. It is recognizable in a glance, a postural change, or a nuance of vocal inflection in the moment at which the therapist has struck the first true note. In the psychoses, this readiness may be quite evanescent and relatively soon destroyed. If we can grasp it while it is still in reach, a rationally precise and prompt human action is worth a hundred shocks.

# Direct Psychotherapy
# in Adolescence

(1942)

A 15-YEAR-OLD BOY entered the psychiatric unit following a diagnosis of schizophrenia at a distant clinic. He had been referred there by the family physician because of a hallucinatory episode in which he heard a gentle sexless voice telling him to prepare to die. Shock therapy was advised, but was rejected by the parents.

Apparently the illness began when he entered high school and began to do poor work. In the third year, scholarship took a more rapid decline and developed fugue-like states which followed a single pattern: he would start toward the high school and find himself, not knowing how, at the grade school he had formerly attended. The first "fugue" occurred following the patient's discovery of a divorced aunt in coitus with a man he had presumed to be her platonic friend. Extremely disturbed, he threatened to kill the aunt's lover. He had been very fond of this aunt who, in contrast to his mother, had indulged him. Now he turned bitterly against her, although at times he vacillated and felt pity for her in her disgrace. His mood darkened; he became seclusivé and irritable, began to feel that people were curious about him and were laughing at him. He complained of failing memory and had bouts of nausea and vomiting accompanied by occipital headache.

The patient was of old American stock, a cleancut, physically healthy and well-developed adolescent. Of superior intelligence, he appeared more mature than his chronological age. He was considered "reticent like his father" and gave the clinical impression of being a bit suspicious and cautious and somewhat tense and uneasy. As an adult he might have been classified as a paranoid type. Nevertheless, he had apparently made "normal" social and educational adjustments until he entered high school. He was the younger of two children. His sister, age 22, left home early to live her own life, unable to tolerate the rigidity and strictness of the mother, who objected to the normal social interests of her children and even forbade the daughter to marry. The father, a meek, quiet man, was unable to deal with his matriarchal wife. The children liked him but could not depend on him.

During his stay at our hospital the boy was quiet, somewhat aloof, and lacking in spontaneity. In interviews with the resident physician, he was responsive but rather shallow and circumstantial. No delusions or hallucinations were discovered, and the sensorium was intact. Striking, however, was the complete acquiescence with which he accepted placement with more overtly disturbed patients. Physical examination and laboratory studies were negative with the exception of the EEG which showed an irregular pattern with alpha waves of undecided frequency, fluctuating between nine and 12 per second in different parts of the record.

Rorschach findings stated: "Patient retreats into fantasy and the affective life is strongly repressed, with serious restriction of the instinctual trends revealed. Inferiority feelings are definitely indicated. The fantasy is of the type found in patients fighting to maintain the integrity of their personalities. The patient is found to maintain his hold on reality within the range of the normal. Occasional alogical responses occur: the intellectual processes are unimpaired but are restricted within limits narrower than his actual capacity. The personality is considered intact, but evidence of a beginning phase of withdrawal is felt to be present, and it is thought that we may be seeing the early signs of a schizophrenic process which may take an insidious course" (S. J. Beck).

TREATMENT SITUATION

Although the boy was not actively psychotic, he was seriously ill. There were no psychiatric facilities at or near the small town from which he came, a thousand miles from Chicago. While hospitalization was not required, there were serious doubts as to the advisability of returning him to his family and to the disturbing proximity of his aunt. His sister was employed in Chicago, and with this as a safeguard it was decided to keep him in the city. A suitable foster home was selected, but after a few days he rebelled and insisted on residence in a YMCA.

It was our intent to have him under passive observation until the stability of his remission was more certain, and the resident psychiatrist was assigned to this task. Unforeseen developments, however, forced the author to undertake active psychotherapy, in the course of which the possibility of a full psychoanalytic therapy appeared; but subsequent external events made the feasibility of this seem doubtful. The technical therapeutic problem, therefore, was to help the patient gain enough understanding and control to protect him from a possible relapse into acute illness, while leaving the way open to the hoped-for psychoanalysis. The following material should be appraised with these points in mind.

TREATMENT TECHNIQUE

The patient was seen two or three times a week during four and one half months, for a total of 40 interviews. He sat in a comfortable chair facing me. Treatment periods were scheduled at regular hours, but varied in length up to an hour. I did not hesitate to terminate a session at the end of 15 minutes if it seemed necessary to allow the boy to escape from an over-anxious impasse. Nor did I refrain from active intervention in the way of positive help or advice. On one occasion when he was ill, I drove him home. At other times I phoned him to insure a new appointment when one had been missed. Once I took his temperature and had another physician examine his abdomen for the possibility of an acute appendicitis. I tried to have him feel that I was available to him for practical needs if necessary. At the same time I carried on what might be called insight therapy, which I buffered with a definite effort to support his defenses insofar as these were necessary for the protection of his sensitive self-esteem.

He was not very productive, often remaining utterly silent. But when "acting" or other nonverbal clues permitted, I did not hesitate to puncture the silence with interpretations which some would call mere hunches. For the rest, the material will expose the technique.

TREATMENT

After placement at the YMCA, the patient got along well until he entered a local high school. Then, beginning during the entrance examinations, he developed violent headaches, showed signs of tension, and finally, one evening, fainted and was carried to his room. That night he was sleepless and restless and kept calling for his parents. An emergency appointment was arranged through his sister.

When seen, he appeared anxious and spoke vaguely of his dislike for the school he was attending. For some time it was not clear what he was driving at. Suddenly he blurted out that he hated to come to see me. Since the day he left the hospital he had feared the prospect of the clinic visits, although he had passively assented and kept his appointments with the resident. I suggested that it would seem he was afraid that if we kept working with him long enough we might find the same "crazy things" in him that he had discovered in the people among whom he had been hospitalized. He admitted this and then, apparently out of context, spoke of his disturbance over 13-year-old girls who smoke and swear, and 14-year-old boys who think only of beating each other out or of making passes at girls. He was not brought up that way! This enabled me to discuss the conflict between his "idealism" and what he had discovered life to be. He did not want to surrender his ideals, and the things he saw around him were threatening.

Subsequently, because the anxiety created in the sophisticated city high school seemed too great for him to tolerate, I agreed to his plan to transfer to a YMCA school. Almost immediately he threatened to quit. The curriculum was dull! He could get well at home as well as here! He was angry and defiant. It developed that there was a woman in his class who reminded him of his aunt. He could not stand her. I assumed an attitude of definite firmness toward his defiance, depreciated his rationalization, and pointed out that he had fled from each new situation. I told him there would be women at every turn who would remind him of his aunt and he could not hope to continue to run away from his own feelings. I showed him how he was using temper in an attempt to control a situation which he was afraid to try to manage otherwise. He then presented a dream in which his feeling of failure as a man appeared, but which, in the few spontaneous associations, was covered by a disparaging attack on the doctors who had thus far shown themselves unable to help him. He seemed to need to equalize his loss of self-esteem in this way, and my comments were directed toward facilitating this. Later he pretended to be attending the classes in which the disturbing aunt-figure appeared, but from his sister I learned that he had transferred to the night session of the same school. When I confronted him with this he was again very angry, but this time it was clearly shame which was the real feeling. This was discussed with him in terms of the conflict between his anxiety and his need to maintain his self-esteem. He would have liked the courage to face the anxiety situation, and this had forced him to pretend he had it. His self-respect was disturbed by the fact that he could not really appear before me as a man, and his anger had only thinly disguised this.

In the end it was left to him to decide whether he continue in night school or return to day school. He was told I intended to stand by him no matter what his decision was. He responded by returning to the day school and remaining silent during the following therapeutic sessions. Finally, after one of his periods of silence, I asked him what he thought of the situation—our sitting there eyeing one another. He replied, "I think it's foolish." "Obviously that is what you would like to make it appear," I replied, "to make it nonsensical so that it should be discontinued." His subsequent comments, characteristically, seemed out of context. He spoke resentfully of the older men at the Y who permitted him no privacy, who made fun of what he was doing, against whom he could not even lock his door. He wished he could move away as some of his friends had done. He appeared jolted when I commented that it would seem he felt that I, too, was trying to batter down his privacy. The tension was broken, and for the first time he willingly accepted the next appointment.

Following this he wrote his aunt a friendly letter, the first since his disillusionment. He spoke of having given up his earlier ambition to become a doctor. Things connected with hospitals now disgusted him. Journalism would be preferable. Again I was able to discuss with him how his anxiety was tempting him to turn from the possibility of understanding himself and life; his letter to his aunt was an effort to clean the slate, to start all over again as if nothing had been changed. Rejection of his medical ambition was a rejection of the interest he must have had to know what adults know. He had found out more than he felt he could bear.

His rejection of the unknown now assumed other forms. He protested against instructors who did not stick to the syllabus but went off on tangents in religion and politics. He disparaged foreigners he had never previously known and whom he did not understand. He objected to the interviews in which I sometimes actively interrogated him on his activities. Then, following an hour in which we simply "talked" in a quite relaxed way, he came in more than usually angry and opened up again on this theme. I interrupted him with something to the effect that I did not understand what his feelings were about, but surely they were not the outcome of the surface circumstances of our last talk. Immediately, he told me that after the last visit he went downtown to a theater. While waiting in the lobby he stood with his arms folded over his chest, protecting the wallet in his pocket. A man came barging through the crowd and ran into him. The man apologized. Later, finding his wallet gone, he thought this man had picked his pocket.

It had previously been clear that he was developing anxiety concerning his passive dependence on me. During one of our discussions he confessed this quite openly, and I deemed it advisable to assure him that his dependence was not the aim of my work, and that I would consider it a failure if that were its result.

Now I ventured a little further. While it was entirely possible that his pocket had been picked, the feeling he had been displaying was clearly directed toward me. Consequently I handled his reaction to the incident as a displacement from me. I told him it was as if he had looked upon my friendly conversation as a means of insidiously "sneaking up" on him to bring him under my influence. Because this was a potentially paranoid boy, who seemed to be projecting his own fantasies of omnipotence on me, I specifically told him that I had no magic power; that we were engaged in a process in which what I learned about him I learned from him; that he became aware of things about himself in the same order as my understanding of him developed.

This interview relieved him greatly. His attitude became optimistic and buoyant. He blossomed out in social activities at the Y. He told me that for the first time in his life he was finding it possible to go up to somebody and start a conversation. He no longer found it difficult to find things to talk about. He began to look forward to the possibility of continuing treatment longer than he had originally envisaged. There was not doubt that he was better able to accept the passive and dependent relationship to me, although he was probably helping himself to accomplish this with his newly developed extroversion which served to dilute his transference feelings.

In the meantime he was truanting from school. Again he appeared at my office with his heavy, sullen mien. And again, with his usual tangential technique, he approached the painful truth. He had been unable to overcome his aversion to school. He had lain awake nights making resolutions to return, but nothing had come of them. Sometimes he had traveled seven miles to the loop only to turn back within a block of the hated destination. In response to my comment that the struggle over school attendance seemed to be a counterpart of his divided feelings toward me, he explicitly admitted conscious awareness of his ambivalence; sometimes he liked me and sometimes he was unable to understand what he felt—some kind of inner tension and an aversion to coming here to which he had not given in. He was able to see the displacement to the school situation very clearly. Again he was told that I did not intend to participate in his decision regarding continuance. He must see where he stood without my "mixing up the picture" for him. And again I assured him that I would stand by him, no matter what.

In the following interview, he spoke explicitly of his mother for the first time, revealing that she was "the power behind the throne," "the iron hand in the velvet glove." The last formulation was mine, and he laughed heartily over it. His father, he said, stood silently by "while mother made the decisions." Following this he quit school.

A week later, barely inside the office, he burst out indignantly, "I seem to have lost my parents' confidence"—specifically his mother's confidence. A letter from her to the sister had revealed that a man at the Y, who was acquainted with friends of the family, had written them to the effect that the patient was "running wild." Actually, this was not true. In reality, the informer was himself a dissolute person whom the patient depreciated. Why should his mother believe someone else and not him? I observed that his indignation seemed justified but that he had well learned by now that there was usually something besides "justification" to stir his feelings to such a pitch. I wondered if he wasn't really reacting to the disturbance of his relationship with mother? His anger, I suggested, might well be a way of avoiding his feelings about that. Only recently, I reminded him, had he found it possible to laugh over his mother's "iron hand." And equally recently was it that his self-assertive tendencies had appeared. Wasn't there conflict between what he wanted to do and what he felt was expected of him? His mother's expectations of him might very well have become his expectations of himself.

Now, for the first time in the therapy, the facts of his illness were specifically taken up. I connected the present emergence of his conflict with his mother to the past "fugues," which had originally appeared in relation to a conflict regarding a woman who was a "second mother" to him. They surely seemed to have been an effort on his part to eradicate the period in his life in which his conflict had appeared; they seemed to serve the purpose of taking him back to a period in his life, when he was still at grade school, during which his own impulses and tendencies had not yet emerged, during which his relationship with his mother and his "conscience" had been disturbed. The patient's reaction was proof of the pertinence and timeliness of my formulation. He burst out, "It wasn't only my aunt I ran away from—it was my mother too!" For the first time he gave explicit vent to his hostility against his psychotically rigid mother.

This development appeared to be a propitious moment for discussing for the first time the psychotic episode which had been the crisis of his illness. I asked him what the content of his hallucination had been, and he told me. Then I said that we could not understand its meaning. His feeling about his mother had become so strong that he had had an acute attack of conscience. The voice was his own criticism of these feelings and his own punishment for them. In order to emphasize his autonomy and to encourage his feeling of capacity for controlling his destiny, I also said, "Now is the time to tell you that you never really were insane in the way you thought," and I elaborated this in the direction of dispelling any notions of magic and external omnipotent powers. He confessed the disturbance such ideas had brought to his self-respect, and his general reaction of relief seemed to indicate that this had been the correct point at which to introduce this topic, when he could see it in dynamic relationship to his whole problem.

It now seemed probable that the boy's extreme anxiety in reaction to the danger of coming under my influence was connected with the relationship with his mother. Therefore I suggested to him that he was afraid of his relationship with me because the feelings were somehow similar to those with respect to his mother. The suggestion met with convincing affirmation. The only thing that had kept him from "chucking" the treatment as he had "chucked" school was the fact that he liked me despite his fears and his anger.

In the 20th hour of treatment he brought the following dream. He was visiting the grade school he had attended and was going around shaking hands with the teachers he had had two years before the onset of the disturbance in his personality. He awakened from the dream with an overwhelming feeling of loneliness.

His only specific association to the dream was, "It looks as if I wanted to go back there." However, throughout this rather long interview, he kept asserting how much he wanted to be on his own. There was no doubt of his regressive nostalgia, but I felt that his strivings toward maturity should be encouraged. I said, "Yes, but to be back there as a man, no longer a child and a subordinate." He nodded spontaneously in confirmation. He could not imagine why he had felt so lonely afterward. I told him that it was the inevitable feeling of loss which comes with renunciation of a relationship which has its attractions and advantages as well as disadvantages. Further, I indicated that the teachers also represented me and that his feelings about me might be the same. He interjected, "Yes, I have learned a lot from you," but again emphasized how much he wanted to stand on his own.

There is no doubt that his strong self-assertive protests were more a reaction to the deepening transference, which he both valued and feared, than they were positive expressions of a wish for real independence. But his anxiety was great, and I felt it necessary for him to sense the strength of his ego even at the sacrifice of fully accurate understanding. In the interpretive comments, therefore, the attempt was to stay in a dynamic middle ground.

After leaving school he looked for employment, and a week after the above interview he obtained a factory job. He missed a number of appointments because of conflict in our schedules, but each time he telephoned to explain the situation. When he finally returned to treatment he stated that now he had a different feeling about it; he felt more like continuing with it. We discussed this in terms of the greater security employment gave to his self-respect. He felt he could now see me on a more equal basis than previously. I put myself in the position of fostering his independence, at the same time encouraging the continuation of treatment by making necessary adjustments in the schedule of interviews. Succeeding meetings, however, were unproductive. Then, one day, a friend of his called to inform me he was ill. When seen again, the patient informed me that he had been having gastrointestinal disturbances of which he had previously not spoken. Because fellow workers were similarly ill, he thought it was due to inadequate protection against chemicals which were used in the manufacturing process. Despite the possibility of "acting," I had the impression that he might actually be suffering from an industrial disease and therefore urged him to give up the job. I told him that if there were more at stake it might be worth taking the risk of continuing, but, after all, he had shown his wish and capacity for assuming responsibility for himself. He showed much relief and said he was glad to find somebody at last who was interested enough in him to advise him.

In the following interview his feelings regarding this sense of obligation to me became acute. He had forgotten to telephone the day before, as I suggested he should, to inform me whether he had acted on my advice to give up his work. (He had in fact done so.) On entering the office he heard a sound in the EEG laboratory with which he was familiar. The sound turned him "cold." The night before, at about the same time that he recalled he had failed to call me, he also recalled the interviews and tests with the resident physician, and developed a feeling of repugnance. All his old aversion to coming to the clinic returned. He affirmed my comment that he had looked upon my suggestion that he telephone me as emphasizing his dependence. The very fact that he had been appreciative of my interest was unacceptable to him. He burst out that he did not like any one prying into his life; he had always resented that; his mother had always pried and wanted to know everything. He became progressively angrier; didn't like the whole "darned business." I suggested that the reason for his mounting anger was that he had recognized the validity of my understanding of him and was resentful of my superior insight. It made him more keenly aware of feelings of inferiority which he could not accept. He could not quite trust me because I was mixed up with his feelings about his mother.

Then I was compelled to be away 12 days. On my return he was "in the dumps" which, he explained, was due to a sniffling cold. It became clear to him, however, in our discussion, that he was reacting to the separation from me. He verified this by telling me that several days before my scheduled return he had had an illusion of seeing me downtown. After that he developed the cold and became consciously depressed. Before the interview was over he understood that depression was the form in which he experienced disappointment and resentment toward me because I had abandoned him. The depression lifted.

In the 33d hour he presented the following dream: He has gray hair. He seems suddenly to have lived a long time. He is very much amused at the idea, laughs out loud, and wakes up laughing. When I asked him what might have happened the day before which might have produced such a dream, he answered that he had written letters to his mother and aunt yesterday and that he had felt older in writing to them, as if much had happened since he had last seen them. The night before, he had seen a hotel (one with a shady reputation) burn down. I recalled that in a recent interview, when I asked him why he was silent, he confessed that he felt like laughing at me and had difficulty restraining himself. At that time I commented that he was enjoying the way he could control the situation and that I was helpless if he wished me to be, despite my superior knowledge and experience. Now, I remarked, everybody at home was treating him with kid gloves on the assumption that the mere knowledge which he acquired in the episode with his aunt and her lover was in itself a tremendous shock to him. The people at home might think this accounted for everything. But, I said, he was laughing at them as well as at me because he had fooled us with his youth. He knew better; it was not the sexual act which upset him, but the feelings having to do with his relationship to his aunt that were really important. Sex, as such, he had known about. Real knowledge would be concerned with how he fitted in and stacked up with others, what he expected of them, and what he felt toward them. What he was afraid of was his own relationship to people. With much feeling he exclaimed, "What makes me mad is that people take me for a dumb kid!" I commented that what he really seemed angry about was his fear of being anything more than a "dumb kid." As I concluded this statement the boy pulled out a magazine he brought with him and had been sitting on, and began thumbing through it absently. It was a juvenile journal called *Youth*. This act had been completely unconscious and I called it to his attention, showing him that with this gesture he had indicated how he held on to his "dumb kiddishness" because he was afraid of what the future (including treatment) and adulthood might bring him to. He laughed heartily, "amazed" to find so much meaning in acts and dreams. That is something he really "learned." He "sees that it is so."

Six more interviews followed, during the course of which we were able to see more and more clearly the conflict between dependency longings which he could not trust or accept and his reactive self-assertion. In the 34th interview he came into the office in a determined manner and announced in a rather loud tone that he had decided to return home. It happened that, for the first time, I had to keep him waiting about 15 minutes. He gave assent intellectually to the possibility that there might be other reasons besides the various "advisable" ones that he advanced, but he remained determined, and I did not stand in his way. In response to his question, I told him I could not say that his continuing with treatment was a matter of life and death. It was something for him to decide. What more did he want for himself? He told me spontaneously that he had never felt better, more confident, freer, more able to express himself without a feeling of holding back. Life had seemed dull previously; now it was interesting. I warned him there might be some change in these feelings of self-confidence if he again found himself in the situation in which his trouble had started.

At the next interview he looked rather sour and reported he had had a gastric upset. The symptoms were such as to raise the question of appendicitis, and I had him examined. Following the negative results of this examination I proposed that we attempt to find out what the feelings were that were expressing themselves through his body. I reviewed the events of the previous visit, when he had had to wait for me while I saw another patient, and I had not interfered with his decision to interrupt the treatment. I suggested that his illness was a protest against both of these facts, a protest that had to emerge by way of his body because his self-respect would not permit him to acknowledge any tendencies on his part to wish to be preferred by me or to wish to continue in a help-seeking relationship with me. I referred to the brave way in which he had announced his determination to go home as an effort to deny to both of us these feelings of conflict in his relationship with me. During the course of this discussion the sourness turned to anger which he admitted explicitly. This, I told him, was his way of asserting that what I was saying was "inconceivable" and "untrue". I warned him against acting impulsively on the basis of this feeling, to which his answer was, in effect, that anything he might decide now, he'd have to change his mind about later.

At this time his room was entered and some belongings taken. His face was heavy with depression and anger as he announced it to me. He had never specifically returned to the matter of prolonged treatment toward which, it will be recalled, he had at one point shown himself favorable. (This refers to the question of a possible analysis.) At this time (June) he stated categorically that he had decided not to return in the fall. Stubborn silence followed. After a while I admitted I didn't understand why he was feeling as he did. I remarked on the fact that he was not merely angry but also depressed. I asserted that the feelings which led to his decision to interrupt treatment were hidden, in his silence, from both of us. I urged him to talk, no matter what he had to say.

He began to speak of his father's aging, of his mother's ill health. He should be with them. I said that it looked as if he were feeling rather guilty toward his folks. Did he feel that the matters emerging in the treatment were coming between him and his parents? Was this what drew him back to them? He replied immediately, "Of course, that is so." He had felt estranged from them. They didn't seem to mean the same things to him they had before. "I have a long life to live. I am young."

Again it was the last, apparently tangential, statement which gave the main clue. I suggested to him, now, that it looked as if he felt he should have his parents for a long time yet. My absence for a week, my keeping him waiting, my leaving him to decide some things for himself must have meant to him that I was undependable. The robbery had touched on these same feelings. Life was not dependable; people could take things from you when you least expected it. He turned toward his parents again, despite everything, because they were at least predictable; he knew from past experience what to expect of them. And that was preferable to the uncertainty he had with regard to me. These statements met with intellectual affirmation, but the actual confirmation of their validity came with the easing of his tension and the lightening of his masked features.

When the railroad pass for his return home finally arrived, he gave himself no time to waver. In the last interview, which came rather precipitously because the pass had not been expected so soon, he laughingly admitted that his attitude was, "Just let anybody try and stop me from going." The boys at the Y with whom he was popular had urged him not to go and had, for a time, hidden the pass. We discussed the evidence of his really wanting me to interfere with his apparent intentions. But, because my practical responsibility for this 15-year-old youngster was great, I did not try too hard to keep him. I told him I felt this was something not to be interfered with; it was something he must go through with and see the ins and outs for himself. We discussed the evidence of what he had gained in terms of maturation over and above the mere recovery from his acute illness. I told him that if things were well with him there would be no practical necessity for his return in the fall. But I also warned him that he himself might decide that there was more work to be done, yet be restrained by his pride from returning. I urged him, in that event, to match his new understanding against his pride. As we shook hands at the door he said he would be seeing me again.

### Follow-up

The patient did not return to Chicago in the fall. During the Christmas vacation of that year he paid me a visit. He was cordial but somewhat tense. We discussed the possibility of his return for further treatment, but his mother was opposed, and it was obvious that he could not insist on it. Reports from the patient's sister indicate that he is free from signs of gross psychopathology. He has returned to school, and while his work is not brilliant neither is it bad. The mother, as described by the sister, exhibits a paranoid picture and has attempted to resume her former domination over the boy. For the first time in his life he has defied her psychotic interdictions, has acquired a "steady" girl friend, and is more active socially than he had been. At the time of completion of this report he had not been seen again.

## DISCUSSION

*Dr. Gitelson:* Treatment of this case was entered upon as a consequence of developments calling for active intervention. My original intention was to manage the problem expectantly. The patient lived a thousand miles from Chicago. He was only 15, and the responsibility for his fate away from home was a heavy one. His 22-year-old sister, herself at odds with the mother, could not be safely regarded as a responsible guardian. It was urgent not to prolong the boy's stay in the hospital among patients overtly more seriously ill than himself, yet I did not feel he was ready to return to his home and the vicinity of his aunt. The temporizing plan was to keep him in Chicago for six months of observation with purely supportive treatment. You have seen in the report of the case how this soon became impossible.

When I began work with the boy it was hoped eventually to bring him into analysis. From correspondence with the parents it appeared that they had arrived at some understanding of the severity of the problem. They seemed willing to consider letting their son attend school in Chicago for a year or two while under treatment. It became progressively evident, however, that while the father had an intuitive grasp of the advisability of this plan, the mother was incapable of accepting it.

The uncertainty of the external situation was such that I had to solve the double problem of giving the boy something of immediate usefulness in managing his life, in the event that treatment might be interrupted (as it was) and, at the same time, lay a foundation for more extensive work, should that prove possible. My first task, therefore, was to help him work through the immediate problem of his acute illness and to sensitize him, without too much attendant anxiety, to the ramifications of his conflicts. My management of the case must be evaluated from this point of view. I was confronted with the following technical problems:

1. The strong fear of his sexual and aggressive tendencies and impulses, from which he had recoiled at puberty, accentuated by the episode with the aunt.

2. The resulting regression to passive dependent attitudes, which, at the same time that they begged for satisfaction, were repugnant to his normal masculine aggressive tendencies.

3. The necessity, in consequence of the above, of sparing his pride while showing him his reactive dependency; and, while acquainting him with the deeper aspects of his emotional tendencies, to re-educate him toward a tolerance of them.

It has been my experience in the therapy of adolescent boys that the therapist must work simultaneously toward these two ends, namely, to strengthen the feeling that the emotions are manageable and need not run wild—the kind of problem one encounters in psychoses—and to dissociate the patient's symptomatic dependency, against which he rebels, from the necessary therapeutic dependence. To accomplish this the therapist must somehow fuse two apparent incompatibles; first, a strong, firm attitude, which, while it lets the patient feel protected against the feared deeper emotions, rouses rebellious attitudes on the level of his own prestige and self-respect; second, a comradely, older brother attitude, which, while it can be used to increase the patient's courage to hope to be as strong instinctually as the therapist, may bring him too close to the emotions he fears. In different phases of the treatment there will be need for different emphases. Throughout treatment the therapist must remain sensitively aware of the patient's tendency to become afraid because of his deeper emotions; to become ashamed because of his fear; to become angry and dangerously rebellious because of his shame.

In general, I can say that I have had relatively little need to assert a fully strict and controlling attitude. I have found it possible to establish, particularly in this case, the feeling that treatment was a collaboration; that the patient himself had the answers to his problem; that it was a circumstance from which he was not barred; that I, having lived a little longer, could catch on a little more quickly, and that whatever I learned *about* him, I learned *from* him. This technique, I believe, serves two purposes. It minimizes the disturbing feelings connected with his own prestige motives, and it strengthens him in his sense of final control over dangerous-seeming emotions through a feeling of alliance with one who provides implicit affirmation of having safely and satisfyingly dealt with such emotions himself.

*Question:* Would you describe the physical arrangements of the interviews?"
*Dr. Gitelson:* We both sat in chairs and sprawled out. I smoked a cigarette or cigar or pipe, whatever I happened to have. There were interviews in which we did not talk much about anything except the State he lived in, or we casually exchanged views. As I said, my relationship with him was quite informal, for I felt that the best way to get along with this boy was by being the "older brother" who had lived a little longer and knew just a little more.

*Question:* How long were these interviews?
*Dr. Gitelson:* They were indefinite in time. If we were getting somewhere, the interview might last an hour. Sometimes, if we came to a logical point in our discussion, I would terminate in 30 or 35 minutes. I felt it was better not to continue building up anxiety in the face of too much obvious tension and resistance. I would tell him, "Well, there must be reasons why we can't get any further today. Let us see where we can get next time." I would rather do that than just bulldog through to the bitter end.

*Question:* I would like to ask if the patient accepted you as the older brother. You said you thought it the best role to play with him. I am interested to know if that was the way he accepted you or was he seeing you as something else?

*Dr. Gitelson:* Of course he saw me in other ways. Sometimes my effort did not work out as I wanted it to, and then I had to deal with him concerning the reasons. For example, I told him at one point that what he was going through was something I had gone through myself. I did not tell him I had been analyzed, but I told him that psychiatrists in the course of their training went through a self-investigation, such as he was then undergoing. This came at a point when he was beginning to sense his first hostile feelings as such. He had to have some feeling that he was not a unique monstrosity, whom he felt I criticized. My technique brought definite relaxation.

*Question:* I noticed that you gave a transference interpretation of his dream. I wonder if you gave any other type of interpretation than that.

*Dr. Gitelson:* No. For example, he brought one dream in which somebody died and he was present at the funeral. That came in a situation in which hostility to the mother was ascendant. I did not feel that I could deal with this attitude explicitly, but at the same time I did not want to bury the hostility. I acknowledged its existence with a comment to the effect, "Well, those are feelings you have, but after all it was only in a dream." His associations to the dream had been that it was just like the funerals of his grandmother and grandfather which he had attended.

In general I did not feel that I could go too far with the boy because of the uncertainty of my therapeutic relationship with him. In any case, even if treatment had continued, I am not sure that I would have made any interpretations to him other than on the level of our relationship and of his real relationships in the life about him.

*Question:* I should like to ask about something on which you have just elaborated. Did you do what you did because of the nature of your relationship, or was it because you felt that if you went deeper into this case there might be anxiety attacks or attacks of panic?
*Dr. Gitelson:* That was definitely the point. As I said, before, this was potentially a very sick boy, although not as sick as he had been described. Consequently, I was handling him with kid gloves. I tried to steer between two extremes—to give him necessary support and yet avoid a repressive process which would tend to be explosive. As previously stated, I tried to give him something that he could handle, even if I had to let him go.

*Question:* Can you give us some idea concerning how deeply you went in your analytical treatment of this boy? You brought up some incest material related to the oedipus situation.
*Dr. Gitelson:* It is not necessary to think of this as incest material. This is a very sick boy, and if in five years of treatment he could come to face the possibilities of such tendencies, if they existed, it would be very satisfactory.
*Dr. Gitelson* (closing): I do not think that in any therapy we can hope to find the indications for our activities precisely, line by line, in the things the patient

gives us unequivocally and overtly. We have to bring to the therapeutic situation all we possess from all of our other experiences: what we understand about the human personality in general, and what we know about the particular *type* of individual we are dealing with. We must act as quickly and as smoothly as possible on the basis of that experience. We may be forced to act blindly in a way that might be called hunch or intuition, but I do not believe this is an activity necessarily to be deprecated. I think we all do such things and often ask ourselves afterward why we did what we did and actually search out meanings as they implicitly exist in our activity.

# Intellectuality
# in the Defense Transference

## (1944)

---

IN *The Ego and the Mechanisms of Defense,* Anna
Freud (1936) has shown that the tendency toward
the recapitulation in the transference of original interpersonal relations involves not only the particular instincts but *equally* the defensive measures which the
person had developed against them. The various libidinal and hostile impulses do not merely reappear as
themselves, but rather in their established distortions
and disguises. "It may happen," she says, "in extreme
cases that the instinctual impulse itself never enters
into the transference at all but only the specific defense adopted by the ego against some positive or negative attitude of the libido. . . . indeed we shall find it
hard to induce [the patient] by an iron insistence on
the fundamental rule [of free association] . . . to expose the id impulse which lies hidden under the
defenses as manifested in the transference" (pp. 19–20).
In this essay I attempt to demonstrate the role of intellectuality, as such, as a defense transference.

---

*Editorial note:* This was the paper Dr. Gitelson submitted for acceptance into the Chicago Psychoanalytic Society and thus into the American. It is his first psychoanalytic paper.

To survey the variety of relationships that people have with each other is to be impressed by the hierarchy which exists among them. First come the more intimate: husband and wife, parents and children, siblings and other kin. Then there are those who are close friends, those who are friendly associates, and those who are neutral acquaintances. Finally, at the periphery, is the mass of humanity. As one moves from the central person toward this periphery there appears to be a progressive attenuation of contact with other human beings: the emotional investment in those who are increasingly remote is correspondingly decreased. Intellectual attitudes and techniques, on the other hand, become more prominent. [1]

It is known that even in the most secure central relationships the libidinal tendencies express themselves only through a system of defenses, the extent of which depends on the degree of anxiety the relationship has left free or has fostered. The principal example of this is found in the normal emotional attitude of the child to the mother. Here, in the beginning the yearnings for contact, for gratification, and for protection, and the reactions to the thwarting of these needs and wishes, gain relatively direct expression. It is known, however, that under the influence of social disavowal such libidinal and hostile expressions normally recede during the latency period, and that their later tendency to reappear during adolescence is concealed in the typical intellectualizations of that period. Furthermore, clinical experience has taught us the difficulties attached to the treatment of older persons: what is described as

---

[1] Subsequent to my writing this paper. Jennings (1943) published a study bearing on this point.

their "rigidity" has really to do with the structuralization of their libido in the defensive system of the ego.

It may then be seen that both biological process and interpersonal experience take the individual progressively further from the possibility of that hypothetically complete gratification of the instincts which belongs to infancy and early childhood. The older the person and the more distant he is in time and space from his original libidinal objects or their surrogates, the less explicitly are the emotions expressed and the more wrapped-up and concealed are they in the person's apparent *modus vivendi*. Because of such defenses, on first acquaintance even the more or less normal person may give the impression of distance and aloofness. His emotional attitudes may be completely masked, or they are revealed tentatively and only in fleeting glimpses. Gradually, if contact with him continues, he begins to display those previously successful life techniques which may again be useful to him in establishing social relations. Should the relationship be sustained, then, within the capacities of the given person, bit by bit the superstructure gives way and deeper emotional tendencies, hitherto concealed, appear. This is the process which can be observed in the gradual assimilation of newcomers to a community. Through such phases, the normal bonds of love evolve in a man and a woman who were originally strangers to each other.

No defense is that alone. The critical emotions can find paths for their expression over and through the very barriers that would confine them, and the defensive technique itself becomes an attenuated expression of the emotional tendency against which it is directed. Even normal love in its beginning is not certain of the reliability of its object and transiently employs defensive techniques to clandestinely sample and test it. This is also the pattern for the chronic deviousness in the interpersonal relations of persons suffering from certain "intellectual" types of narcissistic character neuroses.

Such neurotic intellectuals may live their lives on the periphery of real human relations. Under the circumstances of culture they may attain obvious success and they may appear to have satisfactory object relations. The fact is, however, that they never really come to grips with emotional reality. Theirs is a constant play-acting of friendship and sociability according to accepted standards. One is struck by their lack of genuine commitments and by the extent to which their rich intellectual talents are devoted merely to absorbing their own feelings and to engaging the libido of others. They often waste a mentality whose normal functioning would of itself evoke the very interest and appreciation they crave with such pathological intensity and strive for by pathological means.

The premium placed on intellectual precociousness by parents; their own banal intellectual techniques, compounded of emotional inhibitions and conventionalized hypocrisy which they use in the training of the child's emotions, and the child's fortuitous discovery of the tendentious utility of intellect—all these factors contribute to the genesis of this defense. Add the general characteristics of society as manifested in the intellectualized fictions and conventions of business, professional, political, and social relations, and it becomes apparent why the intellectual defense can remain unrecognized as such and even flourish as alleged normality. It is the mutual usefulness of its common existence in more than one person that makes this possible. It meets its nemesis only in a relationship or in a situation in which the instinct must necessarily function in a franker form. In such instances, the anxiety against which it is directed erupts and forces the adoption of another type of defense.

## CLINICAL EXAMPLES

Excerpts from the analyses of two narcissistic character neuroses are presented here in support of the thesis. The first illustrates a type of childhood situation that is favorable to the development of an intellectual defense. The second presents an opportunity for observing more clearly the relationship between an intellectual "life technique" and the intellectual type of defense transference. Both show the relationship between the libidinal transference and the defense transference and thereby give occasion for discussing some aspects of the technical therapeutic problem that such situations pose.

CASE 1

A highly intelligent male, age 30, came to analysis because he wanted "help in making an adequate adjustment in a competitive society." His relations with people were "too complicated," and because things often "got too hot" for him he would go wandering off on trips culminating in some distant hinterland where he worked as "a jack of all trades." Invariably he returned to the original scene of his conflict.

At 24, for the first time in his life the patient became interested in a girl, a friend and college roommate of his only younger sister. Despite the fact that the sister, for reasons of her own, did her best to disrupt the affair, the patient "proceeded to become entangled" and was married. From the beginning, his relationship with his wife had been highly intellectualized. An adolescent type of philosophical discussion of the nature and implications of their affair continued even after premarital sexual relations had been entered upon. The sexual activity was largely an elaborate forepleasure, ending, for the patient, in *ejaculatio praecox*.

At this time there was a change in the patient's general attitude. Whereas formerly he had taken pride in being a "man of action" who suspected and depreciated the intellectuality of others, now he found himself interested for the first time in ideas as such. He began to read widely and developed political opinions and a social philosophy. However, when with much trepidation he attempted to enter the sophisticated university circle of which his sister was a member, his anxiety became too much for him, and again he fled. Together with his wife, he emigrated to a distant frontier area where he spent several years as a miner and surveyor. There, "direct and simple human relationships" for some time brought him peace. Finally, "frustrated by the narrowness of the life," and having the ambition to become a writer, he returned to the States. In the course of his analysis it became clear that there was a more explicit emotional reason for his having given up the frontier life. With much round-about verbal dalliance, he had approached the possibility of an affair with the wife of a colleague. This time he was dealing with a more forthright woman than his wife had been. In the upshot, he had not dared to respond to her unequivocal feelings and had fled.

Upon his return, he found that his sister had successfully completed a psychoanalysis. Although there were other contributing factors, this became the leading unconscious motive for his entering into analysis. The sister was intellectually brilliant, and the patient had always been strongly rivalrous with her. His disappointment was correspondingly keen when her analyst, to whom he first applied for treatment, referred him to me. He was convinced that his sister had been preferred because of her superior intelligence.

In the analysis his leading defense was connected with the rationalization that he had liked what he had "heard" about my social and political outlook. He felt that similar views of life obtained and that therefore I could understand him better. He hence took it for granted, when he attacked various social institutions and discussed the motives of men in a competitive society, that we were in the fullest accord, even though he assumed that it was not my business to discuss these matters with him. Exercising his fine intelligence to the utmost, he wove intriguing polemics which had as their objective the engagement of my approval. When he realized that I did not participate in his fantasies, when from time to time I made brief comments and allusions which drove him from the course he had set, when he began to feel the personal implications of his generalizations about the social order, he reacted with an anxiety concealed by violent rage. When he resumed his intellectualizations, however, the attached affect reached a somewhat deeper level. He now began a devious discussion of personalized ethical problems. What are the "shoulds" and "musts" of conduct in relations to one's fellow men? What are one's prerogatives and what one's duties? Gradually, as the unconscious libidinal transference went deeper, he came to see that it was his purpose to gain some emotional commitment from me. Let me give an illustration.

For some hours the patient had been discussing the meaning of anxiety and had finally concluded that

Death as an idea is not frightening . . . it's the idea of annihilation . . . of being adrift . . . connected with feelings of frustration. . . . When a person faces death and accepts it there is an expansion of the personality . . . if I could do that, if I could feel that I was not very important in the schemes of things, I'd be sure of myself. It's when you feel that you have to do things about yourself . . . have to keep things under control, and can't, then you're afraid . . . a child is afraid of death and yet knows nothing about it. It is that the things he wants to preserve are the agents of life. It must be terrible when a child experiences a parent's anger. A child has to be sure of his folks. . . . A child doesn't know the whole social setup. All he knows is that he needs the protection of his parents. . . . The feeling is that someone has to stand by and protect you from something.

As my silence continued he went on more and more vehemently, until finally he burst out:

I'm getting sore, going around and around and not getting anywhere. I'm tired of this rationality. I'd like to let go and be goofy instead of reasonable for once. The trouble is, it's all so complex. But I don't seem to get much help. I need a little push, a little contribution!

At this point I interjected with the one syllable, "Boo!" My manner was joking, not sarcastic. The patient laughed with embarrassment. The next hour he brought the following transference dream:

*The patient jumps a traffic light as it is changing from yellow to green. He has the feeling that he was seen by the traffic cop and he pulls up to the curb. The policeman gives him a "talking to," although the patient tries to explain his way out of it. He is very angry.*

The associations to the dream made it explicitly clear that it came in reaction to the failure of the patient's sustained intellectualized effort to evoke an emotional response from the analyst without committing himself emotionally too far. He stated that when I had "booed" him, something had happened: it seemed to him that until then he had been trying to get away with something; only then had it dawned on him that he was "learning something in the analysis," something that he had not realized before, "something non-intellectual, nondeliberate." He confessed that he was becoming aware that his daily life had become less complicated, that he was becoming "more direct" with his wife and his employer. In his relationship to the analyst he now had the feeling that he had a right to know to what he was entitled. During the subsequent course of the analysis, finding himself again involved in one of his long perorations, he would often stop himself with the comment, "There goes the Philadelphia lawyer again."

Gradually the history of his defensive technique became clear. He is the second child and the first son in a sibship of five. Following him by one and a half years is the sister who has been previously mentioned. Then come two brothers, respectively four and seven years younger. The arrival of the younger sister seems to have been the occasion for an outbreak of severe anxiety. A screen memory that the patient associated with the day of the sister's birth, which occurred at home, represents him as cowering with fear while a violent electric storm rages outside; a window is smashed, and the rain pours into the patient's room.

The patient's memories of his mother have been fortuitously verified by another observer, making more certain the reconstruction of her personality. She was one of those false characters who play the great lady on a very slim margin. While maintaining an overt attitude of great refinement and delicacy, she was capable of violent outbursts of rage. It was her pride that she had never been seen nude by her husband, yet she saw no incongruity in discussing this fact with her young son. She made a great parade of virtue and human feeling which was palpably hypocritical. "The right kind of books" were stacked on her shelves unread while she made a show of knowledge on the basis of the blurbs on their jackets. She brought up her children with much serious and earnest discussion and appeals to reason. Anything that could be rationalized could be condoned. For years the patient had escaped punishment for a variety of hostile acts directed against the sister by resorting to an excuse which had once proven highly successful: he had "let fly" with a fork and his mother had accepted the grave explanation that his hand had "slipped."

Of great significance to the thesis was the fact that the mother's self-deluding character made it possible for the patient to indulge himself erotically with her from a very early age. Despite her prudish surface attitude she began the so-called sex education of her children as soon as they could understand anything at all. From the beginning the patient exploited this opportunity to engage her in devious but solemn discussions for which he would prepare himself by reading the books he knew she was using as a basis for her instruction. He told of an episode from his ninth year when he made an overnight trip with her. She had engaged a hotel room with a double bed. After they retired, he inveigled her into a discussion of sexual relations which appears to have greatly stimulated both of them, all of it thinly concealed by the same bland rationalizations that characterized the patient's chief analytical resistance. By way of such erotized intellectuality, he experienced the only emotional contact that he was aware of in his relationship with his mother. Hostility, as well as yearning for contact, were converted into an intellectualized pleasure activity. He recalled his delight in seeing her squirm before his unanswerable logic. His identification with the mother provided him with her own specious intellectuality as a tool to be used in his dealings with her: on the one hand to regain, at least in part, the contact which the birth of the sister had disrupted; on the other hand, to protect him against the anxiety attached to the possibility that his real longings for her might be thwarted and the consequent rage revealed.

The emotional pressure of adolescence proved too much for this defense. During puberty he became ill with mumps and developed a complicating orchitis. His mother nursed him with excessive tenderness. Subsequently the intellectual bouts with her ceased. He became averse to demonstrations of her sentimentalized maternal interest in him. He turned his attention to sports and other conventionally manly things. His associates were exclusively masculine. His depreciation of intellectuality appeared. He first planned to become an engineer, then a geologist. He finally became " a jack of all trades" and a periodic wanderer.

The analysis revealed his interest in the great outdoors and specifically in surveying and mining to be an expression of the repressed hostile curiosity about the body of his mother. *It was this interest which his childhood intellectual philandering with her had both expressed and defended him against.* His meeting with his wife had revived this intellectual defense. It was evoked once more in the affair on the frontier, leading him first to the abortive notion of becoming a writer and finally, out of competitiveness with his sister, to enter into analysis.

The following sequence from a later phase of the analysis demonstrates this formulation. For a time he had been referring to a timid but increasing sexual interest in a woman who had been flirting with him. During this period, he began again to contemplate a return to the frontier. Finally came an hour in which he became aware of how tempted he had been by his mother and how thwarted and fearful he had felt. In the next hour he reported a series of three dreams the last, of which he had forgotten. The first of these dreams referred in its latent content to the theme of the birth of the rival sister and the hostility this had engendered. Here is the second dream:

> I was playing with L's baby, trying to make him laugh, to get some response from him. Out of the corner of my eye I was watching for some sort of response from L. I had the feeling as if we were all in bed together.

The associations to this dream: the baby is the patient himself . . . the analyst's baby, maybe the patient's sister. The feelings were "maliciously calculating," like the feelings he had had about his mother. He had played with M's baby in the same way. [M was the woman with whom he had started the abortive affair on the frontier.] It's some kind of technique; he doesn't like the feeling; it cut him in on something. The night before he had been discussing his mother with his wife, and afterward he had felt funny. His wife had said that his mother was "on the make" for him because the last time the latter had visited them she had gone around in her underthings and been giggly. The last hour had made him feel that he had discovered something important: somehow he felt that he "had the goods" on his mother at last; his formerly vague feelings about her had been confirmed, and he felt relieved. The analyst had once said that his mother seemed to have led him around by the nose. It might be more correct to say that she had led him around by the penis. Now he has regained his self-respect. Last hour he felt somehow that he had been inadequate with her, but now that was over. "The tommyrot she got away with, that sainted mother of mine! There's a lot of relief in that feeling! Yet the feeling about playing with the baby in the dream is different from that: it's a feeling of wanting something and being afraid at the same time; a feeling of not being able to deliver and of avoiding a show-down. Maybe it doesn't all go way back."

At this point I commented, "I wouldn't be surprised."

The patient continued; "Maybe it's a different story today; maybe it has to do with the successful inter-course I had last night." The feeling connected with the second dream now seemed to him to be something sexually aggressive, as if he were about to swoop down on L. Suddenly the forgotten third dream came back to him.

Mary and Jack and my wife and I were riding in an open car like the one we owned when I was a kid. They were in front and my wife and I were in the back. I had a pea shooter that shot oval pellets. There were some birds at the roadside, and I was going to shoot at them. Mary said, "You mustn't shoot at those!" as if she were talking to a little boy. It was like a moral lecture. I said, "I want to and I'm going to!" with the feeling that it was strictly my own business. And I did shoot. I felt good that I did it without concern for the others.

In associating, the patient chuckled, "It's a sort of defiant gesture that I'm going to have sexual relations with several different women; it carries out the idea of here and now, not just talk. Mary and Jack are neighbors of yours. I connect them with you and your wife, and it's you I'm defiant of."

To which I said, "Let's try to understand that."

The patient continued, "The thing I felt good about was my self-assertion. After last hour I was in a good mood. I thought, By gosh, I'm going back to the frontier in spite of you!"

In connection with this last statement, it is important to remember that in the period preceding these dreams he had been talking about returning to the frontier after the analysis was over. Throughout the analysis he had placed in juxtaposition the feelings that city life and relationships with city people were too insincere, involved too much finagling, too much "beating around the bush," while the frontier was direct, honest, and simple. His resolve to return to the frontier had appeared previously in the analysis when he had recognized the connections of his rationalized indictment of "competitive society" with his own envy and competitiveness. When I subsequently suggested that a clearer understanding of his longing for the frontier life was needed, he interpreted this as disapproval of his wish to return there. He felt that I had an interest in winning him to an acceptance of civilized living.

It seems clear that for the patient the issue of civilization versus frontier was the issue of his original anxiety-ridden relationship with his mother—characterized by mutually defensive intellectualizations and circumlocutions—versus libidinal longings which in this phase of the analysis were becoming more direct and were coming more clearly into awareness. *He looked upon business—in which he is engaged—and intellectual activity as a circuitous and dishonest way of getting something that he wanted.* One finagled to take a man's money from him within the boundaries set by the law; or one engaged in intellectual activities to gain something in the way of approval or prestige because one was afraid to be quite direct about it. It was his feminine identification with his pseudo-intellectual mother that he thus depreciated. This had endangered his masculinity in the first place. The frontier again appeared to him as a haven from the danger connected with his real emotions. The basis of his fear is clearly alluded to in this series of dreams: the sibling rivalry and the erotized hostility toward the mother who produced the rivals. For the purposes of this essay, however, I wish to emphasize the longing for contact with the mother which was laden with fear and which was freed from fear only when buffered by the defensive intellectualizations, or when displaced to "nature" during his neurotic wanderings in search of "simplicity."

CASE 2

This patient was a 31-year-old male whose outstanding intelligence was more highly cultivated and exploited than that of the preceding patient. He had been reared with every social and educational advantage, and his erudition was extensive and genuinely profound. He entered analysis because of a work inhibition which threatened his career. He easily obtained profitable commissions, but then invariably neglected them. He was exhausted by real creative effort.

Five years before the treatment began the patient and the analyst had been socially acquainted. While he seemed to be friendly, he had never come emotionally close. Conversations with him tended to become one-sided, with the patient pre-empting all opportunities for speech. The earnestness and validity of his discourse only partly concealed its ostentation; and his intense, glib style seemed aimed to distract one from his underlying need to bind and control the listener. On several occasions the conversation had turned to psychoanalysis. At these times he had, for a while, listened attentively, but the last words had been his. Once in a general conversational group, with the patient holding forth on the general problems of the social sciences, I was rash enough to state rather unequivocally that "the hope of the social sciences lies in psychoanalysis." In the analysis he ultimately reminded me of that evening and confessed that from then on he had disliked me. It was then also that I learned how the patient had exploited his intellectual endowment in the service of his repressed libidinal and hostile aims. Capitalizing on the seductive value of his wide knowledge, his rich imagination, and his brilliant metaphors, he established an aura of considerable charm which secured him a circle of real friends and won him particular success in his affairs with certain types of women. At the same time, those who stirred his anxiety were likely to discover his talent for aggressive innuendo and polemic, a tendency which was often costly to him. His typical underlying tendencies were seen, however, in the instance of a platonic relationship with a motherly woman who had understood the emotional situation of the "bristling, intellectual porcupine" and had therefore been able to outlast his anxiety. Toward her he had gradually developed a dependent friendship, which was sustained by the fact that with her he was relatively simple and unpretentious, while she on her part cared for him as a "charming son" whose actual worth she knew and whose shenanigans might disturb her from time to time but did not take her in.

In the years subsequent to my original contact with him, I met the patient occasionally. He was conventionally cordial, but no more. Then, one day I encountered him again. With some hesitation he informed me that he had been thinking about an analysis and that a colleague—from whom he had been receiving psychotherapy, although he did not inform me of this—had recommended me. Would I care to undertake it? When I saw him in my study some days later, he did not sit down. He walked about the room smoking his pipe and talking continuously. From time to time, he stood over me and talked down to me as I sat in my chair. In this way, with his usual brilliance, he embarked on a self-analysis. Under the guise of seeming self-knowledge, in this very first interview he defended himself, as in the past, against the dangers of his passive emotional attitudes toward me. Finally, when I had said casually, "Do you really have to tower over me like that?" he subsided into a chair and with a wry smile replied that his "restlessness and insecurity" were other reasons that he wished to be analyzed.

The anamnesis which was obtained was quite sketchy because he was so discursive that anything like a complete history would have consumed many hours. His anamnestic style was distinctly reminiscent of his life style as I had previously known it, and I therefore dispensed with further preliminary interviews which would be exploited in this way. For the same reason I did not enter into a didactic discussion of free association or about the unconscious. He was, I knew, intellectually aware of these matters, and any recapitulation by me would have given him an explicit opportunity for their intellectual elaboration in the defense transference. It seemed better that he discover these things in the actual process of analysis. I informed him only of the trial period and specified only that he inform me of the occurrence of somatic experiences at the time of their emergence. Of the trial period I said that it was, in addition to being a diagnostic period, a period for our mutual appraisal of the analytical situation as a human relationship. For reasons which will be discussed in more detail later, I thought it best that he be aware from the beginning that analysis was not merely an intellectual discussion, but that an interpersonal relationship was involved and that there might be real limitations to even real interpersonal relationships.

At the beginning of the second hour, then, I asked the patient to lie down on the couch. He was naïvely surprised that it was expected that he use the couch, although he was aware of the convention. Was it necessary? Could "we not hold our conversations face to face"? [2] When he had taken his place on the couch he curled himself so that he could look at me and talk

---

[2] A question of technique arises here, the answer to which depends on the analyst's appraisal of the degree of anxiety. In this instance it was my impression that the patient's attitude was a maneuver and that it could be safely thwarted.

to me directly. His very first comment, then, was a question: Could I inform him of the "absolutely safest" contraceptive device? Now that he was in analysis it was more important than ever that there should be no pregnancies disrupting his affairs.

More important, at this time, than any possible deeper meaning of this seemingly naïve question was the fact that in it he was revealing his desire to obtain from me the intellectual wherewithal that would protect him against an actual awareness of his emotional attitudes. In short, he wanted to know how he could best protect himself against the feared relationship with the analyst and against the analysis. He had already attempted this in our first professional contact. It therefore seemed indicated to make an immediate interpretation, and I said to him, "Are you so determined as that to keep me from helping you to a new conception of yourself?" His rather shamed reply was that although he had for a long time known about and been interested in analysis, it was only quite recently that he had thought it applied to him. Then he complained of the difficulty of lying down. He could not be sure of himself. When I connected this with the fact that he seemed to be keeping me under surveillance by keeping his eyes on me, he confessed that he had had the feeling that I might hit him on the head. Then he recalled, first, my ancient comment about psychoanalysis as the "hope of the social sciences," and second, the way he had "towered" over me in the introductory interview. His need to control the situation intellectually thus became clear.

From this point his sessions assumed a definite pattern. He began each hour with a precise description of how he had been feeling in the interval, like a medical patient making the necessary reports on his symptoms to a physician. Then he became characteristically discursive. He described his travels; he quoted poetry in languages with which he knew I was unfamiliar; he made abstruse historical allusions; he expatiated on rare art objects—all this with the surface attitude that he took it for granted that common ground was being trod, while it was implicitly clear that he knew his advantage. In other words, he began the sessions with a bid for my benevolent interest and ended them by taking me for a ride.

Like their form, the content of his associations stemmed concomitantly from both aspects of the transference: the hostile intellectual defense and the passive libidinal wish. For example, in one hour he passed from a discussion of classical antiquity to a consideration of the Australian koala bear, which he designated by its taxonomic Latin name but which held its chief interest for him because of its peculiar way of eating and its popularity as a pet. Then, after a moment of silence he announced oratorically, "How sweet to be wrapped in the wings of Morpheus!" and proceeded to narrate the fable of the god Morpheus descending upon Palinurus and covering him with his wings to protect him against the dangers of a stormy sea. It is clear from this example that in his associative style there is condensed: first, the defensive hostile competitiveness of his proud erudition; second, the intention to capture my intellectual interest and thus seduce me into a clandestine satisfaction of his passive yearnings; and finally, in the actual content, by the technique of analogy to express the libidinal wish for love and protection as such. The substance of his technique was to attempt to gain my participation in an intellectual relationship which would indulge his libidinal needs without exposing him to the anxiety of a frank emotional tie. Indeed, it was not necessary for him to evoke any explicit responses from me. The fantasy itself, because it went on in my presence, was autoerotically satisfying to his passive longings.

Some hours later the patient turned to the possibility that an important older colleague and friend who was hostile to analysis would somehow become aware of the fact that he was under treatment. This friend had recently become a father. It became clear that the fear of discovery was delusional and really represented a wish to show the proud father that the patient did not need the relationship which the baby had usurped. This immediately led him to a review of the circumstances of his original contacts with me. He elaborated these into something more than they had actually been and complained that he had lost sight of me as the human being I had been then: a warm, real person. Now he had no genuine idea of me. I was unreal, just somebody who sat behind him. At the end of the hour, when he had risen, I stood before him and suggested that he take a good look at me. I did this for two reasons: first to debunk the omnipotent hostile defense fantasy; and second, to force an awareness of the emotional reality. The next day he brought the following dream, the first of the analysis:

The patient was in his native country, hanging around in a dreary and pretentious living room. He was ill at ease. The carpet kept tripping him up.

Mr. V. popped up. He was the same old show-off, talking in an ancient dialect to show that he was a man of letters. Mr. V. said: "I need to write a book in English and then my reputation is made." The patient responded: "I could write a book in English now, but it would do me no good. I am out of touch and I have no drag in my native land."

His associations were: Mr. V. was an associate at the university which the patient had attended at home. The way he popped up recalled how I had stood before the patient. Mr. V. was also the patient himself. The patient is collaborating on a book which he hopes will contribute to his reputation. The carpet was a rubber mat on the couch. The dream reminds the patient of how I had remained silent for so long and then forced him to face the reality of me yesterday. Finally, the patient confessed his strong feelings of conscious hostility for the analyst during the years preceding the analysis.

Let me review what has happened: The patient originally had suffered keenly at the birth of a younger sister who had come between him and his mother. In the analysis the patient's dependent emotional tension had been similarly stimulated by the fact that he envied the analyst's relationship to the patient's former psychotherapist. Finally, his envy of the place enjoyed by his friend's newborn child had further accentuated the longing to be exclusively loved and appreciated. In the analysis he defended himself against the overt appearance of these feelings for the analyst by recurring to the former intellectual relationship, which he now endowed with libidinal qualities it had not possessed. He thus displaced backward in time the cur-recently developing though concealed libidinal transfer-ence, and denied its existence in the present. The dream demonstrated the patient's unconscious insight into the nature of his chief defense. This insight was induced by the active technique which had been used the day before the dream occurred. In its manifest con-tent, which remained highly intellectual, he retaliated with a depreciatory attack on the analyst. The dream also showed that he was projecting his insight—Mr. V. is also the patient. However, in the typical unconscious dialogue with himself, he presented his awareness of the thwarting of his intellectual technique for obtain-ing clandestine emotional indulgence: "To write a book in English" is to be forthright with the analyst, but he is "out of touch" and he has "no drag."

The next hour showed how the libidinal transfer-ence had been uncovered. The patient brought another dream:

He went to his office. The mail brought a publish-er's letter insisting on material. The office was all upside down with carpentry, mason's work, plaster-ing, and painting. Even the floor was torn up. There was pleasure in reading the letter.

His associations were spontaneous: Yesterday afternoon he had met an old friend for cocktails. This friend had broken away from him a year ago because he had not offered her a complete enough relationship. At the time he had been very angry at her, but could not really blame her now. He speaks of his eyes being sore and of a peculiar feeling in his feet. He has the thought that he would like to elicit the physician in me. He really does not know yet what goes on between the doctor and patient. He finds fear of the unknown in it. His head suddenly feels "fuzzy," and for a few minutes he has no thoughts. Some time ago he had elicited an invitation from a publisher to write a certain essay; but in his usual way, having obtained the assignment, he had let it slide. This morning he had awakened with the determination to go to work on it. There is so much to do. He has been wasting so much time, except for coming to the analytical hour. The analysis is a process of education that he could not get from books. He had had the impulse to get a cup of coffee before coming to the hour, but had restrained it. It would have put him on his guard, and, for once, he would like to be in the open. He thinks he is progressing. Yesterday he had a different feeling toward the people at the university; the idea being, "They can talk what they want to, but I'm getting the real thing." He looks at a portrait of Freud and comments that he had heard that Freud had been a mean man to deal with. This had contributed to his own fear of analysis. People do not seem to realize that the very fact that an analyst understands also implies that he accepts the things that are human. He used to think of analysis as a confession and the receiving of advice, as was the case in the traveling clinics of his native country. Now he sees that it involves his whole life. He describes his excitement and insomnia over the prospect of finally visiting a certain foreign city for which he had long yearned, and how, upon arrival, the obsessive words kept running through his mind, "I am here at last; I am here at last!" A similar feeling has developed in the analysis. It is elation similar to that felt when he was exploring still another city at night and unexpectedly stumbled on a church about which he had read and fantasied, but had never expected to see.

This dream was not interpreted to the patient for the reason that the associations made it clear enough that he was working in the newly uncovered libidinal transference. It seemed best to allow him the experience of it for the sake of the security he needed. There seemed no doubt that the dream was a reaction to the analytical work of the preceding hour. The manifest dream showed this clearly. The patient can dispense with the intellectual defense *to some degree* because of his insight and, furthermore, because the interpretation of it has enabled him to approach a little closer to the defended layers. The new defense which emerged in this hour, the passive submissive masochistic surrender to the analyst as doctor, was at a considerable deeper level and was much more directly connected with the libido and its historical vicissitudes. In subsequent hours, it took the form of fantasies of being operated on by me and of having an abdominal zipper which could be pulled open to reveal the very depths of his "dirty soul." It is significant that it was in this phase of the analysis that he began to talk about his family and about his interpersonal relations with its members.

Because it is not germane to the questions which are dealt with in this essay, there will be no elaboration of the libidinal problem as such. It is, however, necessary to see an example of the connections between the defense transference and the libidinal transference as revealed in one sequence of the analysis:

The patient has been talking about his relationship with a girl with whom he is currently intimate. She is an intellectually complex person who has accepted him at his face value. He is afraid he may lose her. During the preceding two weeks he has had a strange feeling of nostalgia, as though he had cut himself off from something. The fear of losing the girl is somehow connected with this. He has a longing for an attachment, yet he feels nothing to grasp here, although, obviously the analyst is interested in him or he would not be here now. But something separates him from the analyst. The common expression for guilt—dirty conscience—comes to mind. It is very apt. He does not feel straight toward me. He has the thought, "Isn't Doctor G. having difficulties in creeping into me or breaking me down?"

I say, "Perhaps the opposite is what you mean?"

The patient, for the first time in quite a number of hours, begins to create fantasies about colors and landscapes.

I ask, "What's behind the backdrop?"

The patient's response is immediate: Yesterday he had a new idea for a book he would write if the analysis was successful. It would contrast various cultures in terms of their mythologies and religions. For example, the Jews had had their fantasies taken away from them, and the result had been the emergence of Judaism, an unhappy religion of guilt.

The patient is disturbed by my suggestion. He does not like to think of the psychogenesis of ideas. Now he feels blocked and confused. Suddenly he says, "I seldom think of you outside of the hours."

I ask him, "What do you make of that?"

The patient replies, "I don't want to make anything out of it." Then he proceeds to speak of a Byzantine church with a beautiful cloister, to which, in the past, he used to retreat regularly during what he called his cloister hour. He ends the session saying, "What I am saying makes no sense to me but it does to you. If the analysis should end now I would come back a psychotic instead of a neurotic."

It seems clear that the idea for the book was an epitome of the development of the transference as evidenced in the hour just cited. If he gave up his intellectual delusional system he had to confront his real feelings. His nostalgia was for the precarious security of the intellectual character defense represented by his relationship with the girl and reflected in the defense transference. The weakening of this defense had permitted the libidinal transference to emerge, and the idea for the book is a bulwark against this. When this new defense is threatened by my remark, he reacts with anxiety and another regressive intellectual fantasy, as is evidenced by his last statement, despite its histrionic character. Only in "insanity" could he expect to express his deeper emotions and hope to get away with it. He would thus be "crazy" to give up his intellectual defense. The analysis had already damaged, although not destroyed, the intellectual syphon with which he had been able clandestinely to gratify his dependent needs. At the same time, the as yet unanalyzed hostile tendencies made the libidinal transference ambivalent, and therefore brought him in danger of being rejected by the analyst. It was the depth of the anxiety attached to the libidinal transference which made it difficult for the patient to give up his character defense. The character defense was at least a well-tested compromise solution.

## THEORY

In the preliminary discussion of the biological and interpersonal fate of the libidinal and hostile tendencies, an attempt was made to show their gradual assimilation into the ego system so as to both satisfy the instinctual tendencies and preserve the experiencing ego from anxiety. This is, in itself, only a description of the normal adaptive process out of which character develops. The difference between the more or less normal character and the neurotic characters just described is a difference which is determined by how two questions are answered: How much intellectual sublimation has occurred. How much is the person continuing to seek indirect gratification of persistent infantile needs?

In the normal person, one may see a more or less stable system of satisfying interpersonal relations and developed intellectual talents among which emotional energy is shared. In such a situation, mental capacity has its own proper value to the person. It finds its place as such in those peripheral interpersonal relations which normally have minimal emotional importance. It protects the person against anxiety in these relations by the fact that the instinctual tendencies which may be aroused are, in their sublimated form, reality-oriented, and thus are capable of actual mastery of the external source of danger.

The neurotic intellectual, on the contrary, has

flooded his intellectual talent with emotional energy, while its discharge through direct interpersonal relations has been reduced. Whether it is a central person or a peripheral surrogate for a central person, he deals with the interpersonal situation in the same way: if his intelligence is not inhibited together with the emotional energy which could make it effective, he uses it in such a way as to avoid actual emotional contact while securing indirect emotional gratification. Intellectuality thus exercised not only fails to attain its own creative possibilities but also fails to provide real emotional gratification. The fatigue which attaches to its exercise is evidence of this.

Through the accidents of differences in endowment, education, and cultural experience, the two persons I have described appear to have a surface dissimilarity. One had only his peculiar mother with her false philosophizing and ethics as a basis for his clever rationalizations. The other had all the resources of a refined and sophisticated milieu and the benefits of contact with really first class minds. Dynamically, however, they had one thing in common. Both drew upon authoritarian figures with whom they had identified through hostility. Both used as shields in the defense transference ideas that did not really belong to them and that, if worse came to worse, they could sacrifice without injury to themselves.

Thus, at the same time that the first patient was aping his mother's assumed social philosophy, he rationalized, outside of the analysis, his use of scab labor in the work in his factory.

At the same time that the second patient was impressing me with his brilliant self-analysis, he was forgetting to inform me of the series of psychotherapeutic interviews in which he had acquired such an understanding of himself.

This use of borrowed intellectual resources—borrowing they may no more acknowledge to themselves than to others—accounts further for the fact that such persons fail to obtain that degree of actual gratification from the active exercise of their talent that one would expect on the evidence of its overt manifestations. This was seen particularly in the second patient. It was seldom that he got a real "kick" out of his writing. More often it was a burden which he seized every opportunity to escape from.

Only in that exercise of his intellect which involved immediate verbalization in the presence of others was gratification generally experienced. How this operated autistically in his character defense and in his defense transference in the service of his passive wishes has been seen.

The intellectuality of both patients was further characterized, as illustrated, by its tendentiousness. While cleverly pretending to be concerned with a subject, they revealed themselves, on closer scrutiny, to be interested only in themselves. The "psychogenesis of ideas," as a special case of this aspect of the intellectual character defense, was pointedly brought out in that hour of the second patient's analysis in which his idea for a book on mythology, religion, and culture was seen to spring from the dilemma in which he found himself at that time, when his intellectual defense was undermined and his instinctual tendencies were still hampered by fear and guilt. As such, the idea was born primarily as a defense and not as a creative thought. In this connection, it is also interesting that he used to complain that his academic colleagues objected to considering the possibility of ideas as symptoms, and he would accuse them of rejecting this notion out of their own fear of personal exposure.

The intellectual defense seems particularly vulnerable before an increased emotional cathexis of its object. Thus, the first patient gave up this defense and became a so-called "man of action" under the increased pressure of the pubertal libido and his mother's seductiveness at that time. The second patient, with all his sophistication and actual awareness, became a naïve child under the influence of the surge of passively oriented libido when he was asked to lie down on the couch. In both patients the tendency of the defense to weaken before a direct approach to the emotions was seen in their prompt responses to the active technique. This does not mean, however, that one may indiscriminately deflate intellectualization by actively forcing an emotional contact. Nor does it mean that this defense, once breeched, is thereafter abandoned by the patient.

The character defense is a phenomenon of the person's general life relationships, while the defense transference is a phenomenon of the special interpersonal relations in psychoanalysis. But the latter can be seen to be a special manifestation of the former. Despite his best intentions, the patient attempts to accomplish in his relationship to the analyst the same things that he has accomplished in the world at large. In this attempt he follows the pattern he has hitherto found more or less successful. How the more or less normal person tends to progress of himself from peripheral intellectual relations toward more direct emotional contacts has been noted. For such a person, this is possible because he has more or less mastered the previous vicissitudes of his emotional development. The neurotic has failed in this respect. How neurotic characters with an intellectual defense tend to remain emotionally stranded and how they try to make the most of their intellectuality to relieve their emotional isolation has also been seen.

It is the task of analysis to enable such persons to progress from peripheral to real emotional contact in an experimentally limited interpersonal situation—the patient-analyst relationship—so that, on the basis of this special, controlled experience, they are able to accomplish in the world at large what the more or less normal do without help. This is not simply a matter of reductive analysis, but also one of concomitant re-education.

Anna Freud has emphasized the necessity for the synchronous analysis of both the libidinal and the defense transference. But with reference to the therapeutic task here considered, *the management of the defense transference must include active aid to the patient in the testing of the interpersonal reality.* Freud (1917) has stated:

> Let us, furthermore, bear in mind the great practical importance of distinguishing perceptions from ideas, however intensely recalled. Our whole relation to the external world, to reality, depends on our ability to do so. We have put forward the fiction that we did not always possess this ability and that at the beginning of our mental life we did in fact hal-

lucinate the satisfying object when we felt the need for it. But in such a situation satisfaction did not occur, and this failure must very soon have moved us to create some contrivance with the help of which it was possible to distinguish such wishful perceptions from a real fulfillment and to avoid them for the future. In other words, we gave up hallucinatory satisfaction of our wishes at a very early period and set up a kind of 'reality-testing' [p. 231].

Furthermore, it is also from Freud that the classical rule is derived that analysis must be conducted in the state of abstention. This rule is generally understood to emphasize libidinal abstention. It would appear, however, that in the case of the narcissistic neuroses, at least, this emphasis needs to be shifted. While there is no doubt that emotional gratification must be judiciously dosed in the interest of maintaining an optimal degree of pressure from the unconscious, it must nevertheless be recognized that this is quite different in its implications from "withholding."

As shown by the first example, the advantage of the defense technique for the patient rested on the fact that his previous experience had not comprised a direct libidinal relationship with his mother. His defense had served to obtain for him a measure of muffled contact. Consequently it was highly valued, since he had had good reason to doubt his prospects for a more genuine relationship.

The point is that the psychoanalytic situation had to offer the patient the opportunity of sampling a real libidinal object relationship so that the delusional object relationship via the defense could be profitably surrendered. There is no other good reason for any such patient to relinquish even the precarious security and diluted satisfactions of his neurotic intellectuality.

Returning now to the principle enunciated by Freud in the above citation, it may be seen that the emphasis on "abstention" must shift to a systematic thwarting of the patient's delusional gratifications in the defense technique. By producing a failure of the technique to gain its ends, while concomitantly demonstrating in the interpersonal relations with the analyst the possibility of a genuine although reality-limited object relationship, there is recapitulated in the therapeutic situation what Freud has said obtains in normal development, namely: "a kind of reality testing." This has been demonstrated in the examples of technique employed in the cases presented here.

When I jokingly "booed" my first patient I was accomplishing simultaneously a number of things: the monosyllabic response was a thwarting of the surface demand for gratification with words and ideas, while the friendly joking manner acknowledged the deeper libidinal longing and at the same time invited the normal nucleus of the patient's ego into collaboration with the work of the analysis. The policeman dream that followed presented not only the reactive anger but also insight. The dream is the product of the self-critical tendencies connected with originally stigmatized emotions. But with reference to the current analytical situation, it is not really self-punitive. The patient received only a "talking-to," not a "ticket." And he had a "go ahead" signal.

When I stood before my second patient I was in effect saying to him, by way of his unconscious, "Here is the real person whom you formerly actually did not know. Here is a real relationship with him which you formerly did not have."

In both instances, I was frustrating indirect libidinal and hostile gratification through the defense and opening the way for the direct libidinal relationship toward which the patient must be helped.

As I have already said, the tactics I used in these instances are not general techniques as such. The actual procedures of the analyst will vary in their conservatism or boldness, depending on his appraisal of the degree of anxiety the patient can tolerate in a given moment of the analysis.

Conservatism needs to be observed when the libidinal development of the patient is known to have been especially anxiety-ridden; or while the libidinal transference is not yet trusted by the patient; or while the analyst is as yet uncertain of his countertransference, and correspondingly overcautious of his own emotions. The precise character of the technique will also depend on the analyst's particular art. The latter is strictly personal; but the general principle remains the same. What the analyst does and says in those phases of the analysis in which the defense transference is in the ascendency is aimed at explicitly thwarting the aim and uncovering the technique of the defense while implicitly helping the patient to acknowledge the libidinal transference and to move toward its analysis.

Again, as I have indicated previously, the tenacity of the defense tranference will vary in general with the biological and experiential factors, the latter being closely connected with the vicissitudes of the libidinal development. In the analytic situation the persistence or recurrence of the defense transference will depend on the vicissitudes of the libidinal transference. But in addition to recapitulating the emotional vicissitudes of the past, the analytic situation inevitably introduces additional ones. Errors of technique and judgment are among the less serious of these. The point is that the patient seems to be able to tolerate fallibility if it is benign. What the patient cannot tolerate, unless exploited in a neurosis in which masochism is a leading factor, are those disabilities of the analyst which stem from the unanalyzed aspects of the countertransference. Thus, analysis cannot be conducted in the presence of a more or less total negative transference based on a patient's too complete identification with pathogenic figures of the past. This is true for the analyst as well as the patient. The result may easily be an impasse in the treatment in which patient or analyst is bogged down in his respective character defenses.

But more pertinent to the thesis is the problem of the intellectual penchants of the analyst. In this connection, I refer again to the extra-analytical uses of the intellectual character defense as I have already discussed them and their recapitulation in the defense transference. It is a particularly important technical problem to avoid the pitfalls of a countertransference which plays into the intellectual defense transference of the patient by being itself too intellectual even though psychoanalytic. The purposes of analysis cannot be served if unwittingly the analyst and the patient find themselves too much kindred in "intellectual spirit." These are the general principles which led me to begin the analysis of the second patient as I did, although I had particular reason to avail myself of them in the light of my preanalytical experience with him.

# Character Synthesis:
# The Psychotherapeutic Problem
# of Adolescence

## (1948)

---

MY PURPOSE in this paper is to review the problem of psychotherapy during adolescence from the standpoint of the central importance of the ego ideal in the integration of the adolescent. On this basis I shall attempt to describe the task and the role of the psychotherapist.

Clearly, there is a problem on the side of the psychiatrist which must be considered. While this is true regarding all psychotherapy, it is particularly true in psychotherapy of the adolescent. An adult treating another adult has the emotional distance appropriate to the equality of the social relationship and the emotional closeness befitting his status as an accepted helper. In treating a child, the psychiatrist has the emotional position of the understanding and benign parent. In both of these situations there is relative certainty in the relationship and adequate buffering of

---

*Editorial note:* One of the earliest papers on adolescents, "Character Synthesis" has been cited steadily over the past 25 years, perhaps because the advisability and efficacy of psychoanalysis for adolescents are still being questioned.

the most primitive impulses. In both situations the therapist is secure in the feeling tones and outlook of his own generation. The adult treating the adolescent has no such firm ground from which to make his therapeutic efforts. The patient brings little that clearly resembles even his own adolescence. Recent studies by educators have shown that the adolescent's social patterns and values are largely determined by his own group and by his imitation of slightly older adolescents. His relevant adults are kept at arm's length, and only partly contribute to these patterns and values. The result is decreasing knowledge and understanding of him by the adult (Tryon, 1944). In psychiatric terms this means that the psychotherapeutic difficulty is likely to be found in precisely that most delicate aspect of the therapist's equipment—his capacity for empathy with the patient.

Another aspect of this problem is glimpsed by scanning existing therapeutic procedures. For there has been a tendency to shy away from the direct psychotherapy of adolescents. Emphasis has been placed on practical help, steering, environmental manipulation (Church, 1946), and group activity (Valentine, 1943). As a compromise with this inclination to keep the patient at therapeutic arm's length are the familiar prescriptions for interim "suggestive therapy" and, more recently, "group therapy" (Axelrod, 1944; Gabriel, 1944; Janvier, 1943).

Each of these techniques may have its theoretical and practical validity in particular cases and situations. Each, however, may also express a defensive maneuver of the therapist himself, either because of his participation in the adolescent patient's resurgent primitive anxiety, or because of a threat to his own emotional economy.[1] No experienced therapist will deny that he has his own particular limits of tolerance for empathically perceived anxiety. Nor will he in honesty deny that he requires and obtains a measurable if controlled emotional increment from his patient's relationship to him. The emotionally self-centered adolescent, bombarded by anxiety and with his psychic structure demobilized, puts the psychic integrity of the therapist to its severest test.

All of which leads to the consideration that a particular kind of empathic capacity may be needed to deal with the problems of the adolescent. It may also be that it takes particular and different kinds of adults to treat particular and different kinds of adolescents.

As Anna Freud (1936) has shown, the adolescent does not employ the defensive mechanisms in the same ways in which the neurotic employs them to cope discriminatively with particular primitive impulses. Instead there is a massive reaction against all such impulses. This may eventuate in the typical adolescent asceticism, in which case we have the "good adolescent." Or we may witness the envelopment of the instincts by the individual's value system. This may be an intellectual or an action system, or some mixture of both. In either instance we then have the "typical adolescent."

Various therapists have commented on the special difficulties which are encountered in making contact with these patients in interview situations. A number

---

[1] The "pure fantasy" of childhood becomes realizable during adolescence. A 16-year-old, speaking of his father, told the author, "It frightens me that I could now really kill him—a weak little man."

of auxiliary devices have been tried in coping with the problem. Gardner and Wollan (1941) have used what they call the "activity-interview." Delinquent boys were studied through contact and association with them in organized activity groups, as well as in person-to-person interviews which resulted in "more natural and easy rapport." Curran (1939, 1940) has used similar techniques at Bellevue, including dramatics and group discussions. In a Boys' Club situation Martin (1939) has used the device of educating various personnel to avoid the duplication of the attitudes of the parents of the particular boy and to exercise emotionally corrective attitudes fitted to his needs.

Others have focused their attention more specifically on the person-to-person problem which chiefly concerns us here. Topping (1943), discussing the treatment of the pseudosocial boy, emphasized that "the major difficulty is in establishing rapport," and stated that "one has to get into them by knowledge of their lingo, their outlook and their associates. Familiarity with this particular outlook and "tricks or grooves of thinking" can ultimately be used to meet the patient on his own ground and treat him on his own terms. The therapy should seek to utilize adaptive capacities and not to uncover what the author calls "deep-seated conflicts" or to develop insight in the intellectual sense. The therapy needs to be actively sustained by the therapist and must be geared to the patient's need to be understood and accepted from his own point of view.

Eisner (1945), in a study of a sexually delinquent adolescent girl, demonstrated the efficacy of conducting therapy on the terms established by the patient. He carefully avoided so-called dynamic interpretations, placed no emphasis on the patient's compliance with his views, and dealt wholly with the current attitudes as they expressed themselves in the treatment relationship and in the terms in which they appeared. Despite the surface appearance of going all the way with the patient, it is clear that Eisner never permitted the patient to lose sight of the fact that he knew what the real emotional issues were, and that he was secure in his own position.

Mitchell (1944) has similarly seen the necessity for establishing the meaning of the therapeutic relationship on a basis natural to the emotional situation and outlook of the adolescent, while at the same time maintaining unequivocal control.

Blos (1946), writing about college students, states that "ego inadequacy" is the object of his therapeutic effort and "not the infantile conflict." He also emphasizes that the therapist must avoid in his attitudes to the patient a repetition of the parental pattern. He ascribes two characteristic "ego reactions" to the "maturational conflict" of adolescence: "ego restriction" or functional inhibition, and "ego regression." The latter is seen in the reappearance, in sophisticated form, of archaic, magical techniques of mastery and gratification. It is toward these reactions that Blos directs his therapy.

These therapeutic techniques and points of view have one thing in common. All of them are focused on the ego or self-system of the patient; all of them implicitly recognize a qualitative difference in this system from that of the adult; and all of them attempt to make a correction for this difference. Substantially, this amounts to the assumption on the therapist's part of participating responsibility for the purpose of eking out a psychic lack in the patient.

We are reminded by this that psychoanalysts have tended to be cautious about analyzing adolescents. Some have felt that analysis should not be attempted, and the fact is that very few adolescents have been analyzed. From the standpoint of classical analysis, which is best applied to neuroses based on the existence of an organized personality capable of real transference, this position has been justified. But the progress of psychoanalysis has been in the direction of a greater understanding of ego development and function. In the therapy of the narcissistic and so-called borderline cases, which are quite similar to those of adolescence, some analysts are beginning to find it possible to close the emotional gap resulting from the limited transference capacity of the patients (Stern, 1945; Gitelson, 1944). It is in these cases that the "countertransference" in the sense of counteridentification and empathy is of critical importance. The emotional attitude of such patients to the therapist is not merely a repetition of the past. It is real and in the here and now. The therapist must be capable of standing the test of that fact. He must be able to feel and understand how the patient actually sees him rather than how the patient's past is imputed to him.

Considering the psychotherapeutic problems of adolescence from this point of view, it can be said that the therapeutic task is not one of *psychic analysis* but rather of *character synthesis*. If we examine the psychological facts of adolescence (A. Freud, 1936) the reason for this becomes clear.

The adolescent is altruistic and egocentric, devoted and unfaithful, gregarious and solitary, blindly submissive to a leader and defiant of authority, idealistic and cynical, sensitive and callous, ascetic and libertine, optimistic and pessimistic, enthusiastic and indifferent. These oscillations are manifestations of the variable balance maintained between the ego and the primitive impulses which exacerbate at puberty. During early childhood, emotional attachment to and dependence on the parents results in the acceptance of their authority as an undeniable external reality. Ultimately, this authority becomes established as an internal psychic factor which sustains the person in the management of his instincts. In contrast, the adolescent finds himself psychically on his own. The emancipatory strivings which separate him from family figures and their surrogates overreach their developmental purpose and also alienate him from the internalized representations of parental control and parental example.

The typical defenses of the adolescent are of a primitive type which recapitulate those of early childhood before the critical-controlling functions of the personality have become established. These include the magic of thought and act and also, conspicuously, the magic of identification. The latter operates as a means of borrowing, without acknowledgement and without discrimination or assimilation, the strength of those who appear strong. The surface similarity of psychopathic behavior and the behavior of adolescents is due to such ego defenses, which, in the adult, result in the "as if" pseudo personality (Foxe, 1944; Greenacre, 1945). It is as though the adolescent, having arrived at a final disillusionment in the parental ideal, will not again let himself in for such an injury to his sense of security and his self-esteem. The transient identifications which characterize even normal adolescents thus appear to be a constant flight from disillusionment and a constant quest for certainty.

All who work with adolescents have noted some of these specific qualities in their patients. In the Maritime Service during the recent war, it was found that 16- and 17-year-old volunteers were "immature . . . insecure . . . hedonistic . . . intolerant of discipline." They denied or concealed weakness or inadequacy. They formed shallow contacts with their superiors and each other, and were deficient in their capacity for self-criticism and self-control (Marmor, 1945). Case workers have found that adolescents with problems form weak, vacillating, and superficial relationships, yet show a need for acceptance by the adult and at times use an authoritarian relationship as a protection against situations that might lead to delinquency (Beres et al., 1946). Among delinquents in general, conscience and guilt are found not to operate as they do in the latency-period child or in the adult. (Powdermaker et al., 1937). Bromberg, commenting on this fact, considers it inaccurate to speak of the superego of the adolescent as weak or deficient. Rather it is "formless" and "confused . . . because the ego-ideal in early life was confused" (Bromberg & Rogers, 1946).

Hacker and Geleerd (1945) have discussed these problems with respect to the need for an authoritarian milieu in the treatment of more serious cases. They have shown that the adolescent's excessive desire for freedom is quite different from the normal development of the need to be emancipated from family ties. As previously indicated, the process of emancipation overreaches its developmental utility. Not only does it turn the adolescent against the existing and actual controlling relationships but also against the internalized controls which are derived from them. Lacking these, the adolescent finds himself the victim of unbuffered drives. His demand for freedom thus becomes a denial of vulnerability which he feels consciously or unconsciously.

These characteristics of adolescence also define the therapeutic task of those who undertake to work with the problems of the adolescent. The therapist and the therapeutic situation must provide concomitantly, and in nice balance, dependable relationship and emotional freedom, dependent security and developmental stimulation, control and ego ideal.

The literature of the last 10 years shows increasing recognition of such needs. Psychiatrists and case workers acknowledge that the intelligent use of authority, as a means of providing both security and protective control, has a valid place in the therapeutic scheme (Berkman et al., 1939; Bromberg & Rogers, 1946; Hacker & Geleerd, 1945; McDonald, 1938; Slawson, 1938). On the other hand, those who are concerned with institutional cases emphasize the importance of individualization within the general authoritarian set-up (Drewry, 1939; Grossman, 1938; Jenkins, 1941; Topping, 1943). While the formulations of this provision are quite general, its implications are clear; in the therapuetic relationship of the patient with a selected member of the staff, whether it be doctor, case worker, or cottage supervisor, he must find a positive opportunity for growth through empathy, identification, and emotional tie.

It is now possible to discuss more explicitly the dynamics of the person-to-person situation in psychotherapy of the adolescent and consider in more detail the problems of this situation from the standpoint of the therapist.

The patient comes to us in a state of alienation from his parents and from the internalized sanctions and ideals which have been derived from them. Besides this, we may find him in one of several possible positions with regard to his own impulses and emotional tendencies. He may massively have separated himself from them and present a picture of inhibition; he may have entered upon a "schizoid maneuver" (Silverberg, 1947) and "be directing his efforts not towards adapting himself to life but to making life look as if it were adapting itself to him" (Yellowlees, 1940), or he may be ventilating his tensions with the validation and support of a rebellious or delinquent peer group.

The patient comes to us with the same defensive facade as the one he has erected against the parents and their surrogates. He has no a priori reason to expect anything different from us than from those who precede us (Gitelson, 1944; Kilpatrick, 1945). The first test of the therapist is found in his capacity to tolerate this distrust without recourse to self-defensive seduction or sympathy-determined identification. Johnson and Fishback (1944) have stated that "intensive or psychoanalytic therapy of the disturbed adolescent is highly dangerous, not so much because of the strength of the child's instincts and immaturity of ego, but because [the patient] may be the channel through which the parent achieves, unconsciously, [his] own forbidden and thwarted impulses" (p. 202). From the standpoint of the countertransference with which we are concerned, there is the further fact of danger that the adult may also be "channeled" by the impulses of the child. That this is not a needless warning will be verified by all whose therapeutic experience extends far enough back into their own precarious young adulthood. It will not be hard for them to recall siding against the parent in the adolescent's valiant struggle for his so-called freedom, and its futility. On the other hand, to be on the side of the parents is also manifestly futile.

What is the possible alternative in this crucial situation? This returns us to the problem of empathy. Webster (1947) states empathy to be "an imaginative projection of one's own consciousness into another human being." Imagination is characterized by the personality of the one who imagines. The dictionary definition refers to this fact with the phrase "one's own consciousness." In more relevant psychiatric terms, it is possible to say that *empathy is the sensitive perception of another person's state of emotional structure and balance on the basis of the awareness of one's own; and that empathy is interpersonal and requires the vehicle of common language, both verbal and nonverbal, if it is to carry over to (be "projected" into) the other person. This is the real meaning of that much misused word, "contact."* In the sense of this discussion, this meaning comprises comparable experience, comparable anxiety, and comparable emotional directions and tendencies that are mutually sensed but that the therapist has mastered.

The importance of this rests on the fact previously stated: The adolescent is emotionally alienated from all but his developmental peers. And even with them, his relationships have a tenuous quality, being largely self-centered, with only episodic deeper phases. This creates the salient problem in the establishment of a therapeutic relationship. The therapist must succeed in making and maintaining what is substantially a *narcissistic contact* which will enable him to engage the patient more deeply during exacerbations of emotions and attitudes which are really interpersonal (Gitelson, 1942a).

This is the empathic problem. This is why it may be that only particular adults can be therapeutically effective with particular types of adolescents. The psychoanalyst can rely on the universal qualities of his own unconscious as a frame of reference for what goes on between himself and his patient. For those who work with adolescents, the problem is complicated by the fact that the ego of each is the distinct, product of a particular total life experience. This limits the kind of interpersonal adaptation each is capable of. The type of patients each can work with may therefore be limited by his own type of personality.[2]

All this has an intimate connection with the estab-

[2] The author has successfully treated a number of intellectualizing and inhibited adolescents and has failed with the rebellious and delinquent types. Others who have worked with him have been successful with patients whose treatment would have been hopeless in his hands. The psychological principles involved were the same, and the several therapists could understand each other's work. But they could not exchange their therapeutic jobs.

lishment of identification, the reformation of the ego ideal and the final consolidation and reinstatement of the self-regulatory principle which we know as the superego (Flugel, 1945). If we refer again to the picture of psychopathic behavior (Foxe, 1944; Greenacre, 1945), we see that it reflects the failure of the patient to compare himself favorably with that image of himself which his parents have compelled him to adopt. The feelings of inferiority which are characteristic of adolescents indicate that a similar attitude toward the self is present in them. Their sense of disillusionment is connected with not only the dethronement of the parental ideal but with the failure to reach the compensatory goals with which these ideals have been replaced. The paramount importance of the peer group and its subculture (Tryon, 1944) is derived from the fact that it gives the adolescent a chance to recover and preserve his self-regard. He will not easily give up even this tenuous security, or, on the other hand, the security of an ego-restrictive withdrawal, for the prospect of reinstating the old sense of failure in a dubious relationship with even a well-intentioned adult.

Redl (personal communication) has used the concept "optimum distance" to designate the personality differences which can exist among individuals in an equilibrated therapeutic group. From the standpoint of the adolescent and his therapist, we might validly speak of the "optimum ego distance" which would make therapeutic empathy possible. This would consist of that degree of similarity which would make *contact* possible, and together with this—on the part of the therapist—that bearable difference in the direction of integrated emotional mastery which can support the patient and yet encourage him in his own prospects. If this can be established, then the rest follows. While the ego of the adolescent has a much wider range of possible action than does that of the pregenital child, the problems of mastery are substantially the same. His hope of mastery rests on the example of those who have mastered similar problems (Orgel, 1941).[3] The adolescent tends to pattern himself after next older adolescents (Tryon, 1944). Given "optimum ego distance," he will do likewise with his therapist. The therapist thus becomes the model for his ego ideal. *The patient's guiding fantasy becomes not merely what he would be, but, most important, what he can be.*

Nearly all those who write on the direct psychotherapy of the adolescent, stress the importance of a strong, emotionally dependent relationship.[4] This is true if it is qualified in terms of the psychological position of the adolescent. He suffers from a sense of helplessness and inadequacy in the face of biological impulsions toward growth and independence. As has been shown, his self-regard is already highly vulnerable. He comes to us already in a state of defense against this vulnerability. Only the acceptance of the therapist as an ego ideal can overcome this. He must

[3] Oberndorf, in his discussion of Orgel's paper on *Identification as a Socializing and Therapeutic Force* (1941), said, "It appears to be far easier for the child to attain the pattern of one whose physical and mental development is only advanced a year or two beyond that age which [he himself] has attained. Good models of their own age are necessary as objects for identification for all children, no matter what their proclivities may be" (pp. 124–125). Oberndorf notes that where deviants receive psychotherapy, the auxiliary models are a great help.

[4] Some even speak of a dependent regression. While this may confront us as a clinical fact that must be accepted and dealt with appropriately (Gitelson, 1942a), it is questionable whether it should be fostered as such for therapeutic purposes.

offer the patient a ladder to maturity and a confident helping hand when necessary. *The therapeutic situation needs to be dependable rather than dependent.* The various references that occur in the literature regarding the necessity for an authoritative attitude or milieu in the treatment of adolescent problems have meaning only in this sense.

Character has been defined as that which "determines the cohesive unity of the personality so that the individual can maintain his optimum level of integration." It is the "supreme gradient" of personality, the finality of its long development. A crisis in the life of the person will first of all breach his character (Michaels, 1946). Adolescence is such a crisis. But because it is a developmental crisis, we see its effects not only in the disruption of the previous character structure. The potentialities of an unfinished development are also endangered. That is why the treatment of the adolescent cannot merely be directed toward providing a more benign re-experience of his past. The stigmatic factors in that past may in any case make this more or less impossible. On the contrary, treatment must provide the adolescent with a new emotional experience. In the more fortunate instances, a benign parental influence may in part survive and enter into the formation of the new ego ideal. In many less fortunate instances an entirely new beginning will be required.

Treatment may fail, not because it is dynamically inaccurate, but because it is emotionally inadequate. Complete objectivity is not enough. Treatment must be object-oriented and emotion-determined. "It need never contradict science, but it must transcend it" (Yellowlees, 1940). We must not forget that the defenses of the adolescent are also the building stones of human character at its highest potential. Treatment which is concerned merely with the dynamics of the problem may fail because it disregards this fact.

Let us finally return to our original thesis: Character synthesis, with the therapist as catalyst, synergist, and model, is the immediate goal in dealing with problems of adolescence.[5]

In the less serious disorders we may find that we thus attain for the patient a relatively non-neurotic integration that may suffice for the rest of his life. This is by and large the case with the self-cures which occur during the "normal" course of the adolescent phase of life on the basis of spontaneously chosen therapeutic relationships. In this way a great many attain that restriction of instinctual gratification, that recognition of the rights of the community and other individuals, that victory of spirituality over sensuousness which characterize the civilized adult (Yellowlees, 1940).

In the more severe disturbances the therapeutic principles which have been described govern only the first phase of the treatment. Somewhere in the course of the therapeutic activity which we have been discussing as character synthesis, and imbricated with it, reductive or analytical psychotherapy may come into play. When the therapy has developed to this extent, regardless of the patient's actual chronological age, we are no longer treating the problems of an adolescent, but those of a neurotic adult.

---

[5] An 18-year-old, who is completing treatment after three years, said to the author, "I came to you expecting you to treat me like a little boy. Now I find you've been a constant irritant to force me to grow up."

# The Emotional Problems
## of Elderly People

### (1948)

---

THE EMOTIONAL PROBLEMS of elderly people, like all other psychic problems, are problems of adaptation. Adaptation consists of the modifications or changes which occur in an organism in the general direction of more perfectly fitting it for successful existence under the conditions of its environment. The problem of adaptation, therefore, must be considered from two sides. We need to know what the organism's powers and capacities are, and we must also know what are the tasks which the organism needs to perform.

The infant organism of the human species has one outstanding task: it has to survive. Pending the maturation and development of those functions which ultimately enable the individual to exert himself actively to his own ends, vegetative adaptation is of the first importance. The infant's environment is constructed around that fact. It is modified to conform with the

---

Editorial note: This comprehensive essay, originally addressed to members of the medical profession, is among the first in the literature to recognize and describe the specific problems related to the aging process.

limited adaptive capacities of the infant. In the normal course of events we see this situation gradually changing. The successful survival of the infant goes hand in hand with developments which ultimately convert the human organism from a more or less completely vegetative adaptive state into one in which self-initiated active mastery of life is more or less the case.

From the standpoint of the individual, the aging organism of the human species has the same first task of survival. There are, however, these differences in the problem: The infant is developing from helplessness to self-sufficiency; the elder is losing self-sufficiency and becoming helpless. As the child develops, his self-respect and security increase progressively with his personal capacity for mastering the problems of his environment; as age advances there is declining power of mastery and, with it, declining security and self-respect. The child, until his own development toward independent survival is assured, has the continuing security of his dependence. The elder's declining powers of independent survival are not comparably associated with a supplementary secure dependency.

The healthy young child is on the upgrade, his organs are developing; his integrations are becoming more perfect; his external adaptive powers are supported by adequate internal functioning. In all of these aspects of adaptation the aging individual is on the decline. Thus, the factors that maintain homeostasis operate within much narrower limits of variation in the old; we know that the learning curve begins to drop significantly in the early twenties and that reaction time begins to increase then. In terms of the highly refined adaptations of which we are capable, the war experience has revealed to us that a man may be functionally old at 30.

If we state these considerations in psychobiological terms, we see that the helpless dependence of the infant is overlapped in time by the structural and functional maturation of the nervous system and the gradual acquisition of knowledge and experience. As the latter increases, helplessness and dependence decrease. In the meanwhile, the child lacks for nothing. Youth is growth, and growth is hope. On the contrary, with advancing age not only is the person confronted with the experience of failing personal powers, but the involution of the vegetative organs deprives him of the balancing compensations which the infant finds in his vegetative functions. Finally, while the helpless child may be coddled and protected by his mother pending his maturation and self-sufficiency, the helpless grandfather may meet with short shrift. The old man's memory may be full of past glories; his heart may be empty of hope. It is this overlapping of the waning powers of maturity and the increasing helplessness of the second childhood that is the basis for the psychological picture with which old age presents us.

## CHARACTER PATTERNS AND OLD AGE

During the course of childhood and adolescence the individual matures physically and mentally. At the same time the character of the person is developed and consolidated into the form it will have throughout the duration of his mature life. Character is the person's habitual mode of reaction to problems. It is his habitual mode of entering into and participating in relationships with other people. It is his habitual outlook on life. Finally, it is the person's habitual attitude towards himself, his picture of and evaluation of himself, his moral-ethical attitudes and his method of dealing with his primitive impulses and instincts. Character is, in short, the overall adaptive pattern of the person.

Character is in part determined constitutionally. A person's temperament is manifested by his prevalent mood, the relative liveliness or sluggishness of his motor and intellectual behavior, the relative sensitiveness or dullness of his reaction to stimulations. Such factors as these appear to be inborn and determined by the person's heredity. But by far the larger part of the determination of a person's character comes from his experience, beginning with his infancy and depending on the characters of his parents. Prevalent attitudes of security or insecurity, ascendancy or submission, optimism or pessimism, confidence in others or distrust of them, and many less tangible traits may distinguish the various persons we know. The normal individual who has reached old age will have lived his mature life on the basis of a character structure which is pretty well fixed in a pattern that has worked more or less successfully for the total life situation he has found himself in. And in the end the psychological pattern of the aging person will be determined by his mature character.

Let us take an ideal example: A man has been born into a family of good heredity. He has had no unusual crippling illnesses in childhood. He is of good intelligence. With the usual vicissitudes and the normal incidence of failure and successes in his development, he

118 ·

has by and large come out on top and has no particular reason either to doubt his capacity or to have any delusional notions about being invulnerable. Consequently he is confident of himself without underrating the problems of his life. His parents have demanded from him neither moral perfection nor superlative achievement. They have not whitewashed his failings or condoned his delinquencies. On the other hand, neither have they depreciated his assets or rejected him for his deficits. They have respected him, and he respects himself. He knows his own assets and liabilities and is realistically aware of the assets and liabilities of his friends and associates. His life is successful as regards his work and his human relationships. He may be without distinction, but he is good human material. His wife has been fond of him; his children care for him and are loyal without being dependent. We may summarize his life prior to old age as an example of successful adaptation under favorable environmental circumstances.

Now, at last, he is old. He is in good health, but he gets tired rather easily. He is mildly forgetful. His wife has died of an acute infection. His children have married and live at a distance. He sees them and his grandchildren occasionally, but they lead their own lives. He lives in a small apartment which is maintained for him by a housekeeper. He belongs to a club, and he has his acquaintances with whom he plays gin and shares a drink. But old friends are dead and others are ailing or have moved away. He comes to his physician, complaining of his fatigability. He thinks it may be due to constipation, though this is not severe.

What is the doctor likely to find? There may be the

beginnings of a malignant disease, but let us assume that serious illness is ruled out. The diastolic pressure may be a little high, and there may be a mild senile type of glycosuria. Appropriate measures do not remedy the chief symptom of fatigue. Are the etiological findings complete? Organically they may be, but what about the patient as a person?

If the doctor were now to have an easygoing kind of a chat with the patient he might discover that when the patient's wife died a younger daughter had suggested that he retire and come to live with her. He didn't want that. He was a young man still—there were still many years of good hard work left in him. Besides, his daughter had young children—he would only be in the way, much as he knew his daughter loved him. So he set up in the small apartment. There had followed a period during which this new routine made him rather irritable. His housekeeper didn't seem to get the hang of doing things as he had learned to expect to have them done. She was a good cook, but somehow the food she served was different. These were all small matters, but things just weren't right. About a year after his wife's death members of his firm began to suggest that he take a vacation. It was years since he'd been away. He deserved a rest. The business was well established, and he could afford to go.

His business associates were also friends. There was no doubt in his mind that they meant well. Yet he couldn't help thinking once in a while that they wanted him to retire. There had been that deal on which he'd been overruled. He'd been opposed to changing the policy under which the firm had been operating for years—thought the suggestion of a younger colleague was too risky. Anyway, he'd been over-ruled. And the deal had been successful. He still held his opinion about the deal for the long run, but he'd been overruled and it looked as if his judgment had been wrong. Perhaps he did need a rest. Perhaps he would be able to get back in his stride with a little medical help. No surrender. Only a little doubt.

The doctor who can elicit this history will be able to make the diagnosis. Here is an organism that is wearing out; here is a human being who is getting old. To the man I have described, this is an unwelcome and an inconceivable thing. He would like to believe there is nothing wrong with him that a little tinkering won't fix up. For this man cannot really envisage his own death. As an individual he feels only in terms of his survival.

## PATTERNS OF ADJUSTMENT

What does this add up to? As men mature success-fully, they do so on the basis of techniques of mastery which have insured that success. In the upshot, what has worked well for them in their personal relations, in their work, and, as you know, also in their politics, becomes a fixed and rigid habit of adjustment. Conservatism of outlook and action is the older man's reaction to a decreasing tolerance for change. With age comes increasing anxiety before the new and the un-tried. Problems of adaptation which have not pre-viously been mastered successfully become too much of a burden for failing psychological and physical powers. The older person inwardly senses increasing actual inadequacies. Particularly disturbing to him are the even slight failures of memory which may be the first heralds of decline.

The reactions to this are several:

(1) It is a fact of common observation that the elderly gentleman will forget his hat, but will remember the score and the details of the football game in which he made the winning point 50 years ago. The elderly lady may forget her nurse's name, but will remember the names of her bridesmaids and their hair-dos, the wedding presents and their donors.

This dulling of recent memory and sharpening of the remembrance of things past is not the result of organic changes alone. Psychologically these are to be seen as an actual turning away from the painfulness of the present. The present is lacking in both the dependent security of childhood and the independent powers for maintaining security of the mature years. The past carries forever and undeniably the record of life lived successfully, problems overcome, disaster survived. Memory turns backward to periods of highest capacity and greatest security as the elderly person's means of saving his self-esteem and as an attempt to find reassurance that the threats of the present will be as transient as those of the past. It is no inconsistency that this occurs even in the case of those aged persons who may not seem to have much to look back on. The fact is that they had at least survived previous threats to life, that someone at least had once cared for them. And memory is aided by confabulation. Never were such heroic deeds performed as in the memory of an old man's youth.

(2) It is observable that older people may become more emphatically self-assertive, even domineering.

These tendencies are compensatory reactions for the feelings of inferiority and inadequacy which have been engendered by actual physical and psychological decline. The loss of centrality of position in the family group or in the person's work, the sense of loss of social status through actual or relative decline in occupational status, general cultural attitudes toward old age as a period of necessary and actual failure—something which is pitied but without real sympathy by those younger—these are some of the factors that produce the feelings of insecurity and inadequacy that result in the reactive cantankerousness of some elderly people.

(3) Mild depressiveness is a common characteristic of elderly persons such as the one whom I have described. As a basis for this there is the inevitably increasing isolation and loneliness as friends and relatives die or become absorbed in their own lives. Essentially this produces the same kind of desolation as is experienced by the child who feels or has actually been deserted or rejected. The elders are being left behind by life. And they experience this as desertion. Added to this is the loss of self-respect and self-esteem which goes with feelings of helplessness and worthlessness and which further feeds the depressive feelings.

(4) Gradually feeling themselves more and more isolated, older persons turn more and more on themselves. In addition to their increasing preoccupation with a past in which they still felt themselves as having some significance, there is increasing sensitiveness to slights. And because old age may bolster itself by standing tremulously on prerogatives which may be traditional but are in fact little honored, there may be increasing querulousness. Sensitiveness may become

tinged with paranoid attitudes. These do not make the person more comfortable, but they may at least increase his feeling that he counts for something.

(5) The increasing incidence of illness and death among those in their own age group gradually tends to undermine the delusion of invulnerability which all harbor. At the same time, new thought, new techniques, new ways of living make old habits less reliable as bolsters of security. The consequence is an increase in what we call "free floating anxiety." Psychological tensions become translated into somatic tensions. The tendency is for the organism to try to cope with vague general anxiety by attaching it to specific susceptible organs. The elderly person now has an apparently tangible problem which can be dealt with. Constipation or aching joints or paresthesias are matters which can be legitimately looked upon as being of interest and concern to relatives or to the doctor and therefore provide some hope of restoring a little of the lost security. Older people therefore tend to become more and more sensitive to their bodily functions. Infantile body-interest is revived. Actual organic changes tend to become psychologically elaborated and thus become even more severe and incapacitating. Here we can see how the situation in old age is the exact psychological reverse of that in infancy and childhood. The normal child sloughs off his dependency attitudes as his own powers mature. The older person tends to resume dependency attitudes as his own powers become atrophied. The child extroverts more and more of his interest and energy. The older person becomes more and more introverted.

As we have seen, the basic function of that overall

adaptive process we call character is to deal with the person's particular reality in such a way as to overcome its vicissitudes, minimize its dangers, and add to his security, pleasure, and self-esteem. Some individuals are generally recognized to be "flexible." Others we look upon as being rigid. Some are more or less flexible in certain aspects of their adaptive functions and more or less rigid in others. A man may be able to adjust and change with the times in his vocation and become rigid and stereotyped in his social outlook. With another man, the reverse may be the case.

Our discussion thus far has concerned itself with that which is more or less generally true of the psychology of the aging process, insofar as this occurs in even normal individuals. Depending on the character structure of the particular person, the psychological phenomena I have described will be seen more or less overtly. It may be stated that the more rigid the character adaptation has been, the more open will tend to be the signs of anxiety and insecurity as manifested by sensitiveness, irritability and querulousness, compensatory self-assertiveness and stubbornness, depressiveness and hypochondriasis. On the contrary, the more flexible the character structure has been, the more likely are we to encounter that delightful person whom we speak of as never having grown old. In contrast to the latent envy of and hostility to younger up-and-comers manifested in the first type, we will observe in the second type the qualities of generous fatherliness and motherliness that go with security and self-respect.

You will have noted that I have frequently resorted to the modifying phrase "more or less." I have done this deliberately in an effort to adhere as closely as possible to the facts. The adaptive functions are so complex; there are so many internal overlappings and contradictions in any character structure—even those that have been by and large "successful"—that in the upshot we are bound to observe both summations and cancellations in the final observable phenomena.

## EXAMPLES OF OLD AGE REACTIONS

In the case which I have previously described, we saw evidence of mild depressiveness manifested by irritability, fatigue, and constipation in reaction to the death of the man's wife, his increasing isolation, and the change of his status in his business.

In the case of another patient who had been an insatiable go-getter, who had made an outstanding success against many obstacles, and who had been incapacitated by a coronary attack from which he had made a good physical recovery, the final reaction was one of angry resentment accompanied by paranoid ideas. He could not tolerate the fact that he had been ordered by his physicians to slow down and that during his absence his business had gone on quite successfully under the leadership of a younger associate. In an effort to preserve his need for status and his confidence in himself, he had elaborated the delusion that his doctors and his business associate had plotted to get him out of the business and that he was not really as ill as he had been told he was. This is the reaction in a person who was a go-getter because his life had been dominated by hostile competitiveness beginning early in a disturbed relationship to a string of younger brothers. Sensitive to his actual internal helplessness he externalized his problems in a form with which he could feel he had a fighting chance.

Another man reacted to a coronary attack with a refusal to believe the diagnosis. He rebelled against the management of his case and continued his activity in his affairs by way of telephones and visiting secretaries. He finally died in his boots. In this case we see a man who had lived down a relationship with a mother who had rejected him. He could not believe that anyone ever gave anybody anything. After a lifetime of confidence in and dependence on himself only, he could not trust himself to sink into the actual dependence of illness.

Still another coronary case, a man who had successfully operated an old family business, finally presented a clinical picture of unwarranted invalidism and querulous dependence on physicians and wife. Here was seen the collapse of a character which had been largely a facade. Pampered as a child, this man had later in life assumed the habiliments of active responsibility only against inner protest. In the end, he resumed with all the more intensity the dependent claims of his childhood.

In short, the elderly person will present a personality picture which will represent either an accentuation, with some distortion, of life-long character traits, or the breakdown of such traits and the exacerbation of latent tendencies.

## REGRESSION IN OLD AGE

This last fact brings us to some less frequent but not uncommon features of old age. The maturation of the personality is to a large extent attended by the regulation and repression of primitive instinctual tendencies. Outstanding among these is the sexual drive and the infantile interest in the body and its functions. It is notable that some old people lose their former fastidiousness and others their moral scruples. Sometimes we encounter rather tragic forensic problems in this area. The general fact here is that the process of introversion which characterizes old age involves what we refer to as a regression of the emotions. Emotional energy formerly directed externally in such areas as work, friendships, and creative activity, returns along the paths of the person's development to earlier levels of expression. Sexual interest that may have been more or less dormant may be revived in partial or distorted forms. Besides the regressive activation of infantile sexual interest, elderly men particularly may turn to sexuality as a kind of self-therapy—a sort of gesture in the direction of recapturing a sense of capacity and self-esteem.

We must distinguish clearly at this point, however, between regressive sexuality, sometimes in the form of perversion or incest, and sexuality as it may survive in the old in its mature forms. It is a fact that sexual capacity and sexual enjoyment may remain effective until advanced ages in both sexes. Not only do elderly married couples confirm this, but the marriages of widowed elderly persons may be successful emotionally and complete sexually. By and large, however, the involution of sexual capacity and sexual interest increases with age, and its exacerbation is more likely to represent an anxiety-determined protest against old age.

In this connection we can again turn to earlier phases of life to see a complementary situation. Normally, sexual interest and, within the given cultural limitations, sexual activity is greatest during adolescence. As men and women direct more and more of their mature emotional energies to their careers, their homes, their children, or their creative work, the earlier intensity of sexuality subsides. It survives for a longer or shorter time as a harmonious overtone in the lives of normal couples, but it is no longer the theme song. The recrudescence of sexuality as a leading preoccupation in an elderly person therefore provides an index to the degree of involution which has occurred in the mature aspects of that person's character and emotionality.

## INTERDEPENDENCE OF ELDERLY COUPLES

Elderly couples at the end of a long married life will have established a symbiosis on which each of them is dependent, even if the relationship has been something less than ideal according to external standards. It is known that one of a couple may not long survive the death of the other without too much basis for this in the survivor's state of health. In other cases a fairly severe depression will ensue. With couples whose lives together have been marked by an ambivalent mixture of hostility and affection, the survivor will tend to become neurotically ill with symptoms comparable to those involved in the cause of death of the spouse. These are all manifestations of the intensity of the identification which occurs. The dependence on each other of such old people is increased because they remain for each other the familiar landmarks in a life whose course has been changed by age. They lend each other support and security because there survives in at least this aspect of their lives something predictable and capable of being dealt with according to old familiar techniques.

## PSYCHOSOMATIC COMPLEXITIES

One of the striking phenomena in old age is the inextricable relationship of emotional problems and actual organic disease. Illness is much more of a threat to older people, not only because of their decreased constitutional reserves but for such psychological reasons as we have already discussed. Every such blow to failing powers increases insecurity and tends to produce either over compensatory reactions, which burden the failing organism still more, or invalid reactions which enforce the claim of the person for the care and attention which he has felt himself to be in danger of losing.

More striking, however, are those instances in which an apparently healthy person will succumb rapidly to some previously latent organic disease process under the impact of an emotional blow. Physicians are familiar with the cerebral apoplexy which follows the loss of a spouse or some injury to pride. Psychiatrists and neurologists not infrequently encounter cases with signs of rapidly advancing mental deterioration among elderly persons who have remained quite intact up to the time of some emotional blow. We are all familiar with the post-mortem findings in the brains of elderly persons in which there will be considerable discrepancy between the organic pathology and the clinical picture of the person at the time of death. There is no one-to-one relationship between cerebral arteriosclerosis and the degree of mental failure which may be present. Elderly people with more or less well-balanced personalities, such as that of the first case we discussed, are able to withstand a considerable amount of cerebral damage, while less balanced personalities may produce a frank psychosis with a minimum of cerebral pathology. It seems to be the case that cerebral organic pathology is only a final precipitating factor in persons already excessively burdened by such emotional problems as we have been discussing. Even more complex psychosomatic relationships exist in the case of some of the chronic diseases of old age, such as heart disease and arthritis. All such actual organic illness presents us with secondary elaborations based on the person's emotional problems. In some instances it is difficult to be certain that it is not the psychological problem which has primary etiologic significance.

## Organic Mental Diseases

A number of specific mental diseases occur characteristically during the declining years. Alzheimer's disease, or presenile psychosis, tends to develop in the fifties, though it may occur earlier. Beginning with marked failure of memory there is a rapid development of confusion and disorientation leading by way of aphasia and apraxia to complete organic dementia. Even in this undeniably organic disease of the brain, symptoms of emotional origin occur in its early phases and are representative of the person's reaction to the overwhelming nature of the attack on his integrity. Irritability and anxious depression may be attended by compensatory psychic symptoms such as sexual deviations, grandiose business plans, paranoid ideas. Pick's disease, which tends to occur somewhat earlier than Alzheimer's disease and in women more frequently than in men, is also characterized in its early phases by reactive and compensatory psychological phenomena. Here we often see euphoric overactivity and generally uninhibited behavior which is in part to be accounted for by the infantile regression induced by the atrophy of the cerebral cortex and in part a psychological denial of catastrophe.

There are many cases of cerebral arteriosclerosis, with vertigo, tremors, unsteady gait, paresthesias, etc., in which psychotic symptoms never appear. The commonest precipitating factor in the onset of a psychosis with cerebral arteriosclerosis is a major or minor cerebral accident. The psychotic symptoms often date from such an episode, though the onset may be gradual. These symptoms consist of organically determined disturbances of consciousness and mentation and of emotionally determined apprehension and panic, delusions of threats of bodily harm, nightmares, and depression. Restlessness and sleeplessness are common. There may occur episodes of violence against even those closest to the patient, these being dictated by delusions of threat against the patient's person. The emotional symptoms again demonstrate the reaction of the personality to the inwardly perceived threat to its integrity. The anxiety is a direct consequence of this. The violence which may appear is expressive of an attempt on the patient's part to externalize a problem and then to attempt to master it by brute force.

## Functional Personality Disorders

Apart from the general psychological reactions of old age we have discussed and the organic mental diseases we have touched on, elderly people may present any of the various categories of functional disorders of the personality. In order to clarify this it is necessary to digress.

In our previous discussion of character we have spoken of it as the overall adaptive pattern of the personality. We have referred to its function in the repression and regulation of the instincts and drives. Every neurosis represents a breakdown of this function and is an emergency repair job. The neurotic symptom—be it a phobia, a compulsion, a conversion, or a tic—represents the partial breaking through of a primitive impulse which the mature personality repudiates and encapsulates in the symptom. This occurs at a considerable cost of emotional energy and with a consequent decrease in the resources of the personality for coping with its adaptive problems. Nevertheless, the integrity of the personality is thus preserved. Most persons are burdened to a certain extent with neurotic symptoms or traits. Very often these go unrecognized, and for the most part they do not seriously damage the adaptive functions.

But the failure of adaptive strength that goes with age is associated with a weakening of the defenses against the instinctual drives. Thus, it can come about that minor neurotic symptoms which have sufficed to protect the individual against eruptions of the instincts during his maturity may become intensified, and new symptoms may be added as a means of bolstering these defenses. A compulsion neurosis, for example, which first made its appearance in youth and then became latent when an emergent need for it had subsided, may exacerbate in the later years. This may be similarly true of a hysteria or a paranoid or depressive syndrome. We see then that the emotional reactions of elderly people are a reaction not only to the external reality of their adaptive problems but are also determined by the tendency of the internal defenses to be weakened as the strength of the personality declines.

A number of gross functional disturbances are considered characteristic of the later years.

*Involutional melancholia* is mistakenly thought to be a disorder of the female menopause. In its classical form it is an anxious agitated depression with delusions of guilt, hypochondriasis, and nihilism. It tends to appear as a first attack of overt mental illness in women between the ages of 40 and 55, and in men between the ages of 50 and 65. I shall not go into the details of this illness other than to tie it in with the general formulation which I have given to the emotional problems of elderly people. The anxiety is again a reaction to both the internal and external dangers threatening the involuting organism. The depression and the delusion of guilt are reactions to the increased pressure of unacceptable instinctual impulses. Often the delusions are concerned with sexual fantasies and ideas of irreparable injuries done to others. The hypochondriasis is a regressive return of infantile body interest and the fantasies of world destruction that I have called nihilism are simple projections of the sense of failure in the integrity of the personality itself.

*Paranoid states* characterized by ideas of persecution may be representative of the resurgence of primitive hostile impulses and of the reactive resentment of the elder to his unwelcome position in his present life. The unacceptable hostility is projected and becomes the delusion of persecution.

Still other elderly people may be subject to *simple depressions*, with feelings of desolation connected with their actual life situation. Self-punishing attitudes of guilt may be present as a reaction to the resentment and hostility which in the paranoid cases has been projected.

The *senile psychosis*, distinguished from the psychosis with cerebral arteriosclerosis by the lack of, or minimal significance of, organic signs and symptoms, is a final caricature of old age. Its onset is gradual, beginning with an insidious weakening of initiative, loss of interest in things normally of vital importance, reversal of the sleep rhythm, failure of memory and comprehension, general deterioration, with final confusion and delusional formations. What we observe is the gradual breakdown of a personality into what may be compared to the marasmus of an emotionally and physically starved infant. In these cases life has become just too much, and yet the spark lingers on.

## NORMAL ADAPTIVE REACTIONS

It should not be presumed on the basis of what has been said that there is no such thing as a normal old age. Persons whose lifelong stability has been based on resiliency rather than rigidity will live out their years with dignity and decency, though none will escape his share of anxiety and quiet desolation. The flexible person is one who respects himself but has no conceit, who has been guided by principles but has not been the slave of dogma, who has had steadiness of purpose without being hypnotized by an immutable goal, who has bent his energies to making the grade rather than getting to the top first, who has tolerated his weakness while employing his strengths, and who has respected his neighbor. Such a person is buffered throughout his life against both internal and external vicissitudes. Such a person has regulated and diverted his instinctual tendencies rather than attempted to smother them. In such a person the pressure of the instincts will at all times be less threatening. Such a person has applied his adaptive capacities to their proper task of mastering the environment to the end of overcoming its vicissitudes, minimizing its dangers, adding to its security, evolving from it the possibilities of creativeness, and deriving from it its legitimate gratifications. Such a person, having lived within the possibilities, will be less vulnerable to the limitations imposed by the external harsh reality of aging.

It must not be thought that I am advocating a belief in poetic justice. There are the notable exceptions. The tyrannical old man or old woman whose throne goes to the grave together with its incumbent is well known in fact and fiction. On the other hand, the external facts of the case may be too much for the least egocentric and best balanced elderly person. By and large, however, the principles of which I have been speaking do operate.

## Problems of Therapy and Prophylaxis

We come now to the question of therapy and prophylaxis. To die with one's boots on is the keynote for the mental hygiene of old age. Never to know that one is through, never to feel superfluous, never to lack significance, never to be without use, never to be without an outlet for the creative urge, never to be without a word in the affairs of men—these are the other notes. I state them in this negative form because it is the form in which the elderly person feels above all that there are forces operating that would demean and depreciate him. And the emotional problems of elderly people stem from this feeling and are elaborated by these protests.

The economic aspect of the problem of prophylaxis affects by far the largest part of our increasingly elderly population. Financial security after working days are over is an undeniably tangible need. In its details this is a problem for the political scientist and the citizen of good will. But no medical audience can fail to remember its importance as a factor in the emotional problems of elderly people. And even where there is no stringent financial problem, the problem of retirement looms large. All of us must have had the experience of witnessing the rapid decline and death of a man who had retired from his business to play golf in January and catch trout in July. Some of us must have known the teacher who never missed a day at school for 35 years, only to become a bedridden invalid a few months after she had gone on the pension list.

Retirement is often treated ritualistically, like a graduation. There are dinners and speeches and gifts and even certificates of esteem. But no one is fooled—least of all the old one. He's through. Where does he go from there? The fact is that retirement, even though the person survives, is for many the funeral of a living death. Life without purpose is without meaning. And for many men and women, work contains all of the meaning of their life. This fact carries the problem of prophylaxis back into the years of the prime of life. It is then that the person might ideally be expected to envisage his old age and to prepare for it. If he were a business man he would think it only reasonable to diversify his investments in preparation for a crash. But rare is the person who is so reasonable when it comes to preparation for retirement. Such preparation would include the development during the prime of life of collateral interests and activities which could indeed keep one going until one died in one's boots. But then such a person would be no concern of ours.

In the usual situation we are faced with the fact that a person has become too old to work comfortably at his accustomed task; or it may be that he is not so old but his coronaries are; and we must advise him. This is a major medical responsibility. Outright retirement while the person is still ambulatory and has more signs than symptoms is a questionable prescription. It is prescribing boredom to replace interest, uselessness to replace function. If retirement is necessary, it should be gradual and seldom complete. The old one's own pulse will remain stronger and more regular if he can continue to keep a finger on the pulse of his affairs. To the fullest extent possible, collateral interests should be mobilized or revived or created. In other words, retirement should be to something, not from something.

For the financially independent this is feasible enough and requires only the intelligent interest of physician, family, or friends. For the great masses the problem again becomes a social one. There is no doubt that together with old-age benefits we shall have to find some way of providing the elders with opportunities for useful and interesting survival. The war just over demonstrated quite positively that this does not need to be an idle dream. The thousands of men and women who were salvaged from the old-age scrap heap on which they had been tossed before the emergency not only demonstrated the waste of human material which they had represented, but, more important from a moral and ethical standpoint, their opportunity to feel significant and useful and happy and free of aches and pains must give pause to the indifference with which their living burial had previously been treated.

## Conclusion

The treatment of the emotional problems of elderly people falls into three classes—supportive and custodial, medical, and psychotherapeutic.

In the case of the severe degenerative organic diseases of the brain such as Alzheimer's and Pick's diseases permanent hospitalization is necessary. The psychoses with cerebral arteriosclerosis and severe senile psychoses also must be hospitalized.

Two things must nevertheless be remembered: We have learned a great deal about the defective nutritional status of the elderly person. And we know that their reserves are sometimes inadequate to tolerate the additional insult of a cardiac decompensation or of an operative procedure. Many cases that formerly were diagnosed as hopelessly psychotic can now be helped to a satisfactory remission by means of proper medical intervention. In all recent cases of senile psychosis or psychoses with apparent cerebral arteriosclerosis, a thorough attempt should be made to restore organ function as much as possible and to treat the nutritional deficiency, the avitaminosis, the dehydration, the toxemias, and the cerebral anoxia. These are reversible factors which affect the mental picture sharply and which can today be effectively influenced. During convalescence mild exercise, occupational therapy and physical therapy are important. In the general management, sedation must be carefully used. Bromides and barbiturates are in general badly tolerated. The best drugs for insomnia are the old stand-bys, chloral hydrate and paraldehyde, though the latter is difficult to administer. Whiskey can still be depended upon in some cases. And for tension and depression, powdered opium covered with a mild laxative is quite effective.

The depressions of later life respond rather well to electric shock treatment. The risks when properly controlled are negligible. The same applies to involutional melancholia. In other conditions this treatment is contraindicated.

Finally, direct psychotherapy of older people is not so hopeless a task as was once thought. While the disturbances involving specific neurotic and psychotic manifestations require the intervention of the specialist in psychiatry, a large number of the emotional problems presented by these patients can be dealt with satisfactorily by the medical men. If the principles underlying the nature of these disturbances are kept in mind, common sense, empathy, and a little patience will enable physicians to help the elderly to greater happiness and reduce to a gratifying extent the chronic burden of their psychosomatic complaints.

One must give them a chance to talk about themselves. But one must not waste time on sympathy. Whereas some people will lap it up, sympathy will be offensive where sensitive pride is involved. Respectful attention and an attitude of willingness to try to really understand go a lot further toward bolstering self-esteem. Nothing hurts more than the brush-off with a smile. Nothing helps more than to provide a genuine human contact, even if it is on a professional basis.

Knowing that the old ones are really insecure and anxious, the physician will lend them his own strength, not with a pat on the back and a wordy reassurance, but by the living fact of his genuine willingness to stand by and to help in every reasonable way. Knowing that they are proud, the physician will never be patronizing, he will never be condescending, he will never let them feel that they lean on him and that he carries them.

The traditional authority of the doctor will equalize the difference in age and is of sufficient influence, besides, to makes his care-taking role acceptable without affront to the older patient's self-respect—providing that the physician himself lives that role with dignity and with humbleness. There should be no talk about inferiority feelings, no talk about compensatory devices, no talk about anxiety. No jargon of any sort is necessary. One must simply understand how the old person feels and conduct oneself with due consideration for the validity of these feelings.

# Problems of
# Psychoanalytic
# Training

## (1948)

---

T HE PROBLEM of training in psychoanalysis is not a
mere matter of pedagogical technique. How it is
to be done, who will do it, who will be trained, and
how many, are important questions. The basic questions, however, remain: What do we want to teach?
To what end is our teaching to be directed? Unless we
find common ground in the answers to these questions,
there can be no meeting of minds, no resolution of the
other problems presented.

To read the minutes of various conferences on train-

---

Editorial Note: The arguments offered here were in refutation to the
book *Psychoanalytic Therapy* by Alexander, French, et al. (1946, New
York: Ronald Press). The then President of the American Psychoanalytic
Association, M. Ralph Kaufman, had invited Dr. Gitelson to write this
paper, which brought him to the attention of the national and international psychoanalytic world.

The paper is of intrinsic as well as historical interest: the problems
confronting psychoanalysis today certainly differ from those of 25 years
ago, but current demands for speeding up the training period raise very
similar questions.

ing and education that have been held since 1940 is to be struck by the prevalence of a tendency to avoid the issues arising from these basic questions. If we view the contents of those minutes as we do those of a psychoanalytic hour, we notice that the corporate patient is talking all around the point, with only here and there an interposing of something clear and explicit.

We find emphasis on the more or less intangible qualities necessary for being "a good analyst;" such qualities as having an "intuitive understanding of unconscious processes" and "an ability to work with the unconscious." Doubts are expressed over whether an intuitive understanding of unconscious processes can be learned. A need is felt for forming some group to discuss "the fundamental conception of what an analyst is, of what constitutes analytic, healthy growth." Misgivings are voiced lest a scientific society "in a young field" give the impression of being dogmatic by codifying what constitutes psychoanalysis and placing beyond the pale all those who do not adhere to this codification.

At the National Conference on Postwar Problems of Psychoanalytic Training in 1946, the issues became a little clearer. Participants pretty much agreed that high standards, at this critical time, ought to be strengthened rather than weakened. The general view seemed to be that the problem of increased numbers of candidates should be dealt with by an increase in the training load—up to 50 per cent if necessary. But opinion was sharply divided on whether or not training analysis should be shortened. The idea was put forth that candidates be trained and analyzed according to their needs, that many candidates did not require analysis to change their personality structure, but only to familiarize them with the analytic process for their future work.*

This in turn led to a discussion of the adequacy of standards for candidates. Robert Knight, in his comment on the report of his survey of criteria for the selection of suitable candidates, admitted that the replies indicated that no set criteria were being used to qualify or disqualify applicants. One gathers from the discussion that Knight's report was met with a certain concordance of opinion. Candidates were not taken at their face value of apparent normality. The problem of pseudonormality as a defense was recognized. The problems of the orientation of the analyst to his task were brought out.

There appeared to be considerable doubt about the validity of preliminary interviews as a means of determining the suitability of a candidate. Several of the conferees were in general accord that every candidate needed a therapeutic analysis. Differences expressed on this point stemmed largely from practical considerations. Some felt that the transformation of the training analysis into a therapeutic analysis would clutter up the training analyst's time, while others thought that if the analyst who conducts the therapeutic analysis of a putative candidate is connected in the patient's mind with the issue of training, the analyst's therapeutic function is interfered with.

Out of all this arises the following issue: do we have the scientific obligation to continue to develop person-

---

* Editorial note: This idea came from Franz Alexander. Other participants in the various discussions reviewed here included E. Bibring, H. Deutsch, O. Fenichel, T. French, L. Kubie, and A. Meyer.

nel capable of conducting definitive psychoanalysis of patients and of deriving relevant psychoanalytic data from their work, or are we morally obligated to turn out psychotherapists, more or less trained, in as great numbers as possible, in the interest of some mass therapeutic goal? This is not simply a postwar issue. It is an issue for the entire future of psychoanalysis.

Psychoanalysts are in a dilemma. To the extent to which they have succeeded in empathizing with other human beings they feel impelled to do everything they can in their interests. But to the extent to which they have freed themselves from fantasies of omnipotence and become capable of testing reality, they have reason to move with caution. A considerable part of the tendency of psychoanalysts to spread themselves thin is the result of a *real* conflict into which they are thrown by this dilemma. If we add to this those narcissistic attitudes which render them sensitive to their own criticisms and to those of others, we may gain some understanding of the reasons which tempt them to devise new techniques for carrying the burden.

This brings us back to the crux of the matter: What is analysis: what do we want to teach, and to what end is our teaching to be directed? Some of Zilboorg's comments at the Detroit meeting of the Society in 1943 are relevant.

The various conflicting trends with which we are so familiar need not be dwelt upon in detail. Whether they stress the purely cultural, purely ontogenetic, purely physiological, purely reflexological, or purely current factors of human psychology, or whether they elaborate the points on which Freud was allegedly or actually wrong—matters little. They are various facets of the cultural crisis in which we are all engulfed.

This does not mean that I would urge upon psychoanalysis the principle of static and uncritical orthodoxy. Just the contrary. Freud did not say the last word; he could not have and no one can or ever will, for no science has ever said the last word. *But no science has ever survived or preserved its productivity if its postulates were rejected.* This is true of geometry or physics as much as of psychoanalysis. The greatest discoveries or revolutions in geometry or physics never overthrew their fundamental postulates. Psychoanalysis rests on individualism, empiricism, and the inductive method. Much in the libido theory will be revised, but its fundamental postulates will remain. It cannot be substituted by deductive constructions of disindividualized sociologies, or psychophysiologies [1944, p. 83; italics added].

If we accept the relevance of these remarks, then we must ask ourselves whether there have been unequivocally established, recent discoveries in psychoanalysis that would validate a radical change in the fundamental postulates of psychoanalytic instruction, and radical departure from established techniques.

In *Analysis Terminable and Interminable,* Freud (1937) emphasized that deepening analysis rather than shortening it must be the first consideration, and that this depends on the analyst's real mastery over the weak points in his own personality. In respect to this the analyst must be superior to his patient if he is to be an example of what the patient can hope for. At the same time, Freud comes to the sad conclusion that "analysis is one of the three impossible professions," the other two being parenthood and the government of nations (p. 248). We cannot demand perfection from the analyst who is himself a human being, and the training analysis is therefore of necessity incomplete. Nevertheless, Freud says, the training in analysis can accomplish its purpose if it (1) establishes a sincere conviction of the existence of the unconscious, (2) enables the person to perceive in himself psychic processes which are otherwise incredible, (3) provides a first hand glimpse of technique, and, finally, (4) sets up a process which does not cease with the last analytical session, but continues to act so that ego transformation continues.

It would appear that the reason for the notion that a training analysis and a therapeutic analysis can differ is to be found in the fact that the tendency exists to dilute our understanding of what the psychic processes are. There is the inclination to believe that a "glimpse of the unconscious" will really set up that final, continuously integrative process which Freud envisaged. We need only recall the patients who have left us free of symptoms after a hasty glance at these processes, and who continue glibly to parrot their awareness of the unconscious, to see how false this is. If we are really to enable the analysand to perceive in himself his psychic processes to the end that a real reintegration is set in motion, we are compelled, in Waelder's (1945) terms, to eliminate

short-circuit interpretations in favor of an inching downward and backward from a broad basis of character study with a view to thus arriving at more exact reconstructions of unconscious fantasies and of the whole process of neurotic career. . . . The ultimate technical ideal of this ego-psychology is to actually transform the neurosis into its earlier stages, finally into precipitating conflicts—to roll the process of neurosis back along the road of its development [p. 88].

This technical goal has been placed within reach through the elaboration of our knowledge of ego psychology, which has had a very important effect on the technique of psychoanalysis, with the consequence that we can no longer make a valid distinction between therapeutic analysis and training analysis. This seems to have been the basis for the indecision on this point at the Conference on Postwar Problems. Knight's questionnaire failed to reveal a consensus about what factors could be looked upon as explicitly invalidating the candidacy of an applicant for training. The argument was advanced that this was the case because we looked upon these factors psychoanalytically. But as psychoanalysts, how else can we look upon them?

The upshot is that we find ourselves without an alternative to make personal analysis a prerequisite rather than an intrinsic part of training in psychoanalysis. We have, then, to remember what such an analysis must actually be. It must actually give the potential candidate a living experience of the psychic processes. Many will consider this to mean an analysis conducted according to the principles which have been cited. There are nevertheless current trends in the direction of a so-called liberalization of psychoanalysis to which we must give attention.

It appears to be a hopeless task to set up normality as a basis for the selection of potential analysts whose training would be presumed not to take too much time. Psychoanalytically we are compelled to look upon "normality" as a defense, insofar as we are concerned with the person's capacity for empathy with his own and another person's unconscious processes. Often enough it is a defense by way of multiple or of rigid identifications, and of "adjustments" in the shallow sense of that common word. Such adjustments, when examined, are often seen to be examples of the mechanism of "identification with the aggressor" which Anna Freud (1936) has described.

If there are any clinical criteria that might be used to appraise the possibility of a successful training in analysis, they are to be derived from an evaluation of what the person has made of himself despite his neurosis. We need to ask ourselves what has survived of creativity, of useful energy, of emotional flexibility and resonance, and of interpersonal interest—regardless of the formal diagnosis. We have to see what there is of native shrewdness, of wisdom, and of intellectual power. It is doubtful whether there is much more that can be clinically determined from preliminary interviews. There is then nothing to do but embark on the analysis and let its actual outcome be the test of whether or not we have indeed succeeded in the initiation of a psychoanalyst. From this point of view we may seriously ask whether or not we are warranted in saying to a potential candidate that we are first of all committed to what may be accomplished for his psychic health.

Whether we like it or not, there is as yet no short

cut. Those modifications of technique which have been proposed, such as selective therapeutic planning, denial of dependency, circumvention of the transference neurosis, dilution of the analytic schedule, and fractionation of the entire course of the analysis, have yet to demonstrate their psychoanalytic validity. These techniques involve such a degree of activity on the part of the analyst as to eventuate in the encapsulation of large quantities of the patient's psychic forces. They are tactics of penetration in contrast to a strategy of infiltration. They are deficient in that *sine qua non* of psychoanalysis—the process of working through. The patients may produce so-called material. Progress may apparently be made. But if one looks on the consequences in their formal aspects, as one must so often do to understand the function of a dream, one cannot avoid the conclusion that the patient has often borrowed from the analyst the means with which to come to terms with him; and this later manifests itself in the magic-making attitudes of the student toward his own patients.

No one will be unduly disturbed by the fact that under the circumstances of the actual pressure to which physicians are subjected, we are compelled on occasion to make technical compromises which may be practically necessary and symptomatically useful. It is a different matter when the goal is the training of an analyst. Here we cannot compromise. Even if his purpose be utterly pragmatic, the scientific practitioner must be able to operate with freedom of choice and decision. For us this means that the personal analysis of a potential analyst must be comprehensive and thorough. It must take as long as it takes to expose the narcissistic core of the neurosis. There is danger that otherwise we shall propagate and perpetuate the kind of analysts of whom Freud (1937) said, "It seems that a number of analysts learn to make use of defensive mechanisms which allow them to divert the implications and demands of analysis from themselves (probably by directing them on to other people)" (p. 249).

Didactic work with candidates should begin only when we are convinced that the analysand is indeed a candidate for training. This does not mean that we have to await the resolving stages of the analysis. But it does mean that we have to be certain that the candidate has made a bona fide contact with his unconscious libidinal conflicts, with some resolution and integration. Even when an applicant for training earnestly wishes to be analyzed, the narcissistic stake in his neurotic system may prove to be a primary obstacle. For a longer or shorter time the transference will involve all of the characterological defenses with which he has lived previously—including his interest in psychiatry and psychoanalysis. So long as this still characterizes the analysis, the patient is not yet capable of the reality testing which actual training involves. There is danger, when the analysand is from the start considered to be undergoing a training analysis, that the issue of training befogs the defenses in the transference for both him and the analyst.

At the Marienbad meeting in 1936, Glover said:

. . . to judge from earlier controversies it would appear that whenever differences of opinion exist in psycho-analytic circles, two safe generalizations can be made: first, that the original views put forward by Freud on that particular subject are still the best available and second, that as a result of more recent work, these original views are capable of, indeed require, more detailed correlation. I should like to add that in most cases the first of these two generalizations is the more valuable [Glover, et al., 1937, p. 125].

I think this is a fair statement. I believe that many of the so-called "new ideas" are verbal derivatives of earlier psychoanalytic work. It is not enough to say that "students should know psychoanalysis historically." This by itself may simply mean that psychoanalysis becomes a tolerated guest in its own house. Students should be taught *psychoanalysis,* and there should be no doubt in their minds that its derivatives are possible applications of a basis science which are pragmatically useful. Students must learn the meaning of transference in all its ramifications and depths; they must become familiar with its manifestations in their own transference neurosis; finally, they must acquire an earnest respect for its technical implications in the conduct of analyses. I think this is the atmosphere in which institutes of psychoanalysis should teach.

It would appear to be in the best interests of both the student in training and his patient that supervised analysis ought not be undertaken until the student's analysis is in the stages of resolution or is satisfactorily ended. Experience shows that a student's work with patients tends to reflect what is happening currently in his own analysis, and that he may utilize his patient's conflicts as defenses in his own analysis. There are students who do not begin to have a degree of objectivity about their analysands until they have undertaken their second or third case. For that matter, even in their didactic work, many good students experience a temporary inhibition of learning, for reasons related to their own analyses. While there are clinical situations in which the analyst finds technical reasons for advising or permitting a student to undertake a supervised case before the ending of his analysis, such permission may sometimes be dictated by extraclinical considerations.

It seems to be a fact that many students are permitted to choose, as initial patients for supervised analysis, cases which are far too complex for beginners. Cases need to be chosen with due regard for the psychic readiness of the student, and this means that the student's analyst ought to be consulted in the assignment of at least the first case—especially if the student analyst is still in analysis. Supervision should be focused on the student and cannot concern itself only with the patient whose treatment is being supervised. This holds true whether or not the student is still in analysis. The supervising analyst is not intruding on the student's analysis when he calls to notice the bare facts of the student's relationship to his case. And when the student is no longer in analysis, the responsibility of the supervising analyst to be alert to obvious unresolved countertransferences of the student is even greater.

It is a difficult but unavoidable fact that training in psychoanalysis is from its nature an individualized matter of preceptorship. It needs to follow individual indications as to tempo and technique just as does the student's analysis itself. We cannot adapt the schedule of training to suit our convenience or in response to our sense of urgency.

The case seminars are a final consideration. It is puzzling that, in a field in which the defensive process is of such outstanding importance, the tendency is to emphasize formulation. All of us must have noted the penchant of students to turn to schematization and diagrammatics, and how difficult it is to enlist their patience in a study of the analytic process. While individual supervision may to some extent counteract this, it would nevertheless seem that the continuous case seminar or group control has been neglected as a means of further coping with this tendency to foreshorten in the interest of seeming mastery. The single presentation of large blocks of analytic work fosters the trend toward facile and tendentious dynamic reconstruction.

This discussion has had from the beginning no possibility of introducing anything really new. Its only justification is the continuing necessity to remind ourselves that psychoanalysis is not a mere clinical technique but the basic science of man's mental life. Our knowledge of the forces of the unconscious and of their ramifications in the ego is far from exhausted.

Psychoanalysis still occupies a vanguard position. In deference to this responsibility, it must move slowly and cautiously. No current exigencies should be permitted to compel us to give up its refined capacity for discovering, testing, and verifying the new directions which the applied mental sciences can safely and profitably follow.

I have presented a vulnerable point of view, which is at present subject to the frequently heard stigmatization: dogmatic orthodoxy. Is it not possible that the reverse is the case—that we are tending to fly into the study of epiphenomena and into therapeutic improvisations, which we call liberalized psychoanalysis, as an expression of that need for compliant belonging which characterizes our generation?

# The Role of Anxiety in Somatic Disease

## (1948)

---

### STRUCTURE AND FUNCTION OF THE ANXIETY MECHANISM

ANXIETY REACTIONS to organic disease follow the same principles as those which govern the generation of anxiety in general. In a given situation which constitutes a threat to the interests of an organism there occurs a somatic mobilization which is reactive to the danger and preparatory for coping with it. The most easily perceived effects of this are referable to the heart and the respiratory organs. Motor innervations also take part in this reaction. In the human being, awareness of these events constitutes the actual unpleasant sensation of anxiety.

The mobilization of anxiety may be vestigial or quite complete; there may be a transient epigastric sensation, a few extrasystoles, a sharp inspiration, and a slight tensing of the skeletal musculature. Or the heart may assume a steadily increased force and rate, accom-

---

*Editorial Note:* This paper was presented before the Section on Psychosomatic Medicine at Michael Reese Hospital, Chicago. The ideas contained in it have been confirmed over the subsequent years of research in psychosomatic medicine, making them particularly useful for medical practitioners today.

panied by increased ventilation and vigilant explora-
tory activity. If the danger then materializes, the organism is aware of and ready for the alternative—fight
or flight. We thus see that anxiety is not merely a
symptom. It has a very definite function in the interest
of survival. It is, so to speak, a readying mechanism
which clears the deck for action.

Beginning very early, human beings internalize the
objects of the environment and the relationships that
exist among them. Language function and the capacity
for imagery make this possible. In consequence, the
anxiety mechanism operates in response to various
types of psychic representations of danger.

## DEVELOPMENTAL HISTORY OF THE ANXIETY REACTION

The dangers to which the human being responds
with anxiety are derivatives of those that appear and
have paramount importance at successive stages in the
development of the personality.

At the very earliest stage, survival is the outstanding
problem. The inability of the infant to do anything
about this without assistance is obvious. The first anxiety situation is the powerlessness of the infant to cope
with internal tensions produced by the needs arising
from hunger, cold, pain, and postural insecurity. The
first consequence of the mobilization of the anxiety
mechanism is the helpless cry which, together with the
unorganized movements of the infant, serves only to
discharge tension.

At the next stage the child has more or less clearly
identified the mother as the agent of the relief of tension. The leading danger situation then becomes the

absence of the mother. The tensions belonging to hunger, or discomfort need no longer be immediately present to produce the anxiety signal and the infant's cry. Separation from the mother is now enough. The infant's cry is no longer helpless but help-bringing. For the first time, anxiety is seen to be functional rather than simply reactive to tension. Now the infant is able to govern its environment.

In consequence of the further maturation of the nervous system, the powers of perception improve and become integrated with the powers of manipulation and locomotion. More or less active mastery of the environment now becomes possible. The organism becomes more dependent on its own sensory-motor capacities to goven the environment in its interest. The complete elaboration of these capacities goes on until adulthood. With their first appearance, however, comes the anxiety which is connected with any threat to physical integrity. Any threat to the powers of overt activity is now tantamount to a threat of return to the helplessness and dependence which had previously characterized the state of the infant. The adaptive response to anxiety is now characterized by an attempt at physical mastery.

The maturation of the physical powers of mastery brings the individual to the final stage of integration, that which finds him in a social relationship to other people. The social structure, rather than the physical environment, establishes the criteria of survival. By means of the techniques of the particular culture, the person aims at success, security, status, and power. The anxiety stimulus resides primarily in negative factors that militate against such attainments.

To these is added the burden of social disapproval of certain strivings. Such sanctions are derived from traditional prohibitions and regulations which were at first imposed through parental authority. Ultimately they are reinforced and maintained by self-controlling and self-regulating mechanisms which the person experiences as self-esteem and self-depreciation. Together, these factors constitute checks upon the unlimited expression of egoistic impulses. If these checks reach a certain intensity they operate as stimuli to the anxiety mechanism. Thus, the threat of business failure produces anxiety; the threat of loss of reputation, whether it be a matter of ethics or pertains to one's professional capacity, produces anxiety; threats to self-esteem produce anxiety. Dangers of this order are the final social derivatives of the earlier danger of maternal desertion and of the later encountered danger of injury to physical integrity when parental authority and restrictions intervene.

To restate the various levels from which the stimulus to anxiety arises: The threat of complete helplessness derives from earliest infancy. The threat of separation from those to whom we have a necessary relationship stems from the dependence of the young child on the mother. The threat of physical injury originates in the value placed by the child on his self-assertive powers. Lastly, the threat of social disapproval or of the loss of self-esteem derives from the final internalization by the child of taboos and restrictions on his egoistic strivings insofar as these violate the prerogatives of the other members of the family group.

In any given person, depending on various factors which finally make him the personality he happens to be, one or the other of these sources of anxiety will tend to predominate. All persons are capable of deriving the stimulus to anxiety from any of these sources, depending on the circumstances.

## ILLNESS AND TRAUMA AS ANXIETY STIMULI

Illness and trauma constitute frontal attacks on the basic security of the individual. Somatic self-sufficiency is impaired or destroyed; the person is forced back on the path of his emotional development to dependency on other persons. Uncertainty about the reliability of these persons may reach into the deepest levels of feeling and revive primitive anxiety tension. Because our culture emphasizes independence and self-sufficiency as prime virtues, the incapacity and helplessness produced by illness may secondarily affect the person as if he were a victim of retribution for the secret guilts which in one degree or another most people harbor. For similar reasons illness may also be looked upon as a desertion by fate, by luck, or by the particular divinity in whom the person believes. Lastly certain illness may be stigmatized as specifically revealing a person's weakness or unworthiness. Whatever the individual case may be, a quota of anxiety is added to the burden imposed by the disease or injury itself, and the clinical picture is directly influenced by the anxiety and by the particular reactions of the person to it.

Before going further, it is necessary to emphasize the fact that anxiety is not merely an unfortunate complication of somatic illness. Let us assume an ideal condition of somatic illness. The patient feels somehow indisposed, recognizes there is something wrong, decides that he had better lay off for a while before he gets worse, and goes to bed. The next morning he is still sick. There is work to be done, but that will have to wait. There may really be something wrong with him. He permits his wife to serve him his breakfast in bed, tend to him, and finally to call the doctor. The diagnosis is pneumonia. The patient has confidence in his physician, follows his orders, accepts his treatment; he is soon convalescent and back on the job.

If we consider this situation from the standpoint of our discussion we see that here the anxiety reaction to the threat of illness has been minimal, but nevertheless sufficient to serve the purpose of inducing a regression to a level of organic function which established optimum conditions for recovery. The regression to passivity seen here is a flight reaction which is necessary to the survival of the sick organism. It is a sort of strategic retreat. This is a normal psychobiological characteristic of all illness, and demonstrates the adaptive role of anxiety.

### CLINICAL DEMONSTRATIONS OF ANXIETY REACTION TO ILLNESS

Returning now to the consideration of anxiety as a pathological component of somatic illness we are presented with the possibility of deviations in several directions: Anxiety may eventuate in a more than necessary functional regression to passivity and dependence. It may be repressed and produce secondary complicating symptoms. It may lead to reactions against itself.

### EXCESSIVE REGRESSIVE REACTIONS TO ILLNESS ANXIETY

In the first group the cases will run the gamut from anxious agitation about a pimple, through delayed convalescence, to chronic invalidism and complete surrender. All of us are familiar with fearful patients of the first type. These problems belong among the neuroses. The problems of convalescence are somewhat different. As has been shown, every illness induces a certain degree of functional regression. This resumption of childlike helplessness is accompanied by a corresponding contraction of the person's interests. His world narrows down to himself and his immediate needs. He resumes the egocentricity of childhood and becomes demanding, intolerant, and domineering. In part this is a means of controlling his environment despite his helplessness. In part it is a protest against the helplessness which makes him dependent. For the patient is at one and the same time grateful to those who care for him and resentful of the incapacity and insecurity which make this care necessary.

During normal convalescence there is rapid reintegration of the impulse to active mastery. In cases of delayed convalescence psychic reintegration tends to lag behind somatic restoration of function. We have the clearest example of this in fracture cases in which the injured member may be mechanically useful long before the patient uses it. The developmental precursor of this situation is illustrated in the child's learning to walk. Functional capacity may be present here for some time before it is actually exploited. Some children begin to walk earlier than others, not because of differences in neuromuscular development, but because of a different capacity for tolerating the anxiety induced by the new problem of integration. Similarly, patients will tend to cling more or less to the simpler integration which illness induces. They seem to have lost the feel of their former capacity for mastery of a more complex world than that of the sick room. The final result is determined by two variable—the severity of the illness or trauma and the individual's tolerance for anxiety. Convalescence is thus seen to be a process which recapitulates the original problems of development and, with these, the original signals for anxiety.

The chronic invalidism that may follow an illness is an outgrowth of the normal problems of convalescence when these are complicated by a number of other factors. Given equal severity of illness or injury, the patient's tolerance for the anxiety-inducing problems of convalescence will vary with his constitution, with his previous success or failure in mastering anxiety-inducing threats, and, finally, with the secondary gains of illness. Clinical examples will demonstrate this.

*Example 1.* The secondary gains conducive to chronic invalidism generally represent opportunities to escape from situations in which the patient finds himself defeated or threatened by defeat. There are many complicated psychological factors operating in these cases of flight into illness which cannot be explained in the terms of the present discussion alone. Nevertheless all of them have in common the factor of anxiety. The life situation may be characterized by actual insurmountable obstacles or by insoluble neurotic conflicts involving envy, hostility, and guilt. Whatever the case may be, the regression into invalidism serves the comprehensive purpose of protecting the person against the need of coping with the anxiety situation in its own terms.

A 19-year-old man was admitted to the clinic with complaints of weakness, fatigability, vague chest pains. Two years previously he had been hospitalized for pleurisy with effusion and subsequently resided at a preventorium for six months as a tuberculosis suspect. The diagnosis was never confirmed, and he was discharged in apparently good health. Since then he had remained indolently at home, felt unable to engage in any activity, was apathetic, and interested only in his physical condition.

Examination did not reveal any somatic disease.

The social service investigation revealed that he came from a run-down family, the father an alcoholic, the mother a dull woman who submitted to the father's brutalities and took care of a large brood of children. The family was on welfare. The patient had been slow to learn to talk and walk and had left school at age 14 after completing only six grades. He had been a sickly child, had had chronic otitis media and had never been able to hold his own among seven siblings, of whom he was the fourth. After leaving school he had worked sporadically as a news vendor and errand boy until he became ill with pleurisy. At the preventorium he had had a record of exemplary behavior, seemed contented, and was not eager to leave.

The operation of secondary gain is clearly seen here. At the preventorium the patient had for once in his life know what it was to be free from anxiety. For him, to be sick really meant to be safe. His chronic invalid reaction seems largely to represent a consequence of the fact that he had never had enough of the wherewithal to tackle the problems of living.

*Example 2.* A 48-year-old man was admitted to the hospital with a fracture of the femur and general contusions as the result of a fall from a ladder in his store. At the time of his accident he was arranging stock on the shelves. He had a delirious reaction following the application of a cast, and a stormy hospital course. Two years after the injury he was a prematurely aged man, complaining of backaches and pains in his leg, unable to return to work, irascible with his wife, and bitterly resigned to dependence on the bounty of a younger brother.

This patient, the oldest of three boys, had been severely disappointed because, for financial reasons, he had been unable to continue his education beyond high school. He had worked hard, helped support his family, and married at age 28. After numerous setbacks, he finally managed to achieve his ambition of establishing himself in business, only to lose his investment during the depression. Subsequently there had been years of poverty until the outbreak of war, when he recouped his position. At the time of his accident he had been starting out for the second time in a business of his own—with this important factor operating: he was being helped to finance the venture by his next younger brother whose luck had been better.

While various psychic factors in this case made it necessary for this man to injure himself and to remain ill—among them his hostile jealousy of the very brother who was helping him—it is clear that his regression to invalidism was in its comprehensive aspects a surrender to his repeated failures, despite his efforts to master the anxiety stimuli involved in his drive for success.

*Example 3.* Some patients quite literally surrender before the impact of illness. This occurs chiefly in conditions of great seriousness. Most important and most difficult to understand is the fact that this may occur in the absence of the patient's knowledge of what exactly is wrong.

An elderly man who had sold his business preparatory to retirement to California was admitted to the hospital because of complaints of weakness, fatigue, anorexia, insomnia, and cough. These symptoms had appeared after an attack of flu seven months before. A week earlier he had had an attack of pleurisy. Despite the anorexia, he had lost no weight, and under observation he even gained a few pounds.

Apart from marked clubbing of the fingers, the physical findings were negative. Repeated studies of the chest revealed little. Only an undefined shadow in the mediastinum suggested the possibility of an early neoplasm. The Roentgen-ray report stated that "early neoplastic change could not be excluded." But the patient knew nothing of this.

Psychiatric study was requested because he had suffered from a depression 10 years previously and was again apparently depressed. His attitude was one of complete hopelessness. His facial expression and bodily posture were those of apathetic surrender. He had at one time eagerly looked forward to living in California, but this was now a matter of complete indifference to him. He minimized depression and emphasized his fatigue. He repeatedly stated that there must be something the matter with his chest. He had an air of anxious pleading for help, but with an attitude of hopeless resignation. During office interviews, after his discharge from the hospital, he remained uncommunicative or would cry silently and murmur that he expected to die very soon.

Five months after this study, he died. In the interim, weight loss had set in and weakness had become profound. Post-mortem examination revealed a bronchogenic carcinoma with metastases to lymph nodes and intestines.

*Example 4.* Another case of malignant disease presented quite clearly a similar picture of passive resignation and the attitude of a hopeless plea for help. A dream this patient diffidently revealed is illuminating: He dreamt that he was in a house in which everything was rotting and falling to pieces. In cases of this type, illness literally delivers a knockout blow to the patient's psychic resources.

REPRESSION OF ILLNESS ANXIETY

Some patients do not permit themselves to become clearly aware of the specific anxiety tension that illness may induce.

*Example 5.* The classical example of this is the euphoria of some tuberculous patients. A psychiatric patient, whose mother suffered from chronic tuberculosis and was going downhill informed me that on the morning of the day his mother died she talked with him cheerfully before his departure for school about measuring him for a suit on which she planned to start work the following day.

*Example 6.* We are all familiar with the paretic's euphoric megalomania, which masks the actual anxiety induced by the disintegration of his intellectual functions with increased pressure of intellectual activity and grandiose plans. A young man who had been diagnosed as having early syphilis appeared to take the information quite philosophically, only to report on his next visit the appearance of new symptoms: tachycardia and polyuria. A little exploration sufficed to reveal these to be connected with barely apprehended fantasies of an anxious type.

*Example 7.* A patient who had come into analysis because of a neurosis of some 10 years' standing complained also of fatigue. Two months after the analysis began it was suggested that he have a physical examination because of the excessive character of the fatigue. He was examined by a competent physician and was found to have pernicious anemia.

Several aspects of this case were psychologically important: He had postponed the examination for a month after it was discussed with him, during which time he had depreciated the symptom, preferring to attach it to his neurosis. When the diagnosis was established, he insisted that it was of small moment and that there was really nothing to worry about. He showed prompt symptomatic improvement under treatment, and his conscious attitude to his somatic illness continued to be one of optimism. His dreams, however, began to deal with his feeling of helplessness, and while on the couch he began to have intense recurrent visual fantasies in which he appeared as a frightened little boy at whom his father was shaking an admonishing finger. This man had good reason for feelings of guilt and to fear the loss of his status; his unconscious reaction to his somatic illness was governed by those feelings.

FLIGHT INTO HEALTH—DENIAL OF ANXIETY

This brings us to the situation in which anxiety may lead to reactions against itself. In part, the case just cited was an example of this. But there are striking cases in which the patients are even more overt in their denial of the anxiety connected with illness.

*Example 8.* A man of 50 suffered from a coronary attack. Instead of following the regime advised by his doctors he pooh-poohed their caution and hastened his death by transferring his business to his bedside. This patient was one of those who never delegated authority. He had never been able to depend on others and in the end could not allow himself even a temporary regression into the dependency of illness.

*Example 9.* A male patient in his forties was admitted to the hospital for study because of loss of weight, mild anemia, and the occasional appearance of occult blood in the stools. Carcinoma of the gastrointestinal tract was suspected, *but he had not been informed of this.* In the hospital he gave trouble with his complaints about the food, about the nursing service, about everything. He denied the validity of his hospitalization and insisted on going home.

During the psychiatric examination he was responsive, cooperative, apparently cheerful. He gave a coherent life story which did not reveal any unusual neurotic traits, nor did his circumstances reveal evidence of current stress. There was, however, one discrepancy. Since his admission to the hospital he had been having catastrophic dreams. Their content was vague—he knew only that they were distressingly fearsome. He continued to deny the necessity for hospitalization and finally left against advice before a diagnosis could be made.

Three weeks later he was brought back to the hospital in coma and died within 24 hours. Post-mortem examination revealed a carcinoma of the stomach with metastases to the brain.

In this case, one might question whether or not the patient's reaction may have been due in the first instance to the fact that he had organic disease of the brain with consequent impairment. It must be emphasized that there was no clinical evidence of an organic type of cerebral reaction at the time he was examined, and that in any case the reaction of the patient would have encompassed this aspect of the threat to his total organic integrity.

*Example 10.* A chronically neurotic woman of 40, who lived in masochistic submission to a husband she hated, was admitted to the surgical service because of weakness, loss of weight, and pain in the back which radiated into both arms. Difficulty in swallowing was present and had been diagnosed as globus hystericus. In the clinic examination the only positive finding had been gallstones. Because of the psychiatric history, consultation was requested.

The examination revealed the old neurotic problems which had reached a pathological equilibrium. She continued to live her life as it had been at the time when she was last seen some years before. Nothing new had developed emotionally. The old hostilities and the old submissions were still in the picture. Only the somatic symptoms were new. Although description of these new discomforts were consistent, she was curiously unworried about them. Her mood was apparently good. She spoke of the old neurotic situation, but without special intensity. However, although she made inquiries as to when she could go home, her attitude about this seemed quite tentative.

Further diagnostic procedures were advised, and in the end a diffusely infiltrating carcinoma of the esophagus was found. A month later she died in consequence of hemorrhage.

Cases of this type demonstrate the "flight into health."

## ILLNESS ANXIETY AND THE DOCTOR AS MAGICIAN

The history of medicine begins with the history of magic. We are all aware of the attitudes of awe, fear, hope, and veneration which patients bring to a physician's office or to a hospital. The final source of such feelings is to be found in the person's anxiety of the unknown and unpredictable powers which may govern his fate. Even the most sophisticated may turn to religion and mysticism as a final support when medicine fails. The success of quackery is dependent on the survival of such primitive emotions.

The physician is often blind to the magical implications that everything about him, from his white coat to the most imposing treatment apparatus, has for the patient. The doctor is the embodiment of the nursing and protecting mother and the controlling and regulating, rewarding and punishing father. Dependence on the person, the will of God, of fate, or of dark powers, is implicit in the doctor's presence. Whatever augments the mystery—the instruments, the techniques, the scientific jargon—augments the anxiety.

A certain amount of this is inevitable from the very nature of human beings. A great deal of it is artifact produced by the physician and his set-up. Insofar as these attitudes of patients are inevitable, they are insufficiently understood and inadequately exploited in the patient's interest. Insofar as these attitudes are stimulated by the doctor, they are too often disregarded or discounted.

Some patients become "experts" on their own cases as a manifestation of an intellectual effort to cope with anxiety which has been inadequately handled in rational terms by the physician. Some patients become shoppers and wind up with quacks because the physician has adhered too severely to downright rationality.

The art of medicine consists of the judicious exercise of magic and knowledge, or paternalism and maternalism. Such psychological factors as we have discussed are relevant medical data, and insofar as the principles behind them are understood and consciously exploited, the art of medicine becomes a science.

# The Emotional Position
# of the Analyst in the
# Psychoanalytic Situation

(1952)

THE VARIOUS clinical phenomena which have been called countertransference occur in the setting of the analytic situation. The analytic situation may be described as the total configuration of interpersonal relationships and interpersonal events which evolve between the psychoanalyst and his patient. The patient's part in this configuration is understood in terms of the transference as discovered by Freud. The analyst's "normal" role has been regarded from the same standpoint. It has been understood that the analyst so conducts himself that the transference in all its aspects develops in its own terms. Classical technique has been directed not toward its manipulation but toward its systematic resolution through analysis. This has been based on the assumption that the analyst is by his own intention and in the eyes of the patient a neutral

*Editorial note:* The problem of countertransference does not appear to be much clearer today than it was 20 years ago. Subsequent discussions of the subject frequently refer to Dr. Gitelson's contribution.

figure onto whom the patient's centrally significant object relations are displaced.

We have nevertheless long been aware of deviations from this in practice. As early as 1910 Freud (1910b) stated, "We have become aware of the counter-transference, which arises in [the physician] as a result of the patient's influence on his *unconscious feelings* . . . we have noticed that no psycho-analyst goes further than his own complexes and internal resistances permit . . ." (pp. 144–145; italics added). In our students we have been able to identify "errors in technique" as owing not simply to ignorance, but often to intrusions of their own emotions and attitudes onto the patient. Even experienced analysts do not adhere strictly to theoretically prescribed conduct—sometimes with intention and sometimes for psychological reasons of their own. All such instances produce results in the analytic situation which affect its configuration.

Furthermore, recent developments in the psychotherapeutic aspects of psychoanalysis, such as experiences with borderline character problems (Stern, 1945) and with schizophrenic psychoses (Fromm-Reichmann, 1948) have pointed to the significance of the analyst as a real object. It is important, therefore, to attempt a systematic consideration of the actual role of the analyst in the analytic situation.

The term "counter-transference" was originally used to designate the emotional reactions of the analyst to (against) the patient's transference. Countertransference was looked upon as a disturbing factor, inasmuch as it interfered with the emotional neutrality of the analyst which allowed the transference to develop in its own terms. On the other hand, it disturbed the analyst's capacity for the freely hovering attention which enables him to listen effortlessly, to remember, to understand, and to interpret correctly. If the analyst is to see the patient in terms of the latter's history, structure, and dynamics, he must himself be emotionally uninvolved. These concepts were the inevitable complement to Freud's original definition (1905) of the transference: "A whole series of psychological experiences are revived, not as belonging to the past, but as applying to the person of the physician at the present moment" (p. 116). If the transference is to be a truly irrational recapitulation of childhood relationships subject to psychoanalytic interpretation, then nothing in the current reality must intervene to give it concurrent validity. These are still the guiding principles of classical psychoanalytic technique. For these reasons the analyst himself must be analyzed; the maneuvers he employs in the analytic setting are intended to preserve his anonymity and to separate the patient's affectivity from his own.

As I have said, in practice this theoretical ideal is not fully attained. The smooth analytic surface is inevitably rippled by the analyst's humanness and personal "style" (A. & M. Balint, 1939). The transference field is contaminated by such factors as the "before" and "after" moments that surround the analytic session, the analyst's inadvertent or technically intended conduct during the hour, and those unavoidable contacts, direct or indirect, which occur in our tight little psychoanalytic communities. In consequence, it has become difficult if not impossible to be certain of what is being referred to when the term "transference situation" is employed. Strictly speaking, it means "that which is recapitulated from childhood." Yet there is no doubt that it is also used to refer to feelings and attitudes which the patient brings into analysis from other sources. Among these, we have become aware of the possibility that the patient may react, validly or invalidly, to the recognition of the analyst as a person; and that he may react to the analyst's attitudes to him.

These complications of the transference situation and our view of it are paralleled by complications in our ideas concerning the countertransference, as is evidenced by the variety of concepts of it which have been advanced.

Paula Heimann (1950) calls countertransference "all the feelings which the analyst experiences toward the patient." What distinguishes these feelings from those of the patient is "above all the degree of the feelings experienced and the use made of them, these factors being interdependent." The analyst's own analysis enables him "to *sustain* the feelings which are stirred in him, as opposed to discharging them, in order to *subordinate* them to the analytic task. . . . Our basic assumption is that the analyst's unconscious understands that of his patient. This rapport . . . comes to the surface in the form of feelings which the analyst notices in response to his patient, in his 'counter-transference'" (pp. 81–82). The assumption this leads to is that counter-transference feelings may be productive of analytic understanding and good technique, or, if the analyst is in personal trouble, they may lead to defense *maneuvers* which manifest themselves in the overt behavior which is more commonly referred to as a "countertransference."

Fliess (1942) considered the analytic "rapport" referred to above, a "trial identification." He saw this as occurring in four phases:

(1) The analyst is the object of the [patient's] striving; (2) he identifies with its subject, the patient; (3) he becomes this subject himself; (4) he projects the striving, after he has "tasted" it, back onto the patient and so finds himself in the possession of the inside knowledge of its nature, having thereby acquired the emotional basis for his interpretation. . . . In the first phase, in which he is the object of the striving of his patient, an instinctual response will be stimulated in the analyst. This is called the "countertransference," *but it deserves this name only in the case of the further complication that such response repeats an infantile one and uses the patient as a substitute for its infantile object.* The problem of what to do with this induced striving [in the analyst] becomes therefore identical with the problem of "handling the countertransference" [pp. 215-216].

Winnicott (1949) correctly sets aside the phenomena which have been called countertransference in analysts who have themselves been inadequately analyzed. These are merely the manifestations of a neurosis continuing to operate in a new setting. Nor does he regard as counter-transference the idiosyncratic tendencies of an analyst which are determined by his personal history and structure and which make his work different in style and quality from that of his colleagues. He believes that "the truly objective countertransference" is the "analyst's love and hate in reaction to the actual personality and behaviour of the patient" (pp. 69-70). With particular reference to psychotics, he states that "if the patient seeks objective or justified hate he must be able to reach it, else he cannot feel he can reach objective love" (p. 72). The analyst needs to be like "a mother [who] has to be able to tolerate hating her baby without doing anything about it" (p. 74).

Annie Reich (1951) has stated that "counter-transference comprises the effects of the analyst's own unconscious needs and conflicts on his understanding or technique. In such cases the patient represents for the analyst an object of the past onto whom past feelings and wishes are projected, just as it happens in the . . . patient's transference situation with the analyst. The provoking factor for such an occurrence may be something in the patient's personality or material, or something in the analytic situation as such." This she considers "counter-transference in the proper sense." The simplest cases are "those which occur suddenly under specific circumstances and with specific patients" (p. 26). The more complicated cases, which are characterized by the total attitude of the analyst toward a patient or patients, belong to the permanent neurotic difficulties of the analyst. Reich is inclined to believe that most countertransference difficulties belong to this permanent type.

Berman (1949), concerned with what he considers to be the necessity of positively toned attitudes toward the patient for the favorable course of the "therapeutic process," states, "Actually most analysts' positive feelings for their patients involve a wider range of feeling whose totality we shall describe as *dedication*. It is dedication in this wider sense of the dedication of the good leader and good parent that makes an analyst's attitude of kindly acceptance, patience, and so on, genuine and effective" (p. 161). Here the countertransference is presented as the more or less consciously determined therapeutic intention of the analyst.

In a symposium held by the Chicago Society in 1949, a similar view of what constitutes the countertransference was introduced. While recognizing it in the various aspects which have been presented thus far, the position was taken that countertransference is a part of psychoanalytic technique, that a "corrective attitude" can and, in given circumstances, should be taken by the analyst, an attitude consciously based on the emotional needs of the patient as determined by the defects of originally significant figures (Weiss, 1949). A dynamically more important observation was introduced by Benedek (1953) regarding the reaction of the analyst against "recognition" by the patient of aspects of himself as a human being. Her implication that the therapeutic incognito may be used by the analyst as a countertransference defense is clearly important.

It is obvious from what has been said that a wide variety of reactions of both patient and analyst are designated respectively as transference and countertransference. Assuming that he satisfies the basic requirement that he has been well analysed, we see that the analyst may still bring into the analytic situation interfering emotional factors of which the following are examples:

(1) Postanalytic residuals, such as a surviving identification with his own analyst.

(2) Narcissistic power motives characterologically masked, such as the apparently benevolent wish to cure.

(3) Unconscious instinctual aims which may have been analysed in relation to other objects but may nevertheless find refuge in the activity of analyzing.

(4) Surviving vestiges of original conflicts which introduce into the analytic situation the possibility of exacerbations of anxiety in the analyst with the consequent appearance of the classical "blind spots" or of acting out defenses.

(5) Current problems in the personal life of the analyst which have not yet been solved and integrated (Glover, 1955).

Offsetting such "interfering" factors, we find in the qualified analyst:

(1) Intellectually sublimated curiosity about the feelings and behaviour of other people and about himself. It is recognized that there may be a thin boundary between this and unconscious scopophilia as an instinctual aim.

(2) Object-attitudes, including emphatic compassion —as distinguished from sympathetic identification, and helpfulness—as distinguished from 'omnipotence or masochism.

(3) Finally, we expect to find in the qualified analyst an emotionally "open" system of communication among the various aspects of his character and personality. A fluid process of checks and balances operates among his instinctual and defensive tendencies, so that

none is fully isolated, self-operating and self-sustaining. We assume such a person to be in a state of flexible rather than rigid equilibrium and control. Such a person is in a spontaneous state of continuing self-analysis. For him the analytic situation is one in which self-analysis is concurrently integrated with the events and process of his patient's analysis. Thus, a "third ear," directed toward himself, maintains the continuing prospect of resolving the analyst's own interfering emotions while coping with those of his patient. This, perhaps, is the most important technical qualification of the analyst (Fliess, 1942; Glover, 1955; Freud, 1937).

The interaction of these various factors and the possible prevalence of one or more of them produce the final picture of the analyst as a person and as a therapist, providing the basis for the fact that a given analyst may have special therapeutic capacities with special types of patients, and at the same time, he may also have particular therapeutic disabilities. In other words, since the analyst, like the patient, comes into the analytic situation with his own quota of potential nonrational attitudes, the opening phase of any analysis confronts the analyst with problems of social integration similar to those which would confront him in any new interpersonal situation.

The analytic situation is a microcosm in which the analyst has elected to live a significant part of his life. To the extent to which this is true, the analyst is entering a relationship in which his task is to integrate himself rationally in the face of difficulties. The trial analysis is thus not merely a test of the analyzability of the patient, but also contains a test of the analytic situation for the analyst. The problem that the trial analysis needs to solve is thus not only whether the patient has a margin of integrative capacity which makes the analytic situation tenable for him, but also whether the analyst's pattern of social integration includes the particular aspect of life the patient presents to him.

It would seem, therefore, that no analyst enters upon the analysis of another person without residual potentialities for reaction to either the patient, the patient's material, the patient's transferences, or the patient's real attitude to him as a real person. These potentialities for reaction belong, as Freud has shown, to the fact that analysis is interminable. They are the result of presentations by the patient that touch on surviving transference potentials or on still vulnerable aspects of the analyst's narcissism and character defenses. In the presence of these, the qualified analyst can nevertheless exercise his technical capacity because he comes to each successive patient situation with the broad outlines of personal insight and integration. He no longer treasures his narcissistic illusions at all costs, and, as Heimann has shown, he is capable of "sustaining" the blows they are exposed to.

Up to this point in my own discussion of the analyst's reactions to his patients I have attempted to avoid a commitment to the use of the term "countertransference." This has been deliberate, because I wish to attempt to differentiate its use. To this end I shall now speak separately of the analyst's reaction to the patient as a whole and his reactions to partial aspects of the patient.

REACTIONS TO THE PATIENT AS A WHOLE

The qualified analyst brings to each patient situation goal- and object-directed attitudes comprising intellectual curiosity, capacity for empathy, and the wish to be helpful. If an analysis is established, these remain the analyst's compass, his rudder, and his anchor throughout all the vicissitudes of the analytic course. In any given new analytic situation, however, it may happen that the analyst will discover that these sublimations are massively overwhelmed either by excessive intensity or by contrary feelings of indifference, boredom, irritation, or uneasiness.

It would seem that such initial emotional attitudes in a new analytic situation derive their interfering quality from the fact that they emanate from a surviving neurotic "transference potential." They may be less intense and less compulsive than my description would imply, and because of the positive qualifications of the analyst they may be more under the control of the reality-testing attitudes. In some instances they might even be resolvable. This is why it is possible for the analyst to offer himself as a therapist and why he is able to conduct valid analyses with so many different kinds of patients. On the other hand, in special situations, these very facts reveal to him his unsuitability for a particular patient.

*Example 1*

I have terminated my connection with a patient after a trial period, not because I considered the patient unanalyzable but because the patient was not analyzable by me. The eventual proof of this was the patient's successful analysis by the analyst to whom I referred her.

From the beginning I had a vague feeling of uneasiness with the patient, a young married woman who had come because of difficulties in her relations with her husband, and who, from the beginning, presented only complaints of the injustices she had suffered throughout a rather difficult life. There was never, during the eight weeks of my work with her, any dynamic elaboration of these complaints, and it was only when she presented a dream during the final week that I gained an impression as to what she felt about the analytic situation.

In the dream I appeared as myself, while the female colleague who had referred her to me was vaguely disguised. The patient was small like a child, though otherwise herself. The two adults, lying on a mattress, were juggling her between them with their feet. In the childhood background was the divorce of the parents and their struggle for the possession of the patient, which struggle the father finally won. In the dream my appearance without disguise indicated that I had introduced something into the analytic situation which in fact repeated an ancient interpersonal situation for the patient.

Such a clinical experience was the consequence of what was at the time a surviving neurotic transference potential which affected my whole feeling about the patient and which I did not solve until later. It was not an episodic response, but was my reaction to the patient as a person. I think this example makes it possible to say that a person who enters into a therapeutic relationship with overall feelings about and toward the patient is not entering such a situation as an analyst, nor is the relationship thus set up a psychoanalytic situation. The phenomenon it illustrates belongs to the class of displacements which may appear in any interpersonal relationship. It is not a countertransference. On the contrary, the patient has become a transference object for the analyst and realizes it, as is attested to by my patient's dream. This may be true whether the analyst's reaction to the patient is negatively or positively toned.

With regard to a negative reaction, there is not much practical difficulty. Even though my feeling about this patient was obscure to me, it was nevertheless clear enough that I was of no use as an analyst in the situation I have described. More troublesome, because they can be more illusory, are the positively toned reactions to the patient. Nowadays we hear much about "motherly" and "fatherly" analysts and about corrective emotional attitudes (Weiss, 1949). There are undoubtedly genuinely motherly or fatherly people who happen also to be psychoanalysts. However, to the extent to which an analyst looks upon himself as such or is *professionally* classifiable as such, it seems important to consider the possibility that he is presenting a chronic character defense or a surviving neurotic transference potential. As such it may be socially laudable, and in certain clinical situations it may be psychotherapeutically useful, but in psychoanalysis proper it is a gross, interfering factor.

### Example 2

A young analyst responded to a female patient who had occupied her first hours with self-disparagement and the feeling that no one had liked her or could like her with the reassuring comment that he could see no reason for her feeling that way in his case; that, in fact, he did have a good impression of her. In the next hour the patient presented a dream in which she saw the analyst sitting before her with his penis exposed but flaccid. The patient broke off the analysis during the trial period. The problems of the patient which contributed to this denouement do not concern us here. But the "error of technique" committed by the analyst illustrates an attitude of "therapeutic kindness" which represented the analyst's abiding need to reduce the intensity of his own unresolved sadomasochistic impulses.

Students starting a new case will sometimes speak enthusiastically about how much they like the patient. Edoardo Weiss (1949) has spoken of the "resonance feelings" which an analyst may experience in reaction to patients toward whom he feels "technically" well disposed. Some such experience is involved when we find ourselves *feeling into* the patient's subjective state. In such instances it is a contact feeling with mixed intellectual and emotional components. The word "empathy," which carries a note of the familiar and the recognizable, comes closest to explaining it. It touches on something in our own experience and lets us know that somehow we and the patient have lived and integrated similarly (Heimann, 1950; Fliess, 1942). But one must be cautious about what constitutes the subjective reality represented by such "liking" such "resonance." Narcissistic identification and narcissistic infatuation may also produce "resonance feelings." Enthusiasm about a patient masquerading under the cliche "positive countertransference" may be the opposite number of the defensive erotized positive transference with which some patients elude us. Clinical experience convinces one that patients are able to exploit such so-called "positive countertransferences" in the interest of their delusions and defenses.

To summarize my discussion so far: It is my impression that total reactions to a patient are *transferences* of the analyst to his patients and are revivals of ancient transference potentials. These may be manifested in the over-all attitude toward patients of a particular type or may be exacerbated in the "whole response" to particular patients. These attitudes may be positively or negatively toned. They are likely to manifest themselves very early on, and to determine the analyst's attitude to and treatment of the whole case. They may thus operate in determining the analyst's "choice of roles" and choice of patients; and this choice will tend to be rationalized in terms of the patient's "needs." They lead the analyst to think that his personality is the most important agent of the therapeutic process. Finally, they undermine the possibility of the inner reconstruction that analysis can provide.

REACTIONS TO PARTIAL ASPECTS OF THE PATIENT

In contrast to transference, the countertransferences of the analyst appear later and occur in the context of an established analytic situation. They comprise the analyst's reactions to the patient's transference, the material the patient brings in, and the reactions of the patient to the analyst as a person.

I have indicated that unanalyzed and unintegrated

facets of the instincts and of the defensive techniques always remain, and that we can expect only that these be susceptible to further analysis and integration. This will by and large suffice to obviate or, sometimes, to resolve the type of general transference reaction to patients which I have described. But at the same time we know that the patient's productions, his defenses, and his transferences are continually impinging on the unconscious and the defensive system of the analyst. Insofar as the analytic material and the transference of the patient do not open up unanalyzed territory in the analyst, the analysis proceeds according to the art. But when the analysis touches on unresolved problems in the analyst, then we can expect the same type of *emergency response* that we see in patients when they unexpectedly encounter something new in themselves. Again one is impressed that such a development is the inevitable consequence of the fact that analysis is interminable and that no person is finally and perfectly analyzed. I think this means that the analyst remains vulnerable to the need for resorting to *emergency defense reactions* and that such reactions are at the center of the analytic phenomenon we call countertransference. The following experiences will illustrate the point.

### Example 3

Some years ago I was analyzing a schizoid patient. The analysis was progressing favorably when, at the end of about a year, the patient was faced with the prospect of making a public appearance in a capacity for which he was well qualified. Under these circumstances, with the deadline rapidly approaching, contrary to my usual practice, I actively encouraged him. The patient then resorted to a piece of destructive acting out. I made an appointment with my former analyst to discuss the case. To my surprise, I found myself talking not about my patient but about myself. The consultation turned into an analytic hour for me, and I received no specific advice about the management of the case. Nevertheless, I returned to my office, handled my patient's problem satisfactorily, and eventually conducted the analysis to a successful ending.

What I discovered was that certain narcissistic investments, which, under the particular circumstances of the patient's pending task, had become intensified, had produced in me an emergency defense against the deeper meaning of his phobic attitude. I had thus overlooked the passivity problem with its potentiality for panic which was implicit in his doubts and qualms. The defense had taken the form of benevolent interest, and I had been aware only of satisfaction in the fact that a difficult case was going well and of the "benign" hope that the patient would succeed in mastering the particular hurdle he was approaching.

### Example 4

At the beginning of an hour in a going analysis, a young male patient commented to me that I looked tired. I myself was not aware of fatigue. Toward the end of the hour, which he had spent talking about his university activities, he request a change in the time of his appointment two weeks hence, when he was scheduled to present a paper in a seminar. I said I would see what I could do about changing the time. He then withdrew his request, giving as his reason that it would inconvenience me. I told him, however, that the request seemed valid and that I would see what change I could make in his appointment. He left my office looking preoccupied.

The next day he brought the following dream:

He has an engagement with his mother, but it seems to be incidental to a date which he has later with his mistress. He acts as if he were indifferent to his mother and is hurried in disposing of the business with her.

The patient then spoke of how upset he felt after the previous hour. I told him I had noticed it. Then he spoke about not writing home and about his childhood feeling that he was incidental to his mother's career interests. His further comments made it clear that he now ignored the existence of his parents as he had himself felt ignored. When he then referred to my "insistence" on rearranging my programme for him, *even after he felt that he had detected some hesitancy on my part,* something recurred to me which I had until then forgotten: On the morning of the day of my patient's request, I had arrived at the hospital earlier than usual for the purpose of discussing cases with the residents. None of them was around, and none appeared until I was about to leave with only a limited time in which to reach my office. They were disappointed because I could not stay on to work with them. I myself was irked by their lateness and commented on it. But the matter had apparently slipped from my mind.

I shall not go into the personal ramifications of this episode. But it was clear to me that I had displaced to my office my reaction to the hospital situation, and that my patient had detected my latent annoyance with him. I did the only thing I felt I could do; I brought the episode into the open and admitted the irritation which I recognized I had produced, unawares. It developed, however, that what had affected him most was that he had correctly observed my compensatory attitude, which had impressed him as a concern for something in myself rather than for him. That this was more important than my apparent annoyance with him was evident when he told me that his mother had often said that she was doing something for his good when in fact it was something in which she had a personal stake.

There is no need to dwell on those countertransferences that are phenomenologically similar to the emergency defenses of patients. Symptomatic reactions speak for themselves and lead the analyst to try to discover and to analyze their meaning in his part of the analytic situation. Furthermore, the analyst is pretty much aware of his immediate emotional reactions to the overt transference manifestations of the patient, is likely to have fairly adequate access to their deeper sources, and is able to resolve them in his stride before they become interfering factors in the analytic situation. But instances such as those I have just described present more difficult problems. They represent reactions of the analyst to presentations by the patient which touch upon vulnerable aspects of his, the analyst's, surviving character defenses. They are likely to be masked by various rationalizations surrounding apparently therapeutic purposes, whereas they have, in fact, to do with unconscious contents and affects and the unconscious defenses against them.

A countertransference reaction, if the analyst is "open" enough to analyze it, can be an integrative experience along the long road of interminable analysis. For such reactions seem to be defenses against what the analyst discovers of himself in and through the patient. If this is a part of the analyst's deepest realization, both he and his patient are protected against the consequences of nontechnical intrusions which are the end result of an unrealized countertransference. The analyst's real emotional acceptance of the patient consists in his acceptance of his own unconscious community with the patient.

One must conclude that the analyst as a mere screen does not in actuality exist. He cannot deny his personality its operation as a significant factor. He will appear as he actually is: in manner, speech, and general spontaneity. And he will bring into the analytic situation those qualities which I outlined at the beginning. This is far from saying, however, that his personality is the chief instrument of the therapy that we call psychoanalysis. There is a great difference between the selection and playing of a role and the awareness of the fact that one has found one's self cast for a part. It is of primary importance for the analyst to conduct himself so that the analytic process proceeds on the basis of what the patient brings to it. Countertransferences thus constitute an accidental casting of the analyst in an intrusive role in the psychoanalytic drama. Through the analysis of the countertransference, the analyst can reintegrate his position as an analyst and regain a position from which he can utilize the interfering factor for the purpose of analyzing the patient's exploitation of it. In some instances this may mean a degree of self-revelation (by which I do not mean confession). But in a going analysis it may be found possible. In such a situation one can reveal as much of oneself as is needed to foster and support the patient's discovery of the reality of the actual interpersonal situation as contrasted with the transference-countertransference situation.

As an example of this I can again cite the young student (Example 4) who reacted so sensitively to the intrusion of my own narcissism into his analysis. In subsequent hours much emerged about his present status and his early life which demonstrated the central role played by his great wish for unlimited devotion. I think it might not have been possible for me to develop the analysis of this important theme had I not become aware of how my own reaction to a narcissistic injury had eventuated in a transference injury to him. And I think that my acknowledgement of his "recognition" of me was of assistance to him in the realization of the extent of his own narcissistic problem.

In the light of this discussion it can be said that the sustaining psychotherapeutic factor in the conduct of an analysis, the real ego support that the patients need, resides in the actuality of the analyst's own reality-testing attitudes. On his steady and predictable effort to maintain this capacity depends the analyst's function.

It is not only the analyst's capacity to discover himself which is important, however. An analysis can come to an impasse because the analyst is unaware of, or misunderstands, or avoids the issue of a patient's discovery of him as a person (Benedek, 1953). The following clinical instance will demonstrate this:

## Example 5

A competent young analyst had for over a year been conducting satisfactorily the analysis of a difficult case. Then, for external reasons, the supervision of the case was interrupted for an extended period. When consultations were resumed, it became obvious that the patient had not been making progress for some time. There had been a regression to earlier modes of defense; the material seemed chaotic; the contact with the analyst was attenuated.

Interspersed were dreams which repeatedly made reference to the activities of the analyst and to the theme of contact with the analyst. Thus, in one dream, through the rear-view mirror in his car the patient saw the analyst drive up behind him at a filling station. The patient backed his car gently into the analyst's car. In another dream the patient tried to throw balls of fluff at the analyst but could not give them enough impetus to reach him. Throughout was the implication that the analyst was "busy with other things." Finally, the patient presented a dream in which a figure representing the analyst was stalking him but indifferent to him. During the subsequent consultation the analyst made a slip of the tongue. In beginning the report of an analytic session, he said, speaking of the patient: "His dream *for today* was . . ." Then the situation became clear.

Inquiry about this reference to a dream as if it were an assigned task revealed that the analyst had been asked to present the patient's dreams at a research seminar on a special problem. He had devoted himself assiduously to the assignment, with the consequence that, while apparently studying the patient, he had become withdrawn from him. The patient had reacted accordingly.

The resolution of such a transference-countertransference jam depends on the capacity of the analyst to become aware of his own part in the analytic situation. But the problem still remains of how to cope with the patient's part in such a situation. It would seem that here again the analyst may reveal as much of himself as is needed to foster and support the patient's testing of reality. In so doing the guiding questions are: What and how much does the patient need to know in order to correct an illusion or to validate a real insight? How much will be useful to the patient and how much will be a burden imposed on him? One does not ask the patient to share one's own problems. But one does make use of what has palpably intruded into the analytic situation without begging the issue. And of course the patient's reaction to such revelations as need be made to him must be analyzed.

In the case just described, the analyst discussed with the patient the latter's valid feeling that for some time he had been preoccupied with other matters than his analytic work and that this preoccupation had interfered with the proper conduct of the analysis and thus adventitiously affected the patient. The analysis then returned to its previous course.

But there is one position the analyst must be able to sustain without doubt; no matter what he himself brings into the analytic situation which may represent the incompleteness of his own integration *at the moment*, he must nevertheless adhere to the fundamental precept that the patient is there to be analyzed and helped toward *his* integration. Providing he deals with it analytically in himself and in the analysis of the patient, whatever the analyst adventitiously brings into the analytic situation is subsidiary to the patient's needs.

There may be situations in which the analyst might indeed be glad to settle with the patient for the partial truth which the latter has guessed about him, just as the patient on his side may be content to make a similar settlement. Yet when such an issue is joined, the analyst must be prepared either to go through with an analysis of the total analytic situation, including his side of the analytic equation, or to give up his part in the analysis.

Another aspect of the problem of the relationship of the patient's transferences to the emotional position of the analyst may now be considered. An unmanageably intense transference neurosis is likely to be heralded in the patient's first dreams by the appearance in them of the analyst as himself. Such dreams are indicative of the actual recurrence in the analytic situation of an emotional situation which is too nearly like that which characterized an original relationship (Blitzsten, personal communication), and the analyst needs to be certain that it is not his own attitude to the patient that is producing the reaction.*

---

*Editorial note:* This paragraph has been the source of considerable misunderstanding. Psychoanalysts seem to think that Dr. Gitelson wrote

*Example 6*

The following clinical instance was related to me by a colleague: A student had begun the analysis of a young woman who for many weeks spoke very little and was often entirely silent. There were no dreams, and the analysis was at an impasse. Then the patient saw an announcement in the newspaper of a lecture which the student analyst was to give. She reacted with the following dream:

She is in bed with the analyst; she takes his hands and places them on her breasts against his will; she has a strong sexual reaction.

---

a paper on the subject of dreams about the analyst, and that he is responsible for the idea that early dreams about the analyst as himself indicates a poor prognosis. Rosenbaum (1965) took note of this misunderstanding, investigated it, and inadvertently added to the confusion. For although Rosenbaum is careful to state that Blitzsten's ideas "were brought into the analytic literature by Gitelson," and quotes a letter Dr. Gitelson wrote him concerning this matter, he places his paraphrase of the above paragraph with other "literature on the subject," thus strengthening the impression that the "subject" was that of an entire paper. Rosenbaum remarks on the fact that "Gitelson's comments on the problem, even though incidental and quite brief, seem to have left a strong imprint on the memory of many analysts" (p. 436). He even attempts to account for the phenomenon, saying, "We deal with many uncertainties. Therefore is it so surprising that when an experienced analytic clinician *merely mentions* that a certain clinical phenomenon may have a specific meaning for diagnosis, treatment, and prognosis, we seize upon it" (ibid.)?

Rappaport (1959) also cites the paragraph in question and also makes it clear that the idea was Blitzsten's (p. 241). But Harris (1962), in an article called "Dreams About the Analyst," does not mention Blitzsten at all. He gives the impression that Dr. Gitelson's remarks appear in the context of a paper dealing with the subject of his own paper.

Is it possible that Dr. Gitelson himself inadvertently gave support to the misunderstanding? (See p. 225 below.)

In associating, the patient told her analyst how proud she was of him because of his prominence; she used to write her father's speeches for him because of his difficulties with a new language; she is anxious about the analyst's performance and plans to attend the lecture to wish him well; finally she confesses that during the weeks of blocking and silence she had been immersed in sexual preoccupations about the analyst.

In talking about this case, the young analyst revealed that he had decided not to have his work with this patient supervised. This was one case he was going to conduct himself! He had begun the analysis in the context of his own transference rage because it had become necessary for him to give up acting out a sexual relationship that was interfering with the analysis of his oedipal problem. In this context he had the following dream:

> He is in bed with the patient; he puts his hand on her pubis; he feels that he is looking for something, but is aware only of hair and moisture.

In his associations to this dream he speaks of flirting with a girl in his office building en route to the analytic hour with this patient and of his anger at his analyst.

This necessarily highly condensed account nevertheless clearly demonstrates the sensitiveness of patients to the emotional climate of the analytic situation as regards the analyst's contribution to it. It is clear that the student had continued his acting out under the cloak of the analysis which he had undertaken with this patient and that this made the transference "too real."

It is often necessary to refer such patients to another analyst at once, as in the clinical instance just cited and in Examples 1 and 2.

On the other hand, an acute transference reaction to a countertransference occurring during the later course of a well-established analysis can be capitalized on in the interest of the patient if both sides of the equation are analysed, as may be witnessed in Examples 4 and 5. In such situations, the patient's dream in which the analyst appears as himself may be the index to the role which the analyst is playing through a countertransference. And of course the dreams of the analyst which include the patient as a person deserve the analyst's scrutiny for evidences of his countertransference position. In the first instance it is the patient who has discovered the situation. In the second instance the analyst has warned himself.

Finally, experience with students shows that one of the commoner sources of countertransference difficulties is to be found in the pregenital narcissistic and instinctual manifestations of the patient. It is because of the difficulties involved in the treatment of pregenital problems that "active techniques" have gained their recent vogue as a means of attempting to deal with the transferences of such patients. These techniques may at times constitute a rationally chosen and valid palliative psychotherapy. Nevertheless, the therapist's assumption of roles and choice of therapeutic attitudes in the treatment of such cases, while they may be described as techniques, often come close to representing transferences and countertransferences. This is particularly true where activity in the form of intervention is concerned. Influencing actual decisions and life situations may seem desirable at times, but we must remember that it may also constitute *"acting out in the countertransference."* Such intervention may have at least as much to do with the analyst's therapeutic ambitions and his personal outlooks on life as with the dynamic and economic problems of the patient. Whenever the analyst feels impelled to do something "active," it would seem advisable for him to examine his own motives carefully.

Countertransferences, like transferences, are dynamic and economic phenomena. They exist as facts of any analysis. They are a part of the dynamic and economic problem in every analysis. The analyst must deal with them in himself, and, together with his patient, he must deal with them when they intrude into the analytic situation. They are not subject to manipulation and willful control. To the extent to which the analyst is himself open to their analysis and integration, he is in a real sense a vital participant in the analysis with the patient. It is this which constitutes the analyst's real contact with the patient and which lets the patient feel that he is not alone.[1]

---

[1] Since completing the revision of this paper for publication, Margaret Little's sensitive observations (1951) on the response of patients to the countertransferences of their analysts have appeared. The material presented here seems to supplement her views. With these views the present writer is in accord.

# Re-evaluation of the Role
# of the Oedipus Complex

## (1952)

I T SEEMS appropriate that a symposium on this topic[1] should include an analysis of the myths and dramas from which the Oedipus complex derives its name—the more so since Dr. van der Sterren (1952) has also made some re-evaluations, calling our attention to various references in the text to the preoedipal elements in the drama. He has demonstrated how unconscious factors led certain translators to an ambiguity which screened the expression of the son's hostility to the mother as well as the father. He has established the parallelism between Jocasta and the bisexual Sphinx, and has shown the child's need to dilute his ambivalence toward his mother. And finally, apropos of our discussion, he has said: "The question may arise whether the feelings of the positive Oedipus complex are really so very clearly expressed [in the drama] because behind them the enmity towards the mother must be kept concealed (p. 348)."

*Editorial note:* This was the first paper Dr. Gitelson presented to an international audience. He later admitted to having been awed by the occasion.

[1] "Re-evaluation of the Role of the Oedipus Complex," Symposium at the 17th International Psycho-Analytic Congress, Amsterdam, 1951.

This question is of essential importance. In it is latent the issue of the relationship of pregenitality to the Oedipus complex. It suggests also the possibility of pregenital activity behind the oedipal scene as a factor in the major operations of the personality. These are among the problems which we should like to clarify today.

We have looked upon the superego as the heir of the Oedipus complex. Is the Oedipus complex similarly the successor to the several instincts, in a synthesis which focuses on the phallic organization, while subordinating earlier libidinal organizations? Or is it to be seen as the arena for the play of the component instincts? Is it the nuclear complex of neurosis and character formation? Is it only one factor among a series? Or is it possible, as Dr. Lampl-de Groot (1952) asks, that the "central conflict lies in the preoedipal relationship to the mother?"

The last two decades have seen these problems crystallized around the findings and theories of a number of English analysts following the teachings of Melanie Klein. We have heard Dr. Heimann's lucid exposition (1952) of the position taken by this group of workers. Because we are not concerned now with the general metapsychological questions involved in this position, and because the papers of Waelder (1937), Glover (1945), E. Bibring (1947), and others have considered these questions at length, we may dispense with specifically discussing them further at this time and allude to them only as our topic requires.

Now, if one disregards the disputed metapsychological assumptions and the foreshortened chronological scale against which infantile development is viewed by the members of the English school, and if one attends to their content descriptions alone, one is struck by the cogency of their statements with regards to clinical phenomena we all of us observe.

Dr. Heimann (1952) has reported to us that the attainment of the whole-object stage coincides at its inception with the polymorphous perverse condition of the instinctual impluses. While the oral impulses are still predominant and internalizing processes are of leading importance, urethral, anal, and genital strivings are now playing an increasing part. In consequence the depressive position develops and leads in the end to the turning from the mother to the father and the beginning of the Oedipus complex.

With the exception of the putative role of the genitalia, we can agree with Dr. Heimann (1952) that "the most severe conflicts and anxieties relate to the primitive impulses and phantasies" which belong to this stage of development.

Dr. Lampl-de Groot (1946) has described the anxieties of the preoedipal phase in terms comparable to those of the "depressive position". In her paper today she says (1952): "As soon as the mother is recognized and loved as an object outside the self, fear of losing the mother's love will arise in the face of conflicts between instinctual life and the mother's wishes. An important source of anxiety is given in the ambivalence conflict" (p. 538). In her 1946 paper she presents graphic descriptions of two cases in which this is demonstrated.[2]

[2] It was in this paper that she first made the observation, again reported today, that in the process of analysis oedipal material is presented in the fantasies and reminiscences, while, in contrast, the preoedipal material is acted out. It was here too that she demonstrated that the split mother-image had its source not merely in the depreciation of the sexual mother but also in the *survival* of the preoedipal mother-image.

• 203

These considerations bring us to what seems to be the crux of the problem, namely, what is the relationship of polymorphous perverse and pregenital phases of libidinal development to the phallic and genital phases? Dr. Heimann states that the frank Oedipus complex is the final stage (at three to five years) of a process which begins in infancy (at the sixth month) and passes through various stages prior to this. Nevertheless, the general impression she conveys is that of a peculiar telescoping of time relations such as one might obtain from a naïve view of the "chaotic periods" which, Dr. Lampl-de Groot has reminded us, we observe during some analyses. And with reference to Dr. Heimann's statement that throughout its course the Oedipus complex develops *pari passu* and in a reciprocal relation with the development of the instincts, the ego, and the superego, E. Bibring (1947) has helped us to see that in fact this can be true only if the whole rate of development is considered to be much more rapid than any clinical or biological data now available would prove. That is to say, if the oedipal developments envisaged by the English school occur as early as it believes, then it must be assumed that there occurs a much more rapid maturation of compatible ego functions than seems to be the actual case. Thus, while it is possible that the whole object stage may be attained at six months, the familiar figures of the child's environment, according to the observations of Gesell (1940), still have an undifferentiated significance for him as late as the fortieth week, so long as they do not disappoint his habitual expectations of them.

Nevertheless, simply to entertain doubts about the validity of the position taken in Dr. Heimann's paper is no solution for our problem. The clinical facts she has attempted to elucidate from that position have still to be accounted for. We have been accustomed to look upon pregenital material as largely the consequence of regression induced by castration anxiety encountered in the oedipal phase. We consider that the ego may revive from the unconscious the language of earlier phases and may thus present oedipal fantasies and impulses in the disguise of pregenital expressions. It is also agreed that the reverse occurs, and that oedipal fantasies and attitudes may be the vehicles for pregenital impulses and fantasies.

Thus, Fenichel (1931a) in his paper on "The Preoedipal Antecedents of the Oedipus Complex" presents three cases, in all of which pregenital attachment to the mother is carried over to the relationship with the father. In his summing up Fenichel concluded that: The Oedipus prohibition reflects the pregenital prohibitions; that castration anxiety can remain oral or it can be built up out of the dread of losing feces and the mother's breast; that "eruptions" of sensuality can be recognized as the longing for oral incorporation expressed as the female patient's wish for coitus,[3] and, finally, that "Pure genitality seems to exist as independently as urethral and anal erotism. Only because it flowers later does it retain so many of those traces of pregenital origin which are derived from an earlier period" (p. 203).

A year later Freud, in his paper on "Female Sexuality" (1931a), having called attention to the fact that the duration of the passionate attachment of the little

[3] I have analyzed a similar case in a male whose phallic orality included the fantasy of the penis as a sipper and a spoon.

girl to her mother has been underestimated, stated: ". . . the pre-Oedipus phase in women gains an importance which we have not hitherto attributed to it. Since this phase allows room for all the fixations and repressions from which we trace the origins of the neuroses, it would seem as though we must retract the universality of the thesis that the Oedipus complex is the nucleus of neurosis" (p. 226).

Alternative to this viewpoint, Freud suggested the following possibilities: Either the content of the Oedipus complex can be extended to include all the child's relations to both parents; or we can say that women reach the normal positive oedipal situation only after passing through a first phase dominated by the negative complex. Apparently he accepted the second alternative and came to the conclusion that "perhaps the real fact is that the attachment to the mother is bound to perish precisely because it was the first and was so intense . . . the little girl's intense attachment to her mother is strongly ambivalent, and that it is in consequence precisely of this ambivalence that [reinforced by other disappointments] her attachment is forced away from her mother—once again, that is to say, in consequence of a general characteristic of infantile sexuality" (p. 235).

In his further discussion Freud (concurring with the findings of Lampl-de Groot and Helene Deutsch) called our attention to the little girl's transition from the passive to the active attitude, which is inclusive of the foredoomed phallic strivings toward the mother, and came to the conclusion that the same preoedipal libidinal forces are at work in male and female and that for a time these take the same course and produce the same results. Freud emphasized the great intensity of the preoedipal libidinal strivings, "greater than anything that comes later," and gave them neurosogenic status in their own right.

Even if we were to look upon the pregenital situation from the standpoint of Freud's first suggested alternative to the devaluation of the Oedipus complex, that is, if we were to extend our conception of the Oedipus complex to include all the relations of the child to both parents, which is what the English school has done, we would still need to consider that the three-person relationship in its beginnings is nonsexual and noncompetitive in the genital sense.

Ruth Mack Brunswick (1940), on the basis of collaborative work with Freud, distinguished the Oedipus complex as characterized "above all" by the triangular situation and involving the love of one parent and the hostile rivalry with the other. But she went on to specify that in the pregenital situation the father is not yet a rival but simply another obscure figure of the environment who may be pleasing or displeasing; the mother is the central figure; other surrounding figures are not sexually differentiated, and, like the mother, are only objects for passive, and later active, polymorphous aims. In many ways Brunswick's description of this period parallels what Dr. Heimann has described as the "Early Stages" of the Oedipus complex.

In addition to the considerations already entertained, we must also recall the fact that the last two decades have brought to the attention of analysts a large body of material which was originally considered unsuitable for analysis but which our sharper view of pregenitality has enabled us to study more thoroughly.

Whereas Fenichel insisted on the centrality of the Oedipus complex, in contrast to Freud's (1931a) own more liberal attitude, he nevertheless modified his position at least to the extent of making the following statement: "Every single analysis provides fresh evidence of [the fact of the centrality of the Oedipus complex] *except* those cases of extreme malformations of character which resemble a lifelong psychosis and in which . . . the subject's object relations were destroyed root and branch at an earlier period, or because such relations never existed at all" (p. 181; italics added). My own experience leads me to believe that the Oedipus complex may be absent or at best vestigial, that pathological development may be established by earlier constellations of factors, and that there are more primitive libidinal positions which may be of central importance.

In the United States it has been said that at least a third of the cases which come to analysts are borderline cases with just sufficient development and integration of the ego functions to escape outright classification as psychotic. The structure and dynamics of these patients, as discovered in the analytic situation, reveal, however, the extent to which their lives are ruled by primitive operations of the ego and how much they are dominated by one-to-one instinctual object orientations. This applies not simply to their analytic situations but also to their external lives, in which pathological structure and function is often quite successfully concealed by a facade of apparently healthy ego operations. Many of these persons have actually *learned* how to conduct themselves with apparent adequacy in reality on a basis which suggests the early, primary identificatory learning of infants. The analysis of these patients is long and often stormy, yet some of them do mature enough in the end to come at last to what Dr. Lampl-de Groot (1952) has referred to as the "convergent phase" of analysis.[4]

It would be tempting to dispose of the clinical picture of such borderline cases by having recourse to the classical formulation, namely, these patients present a regression from the castration fear encountered in the Oedipus situation. But I am inclined to believe that they have never integrated the phallic position. While they have attained the whole-object stage, this has been at the narcissistic, identificatory, and anaclitic level. I am also inclined to think that the nuclear problem in such cases resides in the primary mother-child constellation. Thus, I have the impression that much of what the English school puts forward is not relevant to the transference neuroses. On the other hand it would seem that a re-evaluation of the material which Dr. Heimann (1952) considers to have phallic and oedipal reference would help to throw a great deal of light on the narcissistically injured pregenital types of cases to which I have referred.

In conclusion: we must be impressed that even the more conservative position of Dr. Lampl-de Groot points up our increased awareness of the importance of pregenital conflicts in determining the structure and dynamics of the Oedipus complex. The very evolution of the analytic process as she has described it indicates

---

[4] I paraphrase her remarks as follows: As the result of successful analysis of pregenitality the mother attachment moves toward the phallic phase; the Oedipus complex then reappears in normal form, free from pregenital material.

that the failure to solve the Oedipus conflict is backed up by unsolved problems of the pregenital phase. When the latter are successfully worked through, the patient can return to the problem of Oedipus, and in a correctly conducted analysis he can now solve this too. The Oedipus complex thus has apical importance, not so much as the nucleus of the neuroses, but as the nucleus of normal character structure and as the basis of mature life.

# Therapeutic Problems
# in the Analysis of
# the "Normal" Candidate

## (1954)

I N ORDER to consider the problems of the psychoanalytic situation in which the "normal" candidate becomes involved, it is necessary to have in mind a concept of mental health. Only when we know what our
goal is, can we consider the technical problems confronting the training analyst. We assume that it is not
simply a question of freedom from symptoms or of "social" adjustment. It is understood that we are concerned with normality from the standpoint of psychoanalysis.

Ernest Jones (1931) approached the question in an
essay originally intended for general readers. He referred to two main groups of definitions of normality:
(a) those depending on the criterion of *happiness* and
(b) those depending upon *adaptation* to (psychological)

---

*Editorial note:* In an earlier paper (see pp. 142-155) Dr. Gitelson
focused on the content and goals of psychoanalytic education. Here,
pursuing the broad subject of how to improve psychoanalysis both as
a science and as a profession—a subject which was of central interest
to him throughout his career—he concentrates on the special problems
involved in analyzing candidates.

reality. The latter "does not necessarily imply the acceptance of the environmental standards, but it does imply a sensitive perception of them, and a recognition of their social significance" (p. 204). This depends on a "feeling relationship" with other human beings, which "is to be estimated by the *internal freedom* of such feelings" as distinguished from surface attitudes of conciliation or self-assertion (p. 210).

Midway between the concept of happiness and the concept of reality-adaptation, Jones introduced the concept of "efficiency," one which depends on a number of factors: Normality cannot tolerate a state of excessive influence by others, nor can it dispense with sensitiveness to others; it is dependent on what Jones calls "gusto"; it is not concerned solely with external success, but it does require the fullest use of a given individual's powers and talents.

Against this background Jones came to the conclusion that the state of balance in relatively stable persons can be "unsuspectedly precarious" and that this applies to "apparently normal candidates" in whom "one is often astonished to observe how a comparatively good functioning of the personality can exist with an extensive neurosis or even psychosis, that is not manifest" (p. 207).

Jones then addressed himself to what is particularly relevant to the topic under consideration here: He stated that while a thorough analysis leads to changes of character and intellect in the direction of increased tolerance and open-mindedness, "There is no motive as a rule to make use of the work done by applying it in detail to the conscious (and pre-conscious) layers of the mind" (p. 207). Hence, the only thing which distinguishes analyzed people, "including psycho-analysts," from others is their greater tolerance in sexual and religious spheres, and the modification of attitudes on subjects directly connected with analytic problems (e.g., mental responsibility for crime). "In other spheres they seem to form their judgements, or rather to maintain their previous convictions and attitudes, on very much the same line of rationalized prejudices as unanalysed people do" (p. 207). In short, in his consideration of "normality" Jones has given us the most difficult of psychological problems, but one which in the training of an analyst we must face, whether we solve it or not, and that is "the assessing in the 'normal' of the relations between the interests of the individual and those of society" (p. 211).

Hartmann, in his discussion of the question of mental health (1939b), was, like Jones, convinced that "the more we begin to understand the ego and its maneuvers and achievements in dealing with the external world, the more do we tend to make these functions of adaptation the touchstone of the concept of mental health" (p. 4). "Psychoanalysis," says Hartmann, "has witnessed the development of a number of theoretical conceptions of health which often lay down very severe standards" (p. 6).[1] These have taken two directions—on the one hand emphasizing rational behavior; on the other hand, instinctual life. This two-fold orientation reflects the two-fold origin of psychoanalysis in the history of thought: rationalism and

[1] He would approach the problem from the empirical side and examine from the standpoint of their structure and development the personalities of those who are actually considered healthy "since theoretical standards of health are usually too narrow in so far as they underestimate the great diversity of types which in practice pass as healthy" (p. 8).

romanticism. Freud recognized both, but the fact is that theory has often assigned undue prominence to one standpoint at the expense of the other. Hartmann is sceptical of the supremacy of biological values. When this criterion of mental health is dominant we approach dangerously near to that "malady of the times whose nature it is to worship instinct and pour scorn on reason" (p. 9). On the other hand, the concept of the "perfectly rational" man presents us with the complication that recognition of reality is not the equivalent of adaptation to reality. "The most rational attitude does not necessarily constitute an optimum for the purposes of adaptation" (p. 9).

Hartmann turned to the coordinating or integrative function of the ego as a solution for this dilemma. "The rational must incorporate the irrational as an element in its design" (p. 10). Progression in one direction entails regressions in other directions. Applying Waelder's (1936b) criterion of freedom from anxiety, he stated that "the mobility or plasticity of the ego is certainly one of the prerequisites of mental health. . . . [but] a healthy ego must evidently be in a position to allow some of its most essential functions, including its 'freedom' [from anxiety] to be put out of action occasionally, so that it may abandon itself to 'compulsion' " (p. 11). In other words, it is neither defense nor instinct which are in themselves normal or pathological, but rather their contextual balance or imbalance which is the criterion. Mechanisms have a positive value for health; withdrawal from reality may lead to an increased mastery over reality; there are progressive and regressive modes of adaptation. The work of conducting an analysis, as well as undergoing it, are examples of the latter.[2] Thus, "A system of regulation operating at the highest level of development is not sufficient to maintain a stable equilibrium; a more primitive system is needed to supplement it" (p. 13). In the balanced operation of the personality we expect to find an emotionally "open" system of communication between the various institutions of the mind, operating through a fluid process of checks and balances among the instinctual and defensive tendencies so that none is fully isolated, self-operating and self-sustaining (Gitelson, 1952a).

It is because we have looked upon health in contrast to neurosis that we have failed to appreciate how active these mechanisms and modes of reaction are in healthy individuals. This is why it is precisely the analysis of conduct adapted to reality which is of such importance (Hartmann, op. cit.).

Hartmann came to the conclusion that "a more attentive examination of the phenomena of adaptation may also help us to escape from the opposition between "biological" and "sociological" conceptions of mental development. There is "an organization of the organism" which in the mental sphere eventuates in the synthetic and differentiating functions of the ego and is a prerequisite of successful adaptation. Adaptations; . . . successful efforts at adaptation toward specific environment in which it develops. It can be "appropriate only to a limited range of environmental conditions; . . . successful efforts at adaptation toward specific

---

[2] In advance of the fuller development of my topic, I suggest that capacity or incapacity to tolerate regression is one of the criteria of mental health which is involved in the problem of the type of candidate we are discussing.

external situations may in indirect ways lead at the same time to inhibitions in adaptation affecting the organism" (p. 16); and the reverse may be true.

It is generally agreed that the neuroses which come to the psychoanalyst today are different from those of 50 years ago. The manner in which the ego admits, repels, or modifies instinctual claims depends on how it has been taught to regard them by the outside world. The changes which have occurred in moral and ethical outlook reflect themselves in the inconsistency of early educational influences on the child, with the consequence that the boundaries between license and deprivation have become blurred and the personality itself has become the carrier of the symptom.[3]

[3] In an extension of a report made to the International Educational Commission in Paris in 1938, Anna Freud reviewed in some detail the psychodynamics of the training analysis in comparison with the therapeutic analysis of the neurotic patient and examined the dynamics as they are influenced by the total training situation. This article ("Probleme der Lehranalyse") was unknown to me until I read it in a translation prepared and lent to me by Dr. Paul Kramer of Chicago some months after the present essay had been written and presented at the 18th International Congress.

There is a degree of overlapping in the theme and in the elaboration of the theme in Anna Freud's paper and mine, particularly with regard to what I have called the "ecology" of present-day candidates. However, in this paper I have given particular attention to the problem introduced into training by the type of candidate who presents a pseudonormal facade. Anna Freud (1950) has said, "In training analyses, the most strenuous efforts are usually necessary to overcome the resistances put up by the ego against the uncovering of the repressed. In the therapeutic analyses of severe neurotics, on the other hand, working through becomes the most important weapon in the difficult battle against the perseverance of pathological instinctual processes" (p. 413).

It is the fact that "seriously neurotic" persons become candidates and that their analyses are further complicated by *ecological factors*, which they exploit and of which the training analyst does not take adequate cognizance, that I am attempting to demonstrate.

The change in the form of the neuroses has been from those of the transference type, based on ego-id conflicts, to the narcissistic type, based on ego-superego conflicts. It has been stated (Alexander, 1930) that the transference neurosis with its intrapsychic symptoms represents an autoplastic regression which is harder to treat than the character neurosis, which is looked upon as directed toward an alloplastic (i.e., "living out") solution of conflict. For example, in a previous paper (Gitelson, 1944) I have described a character neurosis in a patient in whom intellectuality was a leading defense. His mother had brought up her children with much serious and earnest discussion and appeals to reason. Anything that could be rationalized could be condoned. For years the patient escaped punishment for a variety of hostile acts against his sister because of clever explanations which were acceptable to the mother. Despite a prudish surface attitude toward sexuality, the mother's self-deluding character had made it possible for the patient to indulge himself erotically with her by deviously engaging her in solemn discussions of the facts of life. His erotized and barren intellectuality was the end result. This apparent alloplastic conflict with reality is made up of pathological projections and displacements which are connected with the wish-fulfilling orientation of the narcissisticly regressed ego; the conflict is not only *truly* intrapsychic, but in addition is deprived of that impulsion of the instincts toward objects in the outer world which occurs in the transference neuroses and assists in their cure. The very fact that in the narcissistic neurosis the ego maintains its capacity to perceive and to deal "adaptively" with external reality makes it possible for the intrapsychic conflict to be laid out on the framework presented by the environment, and to follow there a course which has the aspect of "normality."

Freud (1924) asked the question: what circumstances were conducive to and by what means did the ego succeed in surviving conflicts without falling ill. His own answers are well known:

> . . . the outcome of all such situations will undoubtedly depend on economic considerations—on the relative magnitudes of the trends which are struggling with one another. In the second place, it will be possible for the ego to avoid a rupture in any direction by deforming itself, by submitting to encroachments on its own unity and even perhaps by effecting a cleavage or division of itself. In this way the inconsistencies, eccentricities and follies of men would appear in a similar light to their sexual perversions, through the acceptance of which they spare themselves repressions [pp. 152–153].

I think it follows that one of the important factors in support of the ego's conflict with the superego, i.e., the maintenance of the narcissistic character defense in the guise of normality, is to be found in the acquiescence of our culture to the phenomena of this defense.

All this by itself would not merit special consideration in a Symposium on Training, for we take it for granted that in the analysis of "normal" candidates we are confronted by the problem of character analysis. However, because the increase in our knowledge of the economics of the psychic structure has greatly complicated the differential diagnosis between normal and the pathological, some analysts have begun to despair of the suitability of "normal" candidates for a career in psychoanalysis. Then too, the recent history of the psychoanalytic movement has literally dropped the problem at our doorstep. And finally, as an aspect of that history, the particular ecology of recent candidates has added special problems.

Sachs (1947) unequivocally ruled out a group with "too few neurotic symptoms," who were well adapted to reality and outwardly well integrated, but whose narcissistic organization produced too firm a repression of conflict. While they might indeed have a good intellectual grasp of mechanisms and be therapeutically eager, he felt that psychoanalysis could not possibly satisfy their ambition or "assuage their compassion," while it was very likely to injure their self-esteem and drive them toward one of the schools of "improved techniques."

Kubie (1948) stated:

Some analysts feel that the persistence of frank symptoms is less important than is the persistence of masked neurotic personality traits. Yet precisely here is where the therapeutic goal becomes most difficult of attainment. . . . It is easy to say that the goal is to spread the domain of conscious control in the student's life, and to shrink to a minimum the domain of unconscious control. But a bright and intelligent student will sometimes unconsciously disguise his subtle neurotic trends and even make them appear as assets. For some the training analysis is like a successful courtship, during which the student feels happy, relieved, and free from tensions; he is on his way toward his professional goal; he is full of warmth and gratitude to his training analyst. Under such circumstances subtle neurotic mechanisms can be temporarily inactivated [sic! I should say: remain concealed] only to reappear in later years after the analyst has faced the stresses of his professional life. This is where the therapeutic leverage of the training analysis [of the "normal" candidate] is so often far less than is the leverage of the analysis which has no training implications, even when the instructor is on the lookout for just this difficulty.

In contemplating this problem some instructors and some institutes feel that the preparatory analysis should be a purely therapeutic venture, undertaken individually by the would-be student . . . and that no application for admission should even be considered until after the candidate has completed a therapeutic analysis. Other analysts feel that we should admit quite frankly that in most instances the preparatory analysis achieves little therapy except perhaps where there have been frank and painful symptoms.

On the basis of an experience with a patient "who gave the impression of being relatively symptom-free and well adjusted" and who wanted treatment "only for professional reasons" Eissler (1953) decided for a time that he "would never again try the analysis of a "normal" person.

Knight, in a Presidential Address before the American Psychoanalytic Association (1953b), said among other things:

Another factor which has been operating in the past decade to alter the character of analytic training and practice also derives from the great increase in numbers of trainees, especially in the postwar period, and from the more structured training of institutes in comparison to the earlier preceptorship type of training. In the 1920's and early 1930's those who undertook psychoanalytic training were of a somewhat different breed from the current crop of candidates. There was, in those days, less emphasis on selection procedures and many analysts were trained who might today be rejected. Many training analyses were relatively short, and many gifted individuals with definite neuroses or character disorders were trained. They were primarily introspective individuals, inclined to be studious and thoughtful, and tended to be highly individualistic and to limit their social life to clinical and theoretical discussions with colleagues. They read prodigiously and knew the psychoanalytic literature thoroughly. . . . In contrast, perhaps the majority of students of the past decade or so have been "normal" characters, or perhaps one should say had "normal character disorders." They are not introspective, are inclined to read only the literature that is assigned in institute courses, and wish to get through with the training requirements as rapidly as possible. Their interests are primarily clinical rather than research and theoretical. Their motivation for being analyzed is more to get through this requirement of training rather than to overcome neurotic suffering in themselves or to explore introspectively and with curiosity their own inner selves. Many have had their training largely paid for by the Federal Government, and this factor has added to training problems. The partial capitulation of some institutes . . . to the pressure arising from numbers of students, from their ambitious haste, and from their tendency to be satisfied with a more superficial grasp of theory, has created some of the training problems we now face [pp. 218-219].

Now let us glance at the social-cultural situation. I have referred to the fact that while character, ultimately, is rooted in the instincts, its formal qualities belong to a large extent to the external reality of the culture in which it develops and operates. We take for granted that the character and personality of the putative analyst are the product of the interaction of his instincts with the general cultural characteristics of his developmental time and place. However, in the context of the problems of training, we must remember that the characters of our present-day candidates are also determined, at least in their secondary aspects, by the particular circumstance that they have grown up in an atmosphere of psychoanalysis. Their pre-analytical training goes on in the midst of psychoanalysts and their "psychoanalytically oriented" colleagues, and under the influence of the various derivations and applications of psychoanalysis, as well as psychoanalysis per se. In short, psychoanalysis has become respectable and "normal"; it has become a part of the milieu.

The consequence is that a number of artifacts enter into the defensive organization of the ego of candidates which, to say the least, create an additional layer of ego-syntonic resistances. Under the influence of reading, lectures, and sometimes "wild analysis" by psychiatric colleagues and instructors, candidates now tend to develop a facade of pseudonormality, due in part to "inexact interpretations" (Glover, 1931) resulting in gratifications and repressions, in part to the development of counterphobic and denial mechanisms, and in part to the intellectualization of symptoms (Reider, 1950). With regard to the last, for example, it is not an unusual experience to encounter applicants for training who will make the most of mild situational tensions and depressive reactions, because of the idea which has gained currency that "it is all right" to have some neurotic symptoms whereas "character problems" are suspect. What may be overlooked is that such an apparent acceptance of the facts of life may actually be the presenting sign of far-reaching character resistances based on submissiveness and acquiescence to authority. It would seem, indeed, that one of the unconscious imagos of authority is now the field of psychoanalysis itself. This appears to be the case even with candidates who sincerely affirm their intellectual acceptance of analysis.

Another artifact which complicates the analysis of all candidates, but I think especially the so-called normal, is the disappearance of the incognito of the analyst. Not only are candidates intellectually immersed in psychoanalysis, but they are also surrounded by analysts during their pre-analytic training and often enough in their social activities. Even more pervasive is the fact that in the small world of the training center the analyst lives in a glass house of gossip, of rumor, and of some known facts. Out of this stem still other consequences:

First of all we encounter phenomena connected with the choice of analyst. To the extent that freedom of choice exists, we see decisions tending to be based on the impression the candidate has had of the analyst in terms of his own neurotic needs. These may be based, for example, on the unconscious recognition of a prospect of gratifying unconscious wishes, or the person of the analyst does not threaten the character defenses—perhaps he even promises to sustain them (Thompson, 1938). "Choice of analyst," however, is largely an academic consideration. In most instances it is not feasible, and the consequences of the pre-analytic situation are reflected in the phenomena of the analysis itself.

It is well known that regardless of the rationalizations presented, the choice of psychiatry and psychoanalysis as a career is in the end determined by the person's search for his own integration. In the early days of analysis this was more obvious. Today, because of the factors I have already discussed and because analysis has been accepted as a valid medical discipline, we see more candidates who cannot be so frank and for whom such frankness is unnecessary. They unconsciously acquire and can consciously maintain the attitude that they wish to become analysts because they are interested in psychosomatic medicine, or because they are interested in human beings and in what makes them tick. As an added fillip, of course, they may add (with unconscious truth) that they are not quite satisfied with themselves and would like to find out why. What it amounts to, however, is that an unconsciously erected façade of professional or scientific interest is now found to be a usual first line of intellectual defense against unconscious conflict.

Then we must consider that the "paranoid" defense and the "manic" defense are more extensively elaborated in the so-called normal character. I have previously alluded to the latter's pseudo alloplastic nature. Under the circumstances of the opportunity given by such realities as I have described, these defenses can attain actual or apparent validation for their still deeper entrenchment. For example, in the cases of candidates with whom I have had professional contacts of the most routine sort prior to their coming into analysis with me, I have seen the largest incidence of first dreams in which I appeared in undisguised form. Such dreams, as I have stated in a previous paper (1952a), are prognostic of a difficult, if not impossible analytic situation, due to the fact that the analyst is quite literally reacted to as if he were in fact an ancient and dangerous imago.* This has been the case when a pre-analytic teaching situation has resulted in anxiety of expected criticism or suspected disapproval. On the other hand, I have tried to analyse former students whose idealization of me became a difficult initial defense which covered a still more serious resistance in the form of identification and omnipotent denial. The apparently "normal" activities of such patients, often characterized by considerable "practical" effectiveness, are displacements *or* denials of the unconscious object to which libidinal regression has occurred. This is per-

---

* *Editorial note:* See fn. p. 196. A further oddity is the complete omission in subsequent literature of all references to this passage. Even Dr. Gitelson seemed to have forgotten about it, for, in 1962, he wrote to Rosenbaum,

I have never written a paper on this subject. I mentioned the problem incidental to my general concern with the "Emotional Position of the Analyst in the Psycho-Analytic Situation." Perhaps there was as much as a paragraph in that paper on the problem. I think that, as stated in your letter, my interest and investment in the subject is a little bit overemphasized [Rosenbaum, 1965, p. 436].

haps most clearly seen among those "phallic characters" for whom the phallus is really an instrument of orality and whose ambition is a substitute for the regression to the oral triad.

The general situation which obtains in the structure of the "normal character" defense is the basis for these consequences. The libidinal and the hostile tendencies, as well as the defenses against them, are assimilated into and fused in the ego system so that the person's way of life aims at once to satisfy the instinctual tendencies, to preserve the ego from anxiety, and to fit in with the pattern of the environment. Among "scientifically minded" medical students, for example, the attitude of "critical scrutiny" is highly developed and valued as an important integrative ego function. This certainly belongs to the realities of a career in medicine. Nonetheless, we know how effective an instrument it can be, often quite subtly used, for ventilating hostility in the service of defense. We are also familiar with those therapeutically oriented and practically ambitious students who live out their reparation and their denial. This makes them more useful citizens perhaps, but their treatment becomes harder. Candidates of this type have great difficulty in surrendering themselves to the uncertain gratification and postponed solutions which effective analysis requires of them. On the other hand, as Sachs (1947) has shown, they become deeply involved in the prospect of the magical solutions for their guilts and anxieties which certain modifications of analysis seem to offer them.

The distortions and disguises through which the various libidinal and hostile impulses express themselves in the character defense are supported by the very common existence of these tendencies in the present day. These defenses favor compromise and *ersatz*. Their mutual interpersonal utility creates a situation in which the character defense can remain unrecognized as such and can even flourish as alleged normality. In a social setting that attaches a high premium to aggressiveness, ambition, and hard work, a gifted analysand can live through his analysis as he has lived through his life, cleverly disguising his neurosis.

To sum up thus far, we see that the analysis of the "normal" candidate confronts the analyst with a situation in which the basic conditions of his work are spoiled:

(1) Normality, a symptom, actually is not suffered from as such. On the contrary, it is capable of earning social rewards, of which the first is acceptance as a candidate. To no other symptom does such a large quota of secondary gain attach.

(2) The defensive system is supported by the general culture and, in addition, is reinforced by the pre-analytic professional experiences of the candidate.

(3) The analytic situation is contaminated and distorted by adventitious external factors which interfere with the normal development of the transference.

We come now to a consideration of some clinical problems presented by these candidates. First of all, despite overt manifestations of anxiety, they enter their analyses with the psychic mobilization which they have maintained in their general life situations. Their emotional position from the beginning appears in the

analysis as a special case of the general character defenses, complicated, as I have previously indicated, by
special current factors. As an example, I may cite an
analysand (see Gitelson, 1944) who had known about
me for some time and whom I had encountered socially on two occasions prior to his beginning analysis
with me. For years the patient addressed me by the
short form of my given name. This familiarity happened to be an index to a general character defense
which, at the nearest level, served against his castration anxiety, and more deeply, as a "handle" by means
of which he negated his separation fear. Characterologically it had entered into his false self-esteem and his
cynical depreciation of others.

Despite the best intentions, which in some cases are
felt as a desire for a better personal integration, the
student-patient attempts to accomplish in his relationship to the analyst the same things that he has accomplished in the world at large. In this attempt he follows the pattern which has hitherto been more or less
successful in mastering the vicissitudes of his emotional
development. An analysand whose previously successful career had been characterized by an attitude of
eagerness to be useful and cooperative presented the
following first dream: *The patient enters the analyst's
office and sees him, as himself. He is suffering from a
toothache. The patient comforts him.*

The various libidinal and hostile impulses do not
reappear as themselves, but in their established distortions. As Anna Freud (1936) tells us, ". . . in extreme
cases . . . the instinctual impulse itself never enters into
the transference at all but only the specific defense
adopted by the ego against some positive or negative

attitude of the libido" (pp. 19–20). Insistence on the fundamental rule of free association is quite ineffectual with these patients.

Fenichel (1938) has stated that the formation of the character traits and their maintenance corresponds to a single definite act of repression which makes possible the later avoidance of separate acts of repression. Thus separate anxiety situations are avoided because such chronic anchorages of instinctual defenses are worked into the ego and not experienced as ego-dystonic. This is what produces the relative constancy of the defensive attitude, and what establishes the "sign" of the personality, no matter how different are the demands from the unconscious and from reality.

Fenichel also has cautioned us against taking at its face value that behavior of the allegedly normal which appears to give the impression of satisfying instincts rather than repressing them. We know how inhibitions may lead to counterphobic attitudes, and these in turn to other inhibitions or reaction formations; the maintenance of the defense of one instinct may involve the expression of another. As an example, we have observed how the ego can assimilate genital sexuality with apparent normality while actually employing it in the service of pregenital instincts which are themselves repressed.

It was Fenichel's opinion that the distinction between the rigid character defense, which I have been discussing, and a mobile transference resistance is dependent, in the first instance, on a fixation on part objects (and indifference to the whole object) which themselves are used only to relieve an endopsychic conflict, and, in the second instance, on relationships to whole objects. In other words, the analysands with whom we are concerned suffer from narcissistic problems which render them at first incapable of developing a true transference neurosis. They are regressed from the genital position, and to begin with they not only continue their defenses against pregenital impulses, but also against the transference, in which these would, of course, have to appear.

A technical digression may be worthwhile here: The resistance to the transference which I have just referred to arises, as Anna Freud (1950) stated, from the threat analysis brings to the ego that it may be deposed from its hard-earned seat on the throne of reality. It is necessary to remember, however, that in such situations the resistance is quite often an id resistance, that is, it is a defense against giving up the clandestine gratifications of the oral triad (Lewin, 1950), which the "normal," in particular, succeed in repressing. This is achieved behind the facade of normality.

Another technical consideration at this point is concerned with the superego's role in the analysis of such candidates. If they are looked upon as students rather than patients, and "active" measures are taken (even if this be only an attitude of "concern" or impatience on the part of the analyst) in the hope of accelerating the analysis, there will be a serious interference with the normal development of the transference neurosis. In effect, the analysand is under a constant superego injunction to be "up and at 'em." The therapeutic split, which permits the patient to regress libidinally in the transference while ego regression remains minimal, is made difficult if not impossible. We find here the chief indication for passivity in technique. All of this faces us with the need for analyzing the "living out" of the neurosis in the atmosphere of the training situation and the "training analysis."

We must now consider the problem which Freud (1937) first discussed in *"Analysis, Terminable and Interminable,"* as it bears on the clinical problem presented by the "normal" candidate. As you will remember, Freud raised certain questions regarding the obstacles to cure. He asked: (1) Is it really possible to resolve an instinctual conflict? (2) Can we inoculate patients against any other instinctual conflicts in the future? And finally he asked: (3) Can a pathogenic conflict be stirred up for prophylactic purposes? His answer to all these questions was in the negative.

But Fenichel (1939b) saw it differently. He felt that instincts are invulnerable only when barred from discharge. It is a question of the relative strength of the instinct, and this can be diminished through the partial satisfactions which occur in analysis. While admittedly it is not possible to resolve all the unsettled instinctual claims of the past, the more insistent remaining claims can be settled. When these are solidified in the structure of the character, then it is necessary to tackle them at the beginning. Fenichel is here referring to the whole technique of ego analysis, *which in the case of candidates includes as a first step the meticulous effort to resolve the part of their defenses which has gained strength from the ecology of their pre-analytic experience. This includes the analysis of the very choice of psychoanalysis as a career.*

For example, a candidate whose training was finally interrupted, had come to his analysis with the common enough claim that he had no symptoms; his family life was satisfactory; he had been very successful in another field of medicine; he had become interested in psychoanalysis while in the army, through seeing analytically trained psychiatrists at work; he had been an avid psychiatric resident. He wished nothing else than to become an analyst and within three months was requesting that he be permitted to start didactic work. This request was chronic throughout the two and a half years of his analysis, despite the fact that there was no dynamic progress and the patient's external gains were based exclusively on identification with me. The focus on analysis as a career constituted a resistance which was not solved. I could not continue the attempt at its solution because of threatening developments which made a compromise advisable.

This brings us to the most serious of the questions raised by Freud: Are we ethically warranted and is it technically possible to turn an unconscious conflict into a conscious conflict? Unless there is already evidence which forces us to decide to terminate the analysis and to advice the patient to give up the idea of training, we must consider the possibility suggested by Fenichel (1939b) that it is not a matter of creating new conflicts but of mobilizing latent ones. Of these there are always *small signs,* even though the ego ignores them. By treating these signs as resistances it may be possible to ultimately demonstrate the fact of conflict and to bring it into analysis. An example is the case of a phallic character who had successfully lived out his denial of castration fear and was looked upon as "normal" by himself and others. His first analysis seemed successful until difficulties in his work, which he valued highly, forced him into a second analysis. Only then was it possible to enlist him in the analysis of a smile which had been the occasional preface to the first verbalizations of his hours. This symptom, previously not admitted as such, now became a source of conscious discomfort. Its analysis led to his previously unconscious hatred and fear of women and the oral-sadistic fixation to his mother.

In recent years various technical proposals have been made to accomplish this end. Most prominent are those that have had as their objective the *active* mobilization of latent conflicts. These have been characterized by maneuvers intended to manipulate the transference, or as Grotjahn (1953) stated, "to change the therapeutic environment as required in order to activate trends in the patient which may lead to the necessary therapeutic experience." Grotjahn proposes that "only thus can we bring the doctor-patient into the situation where he will accept himself as just another patient in analysis." But this type of endeavor leads only to the deeper entrenchment of the narcissistic defenses, since it in effect re-duplicates parental manipulations which in the first place play a large role in the creation of the neurosis of the "normal" adult.

The type of candidate I have been discussing comes to his analysis prepared to deal with its problems in the same way he has dealt with his developmental vicissitudes and with their repetitions in his later adult life. If the analyst is to obtain therapeutic leverage, he must try to correct for the analytic situation the "spoiling" which I have suggested occurs in the pre-analytic milieu. He cannot do this by carrying into the analytic situation the attitudes and techniques of that milieu. The hope of the analytic situation lies in the possibility of effecting a differentiation between it and the atmosphere of the candidate's past life. This idea must not be confused with the idea of the planned creation of a "corrective emotional experience." The latter is narrowly conceived as being directed against the presumed pathogenic effect of a significant figure of the patient's childhood. The correction to which I refer has to be applied against the distortion of reality produced by the culture in which the details of the character defense have been acquired. It is, therefore, concerned with the institution of a learning process which goes on throughout a prolonged initial period of "testing," during which the validity of the analytic situation establishes itself. The patient must prove its *"difference."*

I have seen such testing go on for several years before the patient dared to allow himself to experience the transference situation as we see it in the transference neurosis. One such patient at last exclaimed, "It's a tremendous realization to see finally that you really mean this!" He was referring to the fact that he had in the end not succeeded in exploiting the relationship with me as he had done with others in the past. He had carried concealed in him the deep conviction that analysis was really not what it "pretended" to be, that it was "just another racket," though a fascinating one.

It is during this initial phase of the analysis, but only after the patient's testing of the analytic reality and of the analyst's integrity has gone some distance, that one begins the cautious analysis of the various ego derivatives of the instincts. Only as the patient begins to believe that the analyst "means it" does the analyst begin to stand in the position of an auxiliary ego which *enables the patient to take that distance from himself* which makes possible the analysis of the "small signs" (Sterba, 1934). The "normal" candidate is, to begin with, characterized by the shortness of this distance. He believes that he wants to be an analyst; he believes that he wants to do research; he believes that he wants to help people. He does not feel ill. Nevertheless, one such candidate who came for a second analysis said to me, "This time I want it to be for me!"

Another candidate, in a second analysis, who still adhered to the attitude with which he had gone through the first one, namely, that he wanted to only to qualify for his examination, at last presented the following dream:

> The patient enters the office for his hour. The chair and couch are interchanged, and the foot of the couch is toward the chair. The analyst is already seated, and to his right, in the other half of the room is a class of students. The issue for the patient seems to be whether to lie down with head or feet toward the analyst. The analyst tells the patient that the latter has been tried by others before but that it does not work.

Actually my office is arranged so that there is an "analytic half" at one end of an elongated room and a "consultation half" with several chairs at the other end, my desk being in the center. The analysand knew that students I saw in supervision sat in the chairs of the "consultation half." In the dream the reversal of the analytic chair and the couch has resulted in putting me "in the middle" between the couch and the class of students.

*Associations:* A female patient, who was presented at a diagnostic seminar, had reported that after unsatisfactory intercourse she scratched various parts of her body until orgasm occurred. During the seminar, when the instructor had momentarily left the room, my analysand had acted as if it was immaterial whether he was there or not and had taken up the interrogation of the patient. Looking back upon the episode, it struck the analysand that it would have been a compliment to the instructor had he waited for his return.

When the patient was very young he used to lie in bed with his mother when she was resting, and often she would hold his hand and drum on it with her finger tips. During his early teens, when his mother was resting in bed, he followed the example of an older brother and would lie on top of the bed clothes, with his head at the foot of the bed, and carry on conversations with her.

In a recent conversation with another young analyst, who was also in his second analysis, the latter had said it was practically inevitable that the first analysis should be contaminated by the fact that it was looked upon as a learning process rather than a treatment. Another young colleague had responded to this with a statement to the effect that it was up to the analyst to be aware of this attitude and to force the student-patient to deal with it as a defense.

The night of the dream, the analysand's wife had playfully put her feet on his abdomen. This was the precipitating event for the dream.

Somewhere he had heard an older analyst make an exceedingly keen remark—that it was harder to love

one person than to love everybody. To love everybody means nothing at all; to be able to love one
person fully means everything.

Lying with his feet toward me brings to mind the
idea of stamping on me. As he says this, he jerks his
feet, which reminds him of the characteristic kicking
together of his feet when he has felt annoyed with
interpretations connected with passive attitudes toward me. Then he speaks jokingly of wanting to
play footsie with me, and at this point his left ear,
the one toward me, begins to itch, and he has the
impulse to scratch it—which again reminds him of
the patient who produced orgasms by scratching.
The class of students now reminds him of the times
when he had attended conferences conducted by me.

It seems unnecessary to point out that this patient
has mobilized his old "student" defense against the
classical transference situation that was beginning to
develop in the context of a consistent management of
the character resistances. In this context, too, the hostile denial of the libidinal transference also appeared.

This case example brings up another problem of
particular importance with the "normal" candidate.
That is, there are disadvantages in the effort to deal
with the type of ego defenses they present, when their
analyses are conducted by "teacher-analyst." I have
sometimes tried to deal with this problem by saying at
the beginning of the analysis that I was first of all interested in the patient's health. But I have found that
the candidate has taken this with a grain of salt and
incorporated it into his defensive doubt of my sincerity.

In the end, he has had to discover for himself that I "meant" it.

The problems in the analysis of the "normal" candidate may now be summed up as follows:

(1) There is an actual disturbance in his "feeling relationship" (Jones, 1931). He lives in terms of a façade whose structure is patterned by his environment, providing him with an opportunity to gratify his instincts by virtue of their imbrication with the demands of his environment.

(2) This is the final consequence of the development of an "adapted" personality—"an organization of the organism," as Hartmann put it, whose adaptation is appropriate to its culture and thus passes for normal. But it is not adapted to psychoanalysis, which needs to be free from the gravitational pull of a particular culture and which is incompatible with opportunism and compromise.

(3) It becomes the task of analysis to provide first of all an opportunity to test out a new reality—the analytic situation—to establish its integrity, and to prove its relevance to the basic nature of the person. In this context, and looking upon the culturally determined "normal" behavior as itself a resistance, we may attempt to mobilize conflict made latent by the culture and thus, in the end, analyze the vicissitudes of the libido itself.

This is a large order. We may not be able to fill it. But our candidates, as we find them, are the future of psychoanalysis. We cannot sidestep our responsibility for trying to insure that future.

# Psychoanalyst, U.S.A.

## (1956)

A CREDO is the product of personal experience. Inevitably it is largely of subjective origin. As such it should not have a place in scientific discourse, unless it be as a phenomenon which is itself subjected to study. It is, therefore, with the greatest caution that I undertake to profess what our chairman has called the "Credo of a Psychoanalyst." I am able to do so only because I think I am typical of my psychoanalytic generation and feel that I can present with fairness the outlook which derives from the experience of a Doctor of Medicine in the United States who became a psychiatrist and a psychoanalyst during the course of the 25 years just ending. These are the 25 years which have produced psychoanalysis as we in the United States know it today.

In the early 1930's psychoanalysis was just beginning to make itself at home in this country. The Floyd Dell era of literary and Bohemian adventurings in the

Editorial note: The original title of this essay included the date 1955. Its contents, however, have become increasingly relevant with the passage of time. The editor has hence taken the liberty of removing the date from the title.

unconscious was coming to an end. The first American institutes were getting started. Despite the depression, young medical men were beginning to make a positive choice of psychiatry as a career and were not simply drifting into the "red brick buildings" as an escape. An old mansion in the east and a farmhouse in the west were beginning their evolution from places of custody into centers for psychoanalytically oriented treatment. By the time the United States had entered the second World War, American psychoanalysis had passed through its primary identification with psychoanalysis as it had evolved in Europe; psychoanalytic training had been divorced from control by the International Training Commission and had embarked on a course of development which became distinctively American in its program, outlook, and goals. In effect, all this represented a turning away from what was looked upon as the intellectualistic tendencies of European analysis and a turning toward the pragmatism of medicine, with which analysis now declared itself affiliated. The first manifestation of this was the emergence of psychosomatic medicine. Then came dynamic psychiatry. And out of this, among those trained in analysis, have risen the preoccupations with brief psychotherapy, with group therapy, with hospital management, and with attempts to rationalize psychologically the "beneficial" effects of various physical therapies.

Within analysis itself there were comparable pragmatic developments: "classical technique" has been "modified" variously in the interest of shortening treatment, making it available to larger numbers, and decreasing its emotional rigors. In addition, we have seen during these years a gradually broadening range of the types of patients accepted for treatment by analysts. New technical procedures and devices, far different from those of the basic analytic technique, have tended to be merged with it, so that those who practice them can no longer easily distinguish one from the other. The best demonstration of this is provided in the fact that a few years ago a committee of the American Psychoanalytic Association, commissioned to make an evaluation of psychoanalytic therapy among those who called themselves psychoanalysts, was compelled to give up its task because it could not obtain a concensus on a definition of psychoanalytic treatment which would provide a base line for differential evaluation!

The war provided a capstone for the trend toward making psychoanalysis "practicable." The "ivory tower" of the psychoanalyst was breached by the exigencies of the crisis. Those who were at home found themselves caught up by the demands for psychological first aid in the civilian community. Those of the younger men who went into the armed forces of necessity bent their special knowledge and experience to the maintenance of manpower. Improvisation was of the essence and was warranted. By the time the war was over this had gained such prestige from its merits during the emergency that dynamic eclecticism had become the psychiatric vogue. Another consequence was the great influx of students into psychiatry and eventually into psychoanalysis. Of the many reasons for this I shall refer only to the fact that in contrast to the slowly maturing intellectual and emotional grounds for the gradual increase in the number of students in psychoanalytic training prior to the war, the great burgeoning of interest in psychoanalysis now came from the fact that military experience had demonstrated to practical-minded young men that psychoanalysis (or rather its derivatives and applications) worked; that it could respectably take a place in the armamentarium of medicine, and, last but not least, that it was worth a fee!

There is no doubting the richness of the knowledge psychoanalysis has brought us and is continuing to bring. Despite the many complications which we have become aware of and which cast doubt in the minds of some of the "purity" and "accuracy" of its findings, psychoanalysis still remains the basic instrument for the study of intrapsychic structures and functions. There are at present no other techniques for studying the mind which, one way or another, are not based on an extrapolation of its basic principles. It remains the fundamental referent of all such other techniques. As such, it is a constant, the stability of which, by definition, should remain secure. As therapy, however, the position of psychoanalysis is not so clear. Despite the fact that those who have used it most faithfully are convinced that it is the one technique that is etiologic in its orientation and effectively reconstructive in its goal, we must face the fact that its optimum application and results leave something to be desired; that it poses burdensome and sometimes impossible conditions on those who might benefit from it; that its range of strict application regarding the gamut of mental illnesses is limited; and its social value, measured in purely quantitative terms, is small.

The consequence of this contrast between the social and the scientific positions of psychoanalysis is that the present generation of American psychoanalysts finds itself involved in a real conflict. On the one hand, to the extent to which our own analytic experience has substantially convinced us that psychoanalysis is not a gimmick, we are committed to it as the criterion of effective psychotherapy and the foundation for mental research. On the other hand, despite sharpened awareness of the great complexity of human psychopathology and of the great difficulties connected with its resolution, surviving restitutional needs have left us still sensitive to the great demand for relief of human inefficiency, unhappiness, and self-destructiveness, and discontented with the remedies available.

Apart from this, the social character of this country is conducive to feelings of dissatisfaction with the exercise of a discipline which is so out of step with its prevailing tempo and apparently so tangential to its generally accepted targets. On the moral side there is the fact that Americans, as a people, have distinguished themselves by the promptness and generosity of their response to need, whether this be hunger, catastrophe, or plague. On the intellectual side is the fact that we are first and foremost a practical people, concerned with use and application. Only recently, under the unhappy circumstances which have surrounded atomic fission and fusion, has pure science become an acknowledged element of our daily lives. But the respect we accord it is heavily tinged with almost superstitious and suspicious awe. We seem to condone it because it has dramatically demonstrated that it "paid off." The "mystique," as Glover has called it, with which classical psychoanalysis has been draped, is not different in this respect from the mystery which attaches to all outposts of science, whether in mathematical physics or on the frontiers of biology. Thus, we who take psychoanalysis seriously and whose history has unfolded on the American psychiatric scene, are not so differently situated from the atomic scientists who left their ivory towers under the duress of danger and responded magnificently to a practical need. We know how the latter found themselves caught in the moral and intellectual crosscurrents which were set up when the demands of immediate reality cut across their devotion to the search for further knowledge. Similarly the American psychoanalyst today finds himself tossed between his deeply rooted utilitarianism and benevolence—fostered by a crying need—and his profound conviction that it is the long view which must be kept in mind if man's ultimate dilemma is to be solved.

Basic natural science has been called upon to participate in the "application" of its discoveries and to assume technical, secular, and moral responsibility for the outcome. This has imposed upon it an unbearable burden which seriously threatens the essential characteristics of research born of "general" curiosity and accidental discovery. A similar burden of practical "watering down" now rests on psychoanalysis. Among "classical" analysts there is increasing concern about the lack of understanding of the psychoanalytic method. There is evidence in papers which purport to deal with psychoanalytic problems that the distinction between the psychoanalytic method and its derivatives is becoming increasingly fuzzy.

I have referred to some of the practical consequences of this: The increasing use of "modified" techniques has resulted in office case loads which are generously inclusive of numbers of patients who are quite frankly receiving "brief therapy"; analysts engage themselves in group psychotherapy, are involved in psychosomatic research and in "interdisciplinary" studies; there are attempts to focus the microscopic technique of psychoanalysis on the macroscopic social scene. At the same time a tendency has developed to look down on the analyst who does *only psychoanalysis,* to think of him as a shirker of his social obligations because he will not adapt his technique to whatever material is at hand. An appreciable number of analysts, despite deep conviction of the validity of their method for fundamental research and for the definitive treatment of the neuroses, feel stigmatized by such "moral" criticism.

I do not begrudge the social good that conceivably may result from the many activities which now separate the analyst from his study and his couch and which join his special technique to those of other sciences and disciplines. But I am greatly concerned about the consequence of all this to psychoanalysis as the most refined instrument for research on the structure and operation of the individual human mind. For psychoanalysis is first and foremost individual psychology. This is said without prejudice to the fact of interpersonal and group relationships which surely affect the single person. But it is these *individual effects,* both plastic and reactive, which are the psychoanalyst's central and proper field of study. To speak in terms of physical science, psychoanalysis deals with internal operations on an atomic scale; its results can be and have been *applied* to the more complete understanding of external operations on a molecular scale. But to use the techniques of the sociologist and the physiologist for the derivation of psychoanalytic knowledge, or to use psychoanalytic technique to solve the problems of physiology and of crime is to interchange the cyclotron and the retort. Each has its use and special application, and only the respective findings can be holistically combined.

A definition of psychoanalysis which will finally enable me to make that statement of conviction to which our chairman has invited us is long overdue. Twenty-five years ago it would have been an easy matter to make a clearly differentiating statement about what psychoanalysis is. I could have said that any procedure which recognized the unconscious and attempted to deal with transference and resistance was psychoanalysis. This would have been understood to mean that there are psychic forces operating in an organic matrix; that these manifest themselves an unconscious impulses and fantasies among which there is conflict; that these develop in childhood but are possessed of a permanent tendency to become conscious; that this tendency is opposed by counterforces; and that the analyst, presenting himself as a target for these fantasies and impulses, assists their emergence into awareness by interpreting the counterforces.

Today all this is "old hat." The meaning of transference, repression and resistance, dreams, free associations, verbalization and catharsis, dependency, and regression has passed from psychoanalysis into the public domain of clinical psychiatry. These concepts have all shown themselves to be usefully applicable outside of analysis. They have enabled the psychiatrist to work under the guidance of principles rather than rules of thumb. Psychotherapy today is rational because it is based on what we know about psychopathology and psychodynamics as psychoanalysis has elucidated them. From this standpoint, good psychotherapy looks so much like psychoanalysis that on paper one almost cannot tell the difference! And yet, I believe there are very important differences.

Modern psychotherapy deserves its position in psychiatry because it is in a real sense the psychiatrist's reason for being. Moreover, it has become a truly effective instrument. Nothing I have to say about it is intended to give the impression that I depreciate its validity or its usefulness. Nevertheless, it is not psychoanalysis even when it is psychoanalytic. I state this despite the fact that psychotherapists see the problems of the personality as psychoanalysis has revealed them; that they are aware of and deal with transference phenomena, and sometimes even with resistances; that they are skilled in obtaining verbalization and affective expression; that they often cure symptoms dramatically, and occasionally produce long-lasting, broader effects.

I see the differences between psychoanalysis and the most extensive psychotherapy, first, in the goal which is striven for and which can be attained, and secondly, in the road which is followed toward the end in view. Admitting that psychoanalysis has a significant number of theraputic failures to record, we are aware that it can and does produce an inner unification of the personality and a liberation from both internal and external compulsion, which in some instances becomes evident as "character change." Allowing for the fact that in skilled psychotherapy the technique of "uncovering" may be applied with great sensitiveness, that conflicts may be recognized and even resolved, nevertheless, psychoanalytic scrutiny will disclose that such results have come about on the basis of a massive rationalization. They depend for their effectiveness on what is dynamically a repression of a basic conflict, following on some partial solution of derivative conflicts, and, finally, accepted on the *fundamentally suggestive* basis of an unresolved transference. In contrast, the crucial factor in psychoanalysis which differentiates it from psychotherapy resides in this central aspect of its techniques: *It deliberately provides and maintains optimum conditions for the development, the evolution, and, finally and most important, the resolution of an artificial neurosis,* the transference neurosis, for which the original neurosis of childhood has been exchanged.

The transference neurosis appears under the pressure of the tendency of past fantasies, attitudes, and impulses to repeat themselves. It is permitted to establish itself and to evolve in its own terms toward its own particular denouement. In the relationship to the analyst there thus recur the signficant emotional events of infancy and early childhood. These events do not present as discrete "transference episodes," but are part of a continuous process of recapitulation of the continuous past, in the form of affects, fantasies, dreams, impulses, and somatic sets and tensions.

As therapy, then, psychoanalysis is directed toward the induction, and the subsequent and final resolution, of the transference neurosis. The means to this end is the systematic interpretation of the resistances for the purpose of obtaining explicit verbalization of all thoughts, fantasies, feeling, attitudes, and impulses. To the extent to which this is successful, the patient re-experiences his past in the present; that is, he experiences the transference neurosis with the analyst as its focus. As this evolves, it, too, is subject to systematic interpretation. In the end, the past and present, the once-repressed and the always-remembered, are integrated into the unity of the person. The patient, re-experiencing his past in the transference neurosis as though it were the living present, finds under the new conditions a second chance, an opportunity for a "new beginning." A developmental process which had been halted or sidetracked resumes its course, and the patient "redevelops" while he is reliving.

We see then that while the creation of the conditions for the development of transference neurosis is a suggestive maneuver, the purpose of which is to induce the exposure of the unconscious "material" of the ego, id, and superego, *the resolution of the transference neurois* (which proceeds *pari passu* with its development) *by means of systematic interpretation of its manifestations is the crucial therapeutic device.* The intention and, when successful, the effect are to liberate the person from the nonrationally compelling figures of his past and of his present—including the analyst himself. *The chief qualitative distinction between psychoanalysis and all other mental therapies is its effort to destroy the suggestive influence of the authority of the therapist. It aims to set the patient free.* Despite examples to the contrary, this can and does occur.

As an instrument of research, the analytic situation which I have described is a carefully controlled experiment in human relationship which makes possible the exclusion of many variables that in ordinary transactions obscure the quality of the process which goes on in the participants. Under the conditions of this situation, the process of the transference neuroses constitutes the field which the analyst studies. In this field there reappears the flux of creative and destructive forces that has determined the destiny of the person. The quality and the configurations of these forces is to a great extent known. But there is much yet to learn. As Hans Sachs once said, "Our deepest analyses are no more than scratching the earth's surface with a harrow."

Among analysts of my generation who entered the study of medicine, psychiatry, and finally psychoanalysis in order to understand, perhaps to be able to help, there has occurred a marked shift of goal characterized by aggressive therapeutic ambition. In addition to the external social factors which I think produce this shift, a complementary internal factor seems to be operating. I think we are witnessing a gigantic reaction formation to the consequence of anxiety leading to defensive overactivity induced by the pressures of our time. I think that the *wish to make the patient get well by whatever means* reflects a reactivation of incompletely resolved mandates from the primitive superego which the calm simplicity of the physician's healing impulse no longer seems to satisfy.

Today, when the value of the individual is a matter of doubt to both east and west of the curtains which enshroud the world, when the threat of great danger forces us all together into a frightened huddle, in which elbow-room seems, to many, to be of secondary importance, it is not surprising that "adjustment" tends to become the measure of psychic health and the goal of therapy, while the cost to the potentialities of the free ego is bypassed.

Today, when we are so hard pressed for the quick workable solutions to the problems that beset us, it is not surprising that we think of teams and groups and multidisciplinary studies to share the enormous burden of responsibility that rests on all those whose work bears in any measure on the fate of man.

Under these circumstances the American psychoanalyst of 1955 would be more than human if he did not react with some anxiety and with some self-doubt respecting the validity of his work. We know how persistent are the demands in our culture that we take a part in its daily scene. We know how difficult it is to sustain that balance of mind which Henry Adams has described as "absence of self-assertion or self-consciousness—the faculty of standing apart without seeming aware that one is alone." We see the strong currents which make for adaptation as a substitute for integration. Liberalism as a concept of individualism and of the free mind today moves toward communalism and social amelioration. I do not wish to make a choice between these. In the end they cannot be divorced. But I think it well to remember that psychoanalysis was born out of man's struggle against delusive romanticism, and I am impelled to ask whether or not the present trend in its history is a retreat from freedom and a regression toward intellectual conformity, a conformity which can be rationalized as historically necessary, socially good, and scientifically valid.

With all of this I do not wish to be the advocate of a doctrine of special revelation which is to be faithfully adhered to in splendid isolation. Psychoanalysis, like any true science, must remain open to revision. But at the same time, its fundamental postulates must be preserved.

Modern neuroanatomy, neurophysiology, cybernetics, animal psychology, and the other natural sciences create the climate in which psychoanalysis exists today. Inevitably this affects its context, or, as some might say, the "field" of its operation. We can now have hope that the more recent advances in psychoanalysis, particularly in ego psychology, against this background, may bring us truly fundamental insights into the individual nature of men and particularly into the problem of adaptation as it is related to determinism and free will. To the extent to which we do this, we are also brought closer to a real solution of the living problems whose present insistence evokes our hectic improvisations.

I come, at last, to the statement which, for lack of better, I must call a "credo": Psychoanalysts have a special problem, a special interest in it, and a special technique for studying it. Some psychoanalysts have a special aptitude for the application of that technique. Psychoanalysis has its place among the other natural sciences, and with its technique it has made and can continue to make its unique contribution to the sum total of our knowledge about the nature of man. The psychoanalytic method has developed out of the special nature of psychoanalytic material. The basic psychoanalytic situation cannot sustain extensive modifications without impairing the particular perspective which the scientific ordering of that material requires. Psychoanalysis in its basic form has established the fact of its fundamental therapeutic potential. This does not mean that intermediate therapeutic possibilities should be discarded. Indeed, under the circumstances of the facts of life, the skills of the analyst must be extended as far as they can reach by way of derivative and applied forms of treatment which may bring significant amelioration if not final cure. But this does not permit us to forget that our knowledge of the human mind is far from complete; that basic psychoanalytic technique as a clinical method is at one and the same time our most fundamental psychological research method; that psychoanalysis as therapy and psychoanalysis as research cannot be separated; that there are those whose special capacities and interests lead them to devote themselves to the basic psychoanalytic method, and to some of these it is given to advance the discoveries begun by Freud. The American psychoanalyst in 1955, I believe, must ponder deeply the proposition that unless psychoanalysis as a clinical method is practiced by him in its most developed form we will lose it as a research tool. (Perhaps more important, we will lose it as a bastion of creative individualism.) To preserve the one I see the complete necessity of continuing the other.

# On Ego Distortion

## (1958)

IN OPENING the symposium on Ego Distortion it was
my primary intention to provide a clinical foundation on which the discussion of a difficult problem
might be firmly based. Therefore, whereas this report
begins with some rather discursive theoretical remarks
I shall be chiefly concerned with the presentation of
fragments from the analysis of what I think is a relevant case. And I shall try to pose some of the questions
presented by the clinical material of that case

---

*Editorial note:* When this paper was originally published, Dr. Gitelson
prefaced it with an explanatory footnote:

In its original invitation to me to open the symposium, the Programme Committee at the 20th Congress of the International Psycho-
Analytic Association stated that its concern was with . . . that wide
group of patients known . . . as "borderline cases." Subsequent in-
structions from the Committee specified that it desired the discussants
to consider "learning inhibitions; certain types of neurotically determined eccentricities; passionate interests or hobbies; certain disturbances
of perception or reality testing; 'as if' personalities; impostors and
compulsive liars; and other related conditions." Certainly these more
explicit directions were intended to narrow the field and to sharpen
the view of the problem. Yet, it is a question whether this is really
possible at the present time.

The variety of designations which have been applied to the assorted manifestations of pathology in the ego (e.g., "ego modification," "ego deformation," "distortion," "restriction" and "constriction," "impoverishment," "deviation," "weakness," "immaturity") are indicative of the many singular and combined ways in which this pathology has been thought to come about.[1] Because the disturbance is usually referred to be its chief symptom, our thinking is channeled in a direction which assumes an ego-specific defect. But we soon find that the peculiarity which attracts our attention is embedded in a morass of idiosyncratic adaptations we commonly refer to as "borderline."[2] Compared with the classical neurotic symptoms, the eccentricity in such a patient is seen more clearly as only one aspect of a disturbance which has developed on a broad base in the patient's earliest history (Deutsch, 1942).

Actually, ego distortion is an inevitable consequence of conflict. If, with Hartmann (1939a), we define the ego in terms of its functions, then, transiently or durably, even in the case of the transference neuroses, the ego suffers some impairments. In practice, we tend to disregard such "limited" interferences with the ego's

[1] See Beres, 1956; Eissler, 1953; A. Freud, 1936; Freud, 1937; Reich, 1954.

[2] If one reviews the clinical phenomena presented in the so-called borderline cases, one finds, in addition to the diffuse clinical picture, one or another or several of the specific "distortions" which have been named by the committee.

Indeed, I have seen no case which presents these clinical features in isolation. They would appear to belong, instead, to that group of which Freud (1924) has said, "It will be possible for the ego to avoid a rupture in any direction by deforming itself, by submitting to encroachments on its own unity, and even perhaps by effecting a cleavage or division of itself" (pp. 152–153).

functions, inasmuch as they are clinically insignificant, in many ways well compensated, and the ego as a whole continues to operate according to the reality principle and the principle of multiple functions (Waelder, 1936a). But the point is sharper if we consider the ego of the presumably "normal" adult. Here, though not all ego functions have attained equivalent degrees of autonomy and stability, a significant number of them have attained virtual independence from conflict and regressive pulls. Adaptive functions are sufficiently separated from those of defense and are thus practically uncontaminated by primitive drives. Nevertheless, some instincts have fused with some autonomous functions and have come to operate as (sublimated?) ego interests. And while typical (that is, habitual) methods for avoiding danger and anxiety have become established, adaptive crises occur in which these may fail. We then observe discrepancies which are determined by variations in tolerance for anxiety, or for the nature of the emergency regression which anxiety has evoked. Thus, while thought, action, anticipation, and objectivization have been integrated according to the reality principle and the secondary process, facultative regression has also become one of the ego's functions (Hartmann, 1952). In short, the "normal" ego is balanced in its several functions or is, as it has been called, flexible; it is adaptive in its relations to the id and superego, to itself, and to external reality. That is, while it has objective constancy and predictability, and on the subjective side it has identity, in certain cross sections of adaptation, when a shift occurs from the typical balance of functions and defenses, the ego of the "normal" person may appear "distorted."

This is an idealized picture. A little shift in the point of view reveals that what I have described has only relative quantitative value. In the interest of accuracy, every statement I have made about the normal ego must be modified by the phrase "more or less." On the one hand, each of these aspects of the "normal" ego can move toward the pathological end of the scale. On the other hand, no one of them is independent of processes in the id and superego or of external reality. We are compelled to look upon the entire psychic process holistically (Menninger, 1954a). Viewed externally, this is the human personality. As Hartmann (1939b) has said, the adult sometimes has no choice but to fall back on the earlier adjustive process. Symptoms may be basic signs of health (Eissler, 1953). Childhood neurosis may be adaptively "normal." When viewed against the background of the transient incapacity of the immature ego to master certain of the internal and external integrative tasks it encounters, the neurosis of childhood may be merely the period of truce which is required for the maturation and development of the ego organization as a whole. And the same principle may be applied to the "cross-sectional" distortions of the "normal" adult ego. Thus it may be necessary to define the "hypothetical normal ego" (Freud, 1937) in negative terms as an ego characterized by the absence of specialized defenses, attitudes, or properties, yet, as Freud has said, capable of a certain mode of behavior in the comprehensive situation of the analytic treatment (Eissler, 1953).

It seems difficult indeed, except for heuristic purposes, strictly to delimit ego distortions as such. Exceptions to this may occur in those clinical situations which bespeak defects in such modalities as intelligence and memory and in other adaptive instruments of the mind. Here we may find deviations which are hereditary, or have been somatically acquired (through disease, injury, or other external interferences with maturation and development), or which have been produced by specific neurotic conflicts and inhibitions. Certain types of mental retardation and so-called "functional" physical incapacities are examples.

Such "ego centered" unique defects, however, do not concern us in the present context. Rather it would seem that here the entire psychic apparatus becomes rigidly integrated into what is preponderantly a defense-oriented pattern of adaptation (Fenichel, 1945). The ego thus becomes involved in a diffuse process of adjustment to the other psychic forces, to the self, to objects, and to external reality. While this process of adjustment preserves the formal integrity of the ego organization as a whole, it also more or less affects all ego functions. From this point of view the various specific ego distortions may be seen as single instances of the general process of adjustment and adaptation.

I follow Brenman (1952) in suggesting that as a class "ego-distortions" are highly organized clinical phenomena whose etiology is not assignable to any one of the major psychic institutions. Each case represents a way of life, a method of adaptation demanded by particular deviations in the internal and external environments which had been impressed upon the whole development of the personality. We find in these cases various defenses, various channels for the discharge of tensions emanating from the id, ego, and superego, and various ego-adaptive functions which have become modified in accordance with these pressures. The consequences of the interplay of all these factors and forces are inadequacy, hypertrophy, and/or atrophy of ego functions as such, and an apparent imbalance in the picture of the total ego.

We must ask, therefore, if we are warranted in designating the type of case with which we are concerned in terms which imply ego-specific pathology. Such terms emphasize a structural delimitation of the pathology which does not conform with the observed contingency of the ego's functioning on all of its relationships with all the other internal and external psychic factors (Hartmann, 1952). It would therefore be preferable to view our problem as concerned with disorders of the total personality. Adopting Fenichel's clinical approach (1945), we may conceive of our cases as instances of "character disorders" in which adaptive modifications of the ego (i.e., ego dysfunctions) have developed. Regarding these patients as suffering from ego disturbances, it is possible to recognize in the fixated and/or regressed pictures that they present, features which on the one hand have the metapsychological characteristics of the infant and the young child at various stages of development, and on the other hand have qualities of the schizophrenic.

When we compare these cases with the clinical types more commonly referred to as "character neuroses," we are impressed with the fact that the developmental vicissitudes which have eventuated in each type are different. Both types represent "an adjustment to neurosis, an attempt to make the best of established neurotic conditions" (Fenichel, 1945), a defense against the further extension of the conflict and its consequences. But one group, like the transference neuroses, is determined genetically by the preponderance of vicissitudes in psychosexual development and by the intensity of the ego-superego-id conflict. *The oedipal conflict is distinctly at the center.* The other group follows the genetic pattern of the narcissistic neuroses; the vicissitudes which have been most fateful appear to have occurred largely in relation to external objects; the most intense conflict has been between ego and reality; and aggression figures more extensively than libido. *The oedipal conflict is highly coloured by pregenital conflicts* (Greenacre, 1952). In other words, it would seem that in terms of the evolved pathology, the attendant ego disturbance in this group of disorders approaches, in appearance, the disturbance in the ego of the schizophrenic.

This does not imply a commitment to the debatable thesis that in any one person there is a potential transitional series of ego states ranging from hebephrenic deterioration to assumed normality (Bowlby, 1942; Menninger, 1954a; Zilboorg, 1933). The biogenetic factors in schizophrenia make such a point of view quite risky, for here we may be presented with some kind of bona fide ego defect. But there is the clinical fact on which Freud (1937) may be quoted: "Every normal person, in fact, is only normal on the average. His ego approximates that of the psychotic in some part or other and to a greater or lesser extent, and the degree of its remoteness from one end of the series to the other will furnish us with a provisional measure of what we have so indefinitely termed an 'alteration of the ego' " (p. 235).

Taking into account what I have emphasized with regard to the imbrication of the development and maturation of the ego with other contemporaneous factors, it may be considered that various pathological ego states, in intimate combination with genetically related states of superego and ego ideal and in typical relationship to the body ego and id, form configurations which I would call "narcissistic personality disorders." In these patients we observe features characteristic of the infant and the young child. The ego is not weak; it is intrinsically strong (Menninger, 1954a); it is not defective; rather it is effective in an arrested state of development.

The patient I shall now present as an example may enable us to attach these and other theoretical considerations to clinical realities. He is a 26-year-old man, a graduate student of nuclear physics. At 18 he had been forced into psychotherapy by his father because of a single symptom, annoying to the father but not to the patient: hair plucking. He chewed and swallowed the hair he pulled out. When I first saw him he had three bald areas on his head. This had begun at 14, following a short period of plucking at the pubic hair. Despite his denial of personal concern he had become aware of his conspicuousness and had developed a manner of acting mysteriously and letting it be understood that his appearance had something to do with having been associated with a "classified" project. This pose had succeeded so well that he felt there was no longer even an external need for his being in analysis.

The psychotherapy was without result. He had simply complied with his father's wish. Subsequently, having entered upon his advanced academic work in another city, he accepted the psychiatrist's advice and began an analysis. This continued for a year and a half. He had then insisted on interrupting and had returned home. Then again, on the advice of the first analyst and of his father's wish, while denying any personal feeling of the need for help, he had entered into analysis with me.

Though at first he had disliked his former analyst, he told me, ultimately he had come to "respect" him. But he denied that anything had happened in the analysis. He particularly denied that he had any of the feelings for the analyst which he was "supposed" to have had. He came to me because he had confidence in the honesty of the advice he had been given. But he did not accept the concurrent recommendation, which the first analyst had made, that he live independently. Instead, his parents now being divorced and each remarried, he arranged to divide his residence between them. He thought of and called his mother's husband and his father's wife "father" and "mother" respectively. Despite their social and emotional estrangement, the two families constituted for him a single emotional menage.

The outstanding fact about the first analysis was that a transference in the classical sense had never developed. Besides this, the former analyst had felt that the patient "required cautious handling because a psychotic break was always potential," with a suicidal attempt likely. In his view, the "life-saving factor" was the patient's relationship with his dog, "the only living object which escaped his otherwise universal affective isolation. This relationship [the analyst felt] represented a beachhead from which [the patient] could perhaps extend his object cathexis as a result of therapy. These excerpts from a communication to me emphasize the relevance of this case to the problem we are discussing. It was a transference development, after more than a year of the second analysis, which in other respects was similar in pattern to the previous one, that is of special interest. I shall describe this in the course of what follows.

The patient is an only child. He was 14 when his parents ended a chronically stormy marriage. The father's business in the engineering field had taken him away from home frequently and for long periods. The boy had been reared largely by the mother and various domestics. During the mother's frequent absences he had lived with the paternal grandmother. At the time of one of these absences, at the age of six months, he had an asthmatic attack. Subsequently he suffered from a variety of allergies which became the basis for an intensely close relationship with the mother.

The mother fussed over his diet and his medication. She habitually joined him under the steam tent during nocturnal respiratory crises. I have had a number of telephone conversations with this woman—a consequence of her wish to get "into" the analysis with the patient. On the basis of these contacts, as well as the patient's information, I can say that she is a vacuous pseudointellectual who knows the correct words and gestures and whose emotions are maudlin. The patient has referred to her as a "pollyanna" and a "shrike." I have sometimes thought of her as a Helen Hokinson type. She habitually permitted herself and the boy to be nude together and to use the bathroom in each other's presence. When she noticed his first pubic hair, she abruptly terminated this form of intimacy. Concurrently with this his allergies disappeared. She responded to the youngster's searching intelligence with distortion of the facts, garbled information, and fantastic opinions. Even today she has her muddled say about research problems he happens to be discussing in her presence. The patient's childhood memories are full of her doting attention to him, her shallowness, and her "silly notions."

It was only after the divorce that the patient received any real attention from the father. The patient thinks he may have been afraid of his father's impatience and temper. In addition to his frequent absences, the father seemed resentful of the patient's existence and was withdrawn from him even when he was at home. The boy's attempts to reach him with questions intended to correct the mother's distortions were met with indifference or brusque refusals.

To the casual onlooker, except for bald spots the patient looked normal enough. With his sloppy attire and clumsy movements, his careless posture, he appeared younger than he was. He was likely to walk down the corridor in which my office is located at a lumbering but brisk gait, loudly whistling a tune from an operetta. Though bold and tactless in his address, he was likeable; his social defects were striking only in view of his stuffy middle-class background; he carried off his gaucheries with a kind of boyishness which people accepted. He referred easily to a variety of people as "friends." Indeed, while he was looked upon as an "original," he presented a tacit invitation to friendship which others responded to. Except for occasional argumentative vehemence, he was affectively shallow. His speech tended for a long time to be recitative, and ordinarily he was remarkably literal in his intellectuality—a trait rather difficult to describe. Perhaps its former heavy seriousness may be the quality which distinguished it from its ultimate liveliness and occasional exacerbations of intellectual intensity. In a field in which "objectivity" is so highly prized, it went unnoticed by his colleagues. But, paradoxically, despite undoubted respect for his intelligence, his professors commented on his "disorganized and unobjective" thinking, to the extent of holding up final approval of his candidacy for the doctorate until his preliminary work on his thesis had been reviewed. He is socially conservative and politically dogmatic like his father. During a political campaign he went around plastered with campaign buttons, gratuitously and tactlessly criticizing his instructors for their divergent political views.

Since the late teens he had been going with a girl three years his junior. Over the years a sexual relationship had developed consisting of "necking" and mutual masturbation, sometimes, more recently, with the girl bare to the waist, the patient naked and in the coital position. He professed not to know whether he loved her or not, since he did not "know" what the feeling of love was. But he thought she loved him. Their sexual activity occurred on a sort of taken-for-granted schedule, on the Saturday nights of their weekends together, which were spent at his mother's home. From time to time the girl would interrupt this schedule; sexual contact was a privilege which she could grant or withhold. The *pro forma* character of the patient's feelings about the relationship was striking. His assumption was that boys and girls were "supposed" to go together and marriage was the natural and convenient climax of this. An onlooker to their weekends would have had the impression of an old, established married couple who had long ago shed their sentiment and romance. No other girls attracted him; there had been no other companionate or sexual relationships.

A friendship with a young man of his own age went back into early adolescence. He described his feeling in this relationship as "fellow-feeling." They "think" alike and were in fact sufficiently similar to have been taken for twins. The other boy is less intelligent but also emotionally isolated; he is a chemist. The high points of their friendship occurred on camping trips. On one such trip the patient "thought" of doing something homosexual, but there had been no real impulse, and the "thought" never recurred. Other young men and younger boys had sometimes stimulated this "thought." Asked about his *feelings* on such occasions, he answered with asperity, "I have no feelings! I see them, then I get a constriction in my throat, or a sensation in my belly, and I think I would like to know them better. That is all" (Schur, 1955).

Generally, he masturbated, without fantasy and without pleasure, to induce sleep. Quite frequently, however, there had been pleasurable masturbation, associated with sadomasochistic fantasies, of which the following are typical: He is commanding a powerful airfleet which is executing a bombing mission. He is in an underground country where people cannibalize each other, especially eating each other's genitals, which preferably are torn from the living person. He is a ten-year-old boy and an older girl is about to do this to him. Another boy kills the girl by stabbing her in the rectum or vagina.

The latter type of fantasy occurred more frequently. Sometimes it was he who was being stabbed in the rectum, and there were other variations in detail, but the main theme was recurrent. The fantasies could occur without erection or masturbation. Neither anxiety nor guilt was attached to their occurrence. Queried about this he said, "Well, in the first place, I don't do it myself in these fantasies. Yet I can get sexually excited about it. My instinctive acts don't seem to follow my reason. Robots are logical but not reasonable. They can't discriminate among premises. They can only start from a given premise and work logically from there. But it's all unpredictable!"

Now, to complete the clinical picture, I shall describe an aspect of it I did not learn about until after the occurrence of the transference episode which I have mentioned but shall not relate until later. He was telling me about his extensive reading (science fiction) as a means of separating himself from others. He then went on to say that he does not know exactly how to "be" with people and has recognized in himself "a great tendency to imitate anyone" with whom he has sustained relationship, so that in a very short time he begins to talk and act like that person. He has succeeded in making a place for himself by being very sensitive to clues as to what the prevailing mood, preoccupation, and point of view is. He feels that it is because he has become skillful in merging himself with what he finds that he has been accepted. The only time he has cried since he was a young child was when Boots (the pet mentioned by his previous therapist) died, and then it was not until some hours later when "suddenly it hit!" But generally the case is: "I experience something; then I think of something I have read and compare it with the situation I am in; and then I know what the feeling is." Or again, it may be that "I let myself appear to be, and I get to feeling like, the crowd I'm with as a way to get along." Further to this, "I put people on a stick (like an insect on a pin) and look them over," and, with great (though unrecognized) feeling, "I like to have a relationship of confidence with people; I like to be liked by them; but I cannot feel them or for them!" This has been the situation since early adolescence.

The similar situation in the transference is illustrated in the following quotation: "I'm afraid I sort of regard you as I do a professor. I have no emotional attachment to any of them. I just find out their idiosyncrasies and what they want me to do and I do it. Maybe I don't transfer [he was familiar with the term from a recent popular article] because I didn't have the emotions in childhood."

Perhaps as much as 90 per cent of the material of the analysis was concerned with the thoughts, problems, and activities of the patient's work in physics.

For the rest, there was the emergence of the anamnesis as I have outlined it, interspersed with the daily trivia, the reporting of the fantasies I have described, and of occasional dreams, to which he seldom offered any explicit associations. For over a year there was a nearly complete absence of the usual manifestations of transference. He viewed me as a sort of IBM machine, with him providing the raw data from which I was to derive the answers. He continued to deny having any real stake in the analysis, saying on one occasion that he didn't like to be "in the grip of forces [he] can't control; it hurts [his] pride, which isn't too great anyhow." Nevertheless, the impression gradually deepened that the patient, like a child, had become attached to the analytic situation and to me personally. This showed itself chiefly in the boyish eagerness with which he entered the consulting room, the "openness" which gradually came into his manner, his occasional thoughts about having lunch with me ("but that doesn't go in analysis"). And, as with a child, it had been my spontaneous response to be far from formal with him; I answered his "openness" with my own.

During the first month of analysis with me he would from time to time report crawling or tickling sensations in various skin areas. On inquiry, he once stated that this was another way in which he had "feelings" when he had homosexual "thoughts." But he vehemently denied that any particular thoughts occurred to him on the couch (Schur, 1955). For a longer period there was another "couch symptom" which was chronic. This was a continuous, rapid, and sometimes quite violent rotatory jerking of the legs which were held in abduction from the hips. When, finally, I remarked that it seemed possible that the feeling he denied was being expressed in these movements, he gave vent to a shout of astonishment and became for some time completely motionless and silent. This symptom then disappeared, though lesser leg movements exacerbated from time to time.[3]

Some two weeks following this intervention, the patient was telling me something his mother had spoken of recently: When he was four years old she had noticed that his penis was so long that it protruded from his shorts, and she had had to get him longer ones. At this point in the story the patient fell silent. A moment later he became flushed. Then he reported that a "wave of heat," starting at his toes, had "marched up [his] legs and torso to [his] head." He was quite matter-of-fact about it, and was unaware that his face and neck were, in fact, flushed (Schur, 1955). The next day he reported the following dreams:

(1) He is in a toilet which is for both men and women. There are no doors on the cubicles. He is having a bowel movement. A young woman walks in and ridicules him.

(2) He is on a beach running for his life from a tidal wave which threatens to engulf him.

---

[3] Subsequently, after the explicit appearance of transference reactions, I once detected a particular rhythmic quality in this movement. I asked him, "What is the melody?" His prompt response was, " 'I have often walked down this street before,' from *My Fair Lady.*" The rest of this part of the lyric runs, "People stop and stare but they don't bother me; there's no place where I'd rather be—standing in the street where you live."

The first dream recalled the tale his mother had told him and reminded him of their common use of the bathroom. The second one recalled an incident of mutual inspection with a little girl, on a beach, when he was four. "Ordinary waves have no transverse movement of particles, but this must have been occurring in the wave in the dream." He thinks of the Greek letter psi. He refers to the "psi phenomenon" which he says some physicists are willing to believe. Analysis must have something to do with it. Until adolescence he had believed in omnipotence of thought; it still seems possible. Until he was six or seven he used to point an index finger at someone and think, "What if I should let go and kill him?" I remind him of the wave of heat he had felt in the previous hour, and he bursts out, "That was a wave of feeling!" With this, for the first time, he experienced anxiety, identified by him as "a feeling of fear" and corroborated by his rapid breathing and tachycardia (Schur, 1955).

I cannot quite convey the quality of this hour in which manifest anxiety and a simultaneous aspect of relief appeared in a curious blend. At any rate, it now appeared clear that it was the threat of being flooded by feelings in psychotic proportions that the patient defended himself against in his denial of all emotions. The affect, which previously had been discharged in the violent leg movements and which had now expressed itself in the "heat wave," the "tidal wave" dream, and in dreams of the preceding two weeks (which he now reported for the first time—dreams in which the theme was anxious flight from various dangerous "war zone" situations) was composed of massive rage and destructive impulses, connected with the helpless oedipal erotic wishes.[4] In connection with this it is significant that his original interest in physics had been of a practical nature until his parents' divorce. Then his present theoretical interest arose. He now spoke of this specifically as possibly being a manifestation of his earlier preoccupation with psi phenomena. "After all," he said, "the forces of physics are intangible, but they are effective in reality." Notable also is the overt somatization of affect which previously had been only implicit.

Following this episode the analysis subsided into its typical course. Three months passed before the patient revealed that throughout adolescence the "thought" had been recurrent that people around him on a streetcar or bus were making "peculiar remarks" about him. He never took the experience seriously, however, because he had considered that they were only "poking fun" at his clothes. And it was some months still later that he told me that until the time of the parents' divorce he had lived with the *chronic feeling that nothing was "real" except himself;* everything else was "put on" for him by his mother for his special benefit; "She made things seem to be as they were, but they were not really so." His father and his paternal grandmother were figments of this "feeling-fantasy."[5] He responded

---

[4] In his communication to me, the former analyst had said, "During his treatment with me a major problem had been his tendency to act out aggressive impulses in a self-destructive way, but these were limited to small accidents and minor bodily injuries. Several times he seemed to realize his closeness to loss of reality and become very frightened with the repeated vivid visualization of massive regression, in which he pictured himself vegetating in the back ward of a mental hospital." Such episodes did not occur during the course of the present analysis.

[5] After the emergence of the transference, typical fantasies of the "family romance" appeared.

promptly with denial to my comment that possibly the fantasy expressed doubts about the reality of his mother's love. Still, several hours later he returned to the idea with the statement that it might be that his father's brusqueness and criticisms were "more real."

The second year of the analysis began with preoccupation about the possibility that his thesis work might make it necessary to stop treatment. Anyhow, the analysis was getting nowhere. In this context he began to talk about moving into an apartment of his own. The patient had raised this question with me during his referral interview, but I had not pressed it at the time because of my uncertainty about what he could then tolerate. Now I gave the idea tacit but clear encouragement. Following the hour in which this happened, he reported the first clear transference dream:

He is attending a meeting of the officers of his sea-scout "ship." The captain says that the patient is one of a number of officers who are no good for the ship.

As background for this dream I must admit that I had indeed become "inwardly" discouraged about the progress of the analysis. The patient, however, now said that he would be very disappointed if he had to give up his scout work, and further, "According to analysis the captain must be you." Responding to this, I suggested that perhaps the analysis really meant more to him than he could admit. Perhaps he had been considering living on his own as a matter of meeting a condition for remaining in analysis. The patient reacted with unusually violent denial. He had no such feelings about me or the analysis. It is just a technique. He does not have any fear of feelings. "The only conscious fear I have of emotions is my fear of what I would feel if my mother and father died. Maybe that would be like what I would feel if my dog died." [6]

Several times during this session the patient turned over on his abdomen and talked directly to me. At the end of the hour he remarked, "Something has been going on here, but it will be gone tomorrow." Ordinarily this might well have been the case, except, I believe, for a fortuitous episode.

I was late for an important appointment. I had the choice of waiting for the patient to leave the building well ahead of me or of doing the "natural" thing. I decided on the latter. For the first time we were together outside my office. We went down on the same elevator and walked together to the door of the next building, which was my destination. We talked about the election campaign (he did not know my political position), a handy topic made available by a very noisy sound truck. The next day he reported that he had been upset. His mother had told him he did not look well. He had, for the first time, felt overwhelmed by the burden of his academic work. It had been nice to see me outside the office, but it hadn't affected him in

[6] His dog is indeed the only creature in the world for which he has a *living* feeling. During his previous analysis, when a mongrel pet died, he had gone into a state of agitation from which he had found relief only by returning a thousand miles to his mother's home. The former analyst's impression of the meaning and importance of this pet, which I have already noted, had been corroborated by me. The puppy which replaced him had been named "Photon" because "he is the light of my life"; and because like light, "his nature is indeterminate" (that is, a particle or a wave).

any particular way. Nevertheless, he felt "churned up" on the couch. He felt as if he was "doing things under water—a kind of foggy feeling of unreality." He mentioned for the first time the occurrence of temper tantrums during his childhood. Suddenly, he felt "a tingling, numb feeling" in his body. He felt like turning over on his left side, facing me, and going to sleep. I said, "Perhaps you cannot decide whether to turn toward or away from feelings connected with me and the analysis?" To which he replied, "What good does that do me?" He was quiet for some time and, as the hour ended, said, "Maybe I'm afraid I'll hate you."

It seems clear that the patient had experienced an acute withdrawal of cathexis, induced by the anxiety of the dawning of affect in his relationship to me. But the narcissistic withdrawal did not endure. In the next hour he felt much better, and he was emotionally more "open" than he had been before. The material which now began to emerge exhibited the importance of object-libidinal vicissitudes in their relationship to ego disturbances (Jacobson, 1954). He began to report the details of his pathological feelings (or rather lack of feelings) for himself and others. Some of these (the "as-if" phenomenon and the earlier feelings of unreality) I have already presented. Others I shall describe now.

He informed me that as far back as he could remember he had been aware of the schism between his parents, a schism his mother had sometimes denied. At other times she had made light of the situation: "Father is tired; father didn't mean to be angry!" In connection with this, he asked me if "maybe" his logical talk and the comparisons he had been making between theoretical physics and psychoanalysis denoted to me his "way" of reaching out emotionally to me. When I answered that I thought this was indeed the case, he went on to say that this had been his way of reaching out to others. His mother had always had an answer, an unsatisfactory one; his father had appeared bored, or, frequently enough, had simply told him to "keep quiet."

The question arises whether the patient's impaired sense of identity and reality might have stemmed from the mother's unreal attitudes. Did they serve him as a means of "fading into" the false picture of the severely disturbed family situation which the mother had tried to maintain? For it had now become manifest that it was the father who had the clear mind and the positive tastes which the patient tried to emulate. On the other hand, it occurred to the patient that the disorganizational tendency in his thinking might be a reflection of his mother's confusions. Indeed, it would appear that in his resistance he had structuralized both his father's rationality and his mother's simplicity.

The bisexual problem presented itself openly. His former analyst, he said, had once commented that he didn't know which sex he belonged to, but the patient had thought this "nonsense." Now the patient revealed dreams in which he appeared anatomically as a female, while his girlfriend was a hermaphrodite. In other dreams his mother had appeared with a penis. Then, in a vivid fantasy on the couch, as he lay in one of his typical positions, the right ankle crossed over the left, he felt as if a nail were being driven into the shin at the point of contact while another seemed to be piercing his right thigh near the groin. He thought of Christ being put on the cross. Perhaps, he said, he was less afraid of the complete sexual act than indifferent to it; perhaps he was "sexually self-sufficient?"—he is referring here to his bisexual fantasies and his masturbation. He also "weighs" the possibility that in this way he might be maintaining the feeling of union with the mother of the steamtent as a means of dealing with the threat of losing her.

He has an erection on the couch, and that night he has a dream in which a boyhood friend (one of the people at whom he used to point his omnipotently destructive index finger) kissed him affectionately ("not sexually," he says) on the cheek. He asks, "Why is it that I have so much trouble with affection when I want it so much?" He distinguishes between affect and "lust," saying, "I must have had some violent feeling toward you yesterday when that [i.e., the erection] was happening. Maybe the dream means that I want to make up to you." For he associates the figure in the dream with me.

In the subsequent hour he speaks of feeling, during periods of silence (I have not sustained long silences with him), as if there were radiations passing between us. This is a metaphor, definitely not a delusion. Still, it is reminiscent of the paraesthesia which he formerly used to report and which I have previously mentioned. And it is connected with his feeling that there may be something untouchably destructive in him which might explode on contact. Again he mentions the very violent temper tantrums he used to have as a child. And he recalls a recent incident when he found a ship model slightly damaged by a careless domestic: "I felt peaceful in my mind," he says, "but my body felt violent, as if my arms would like to smash things."

For many hours he kept returning to the problem of living alone. I myself had not reopened the topic. Repeatedly he came up with logical reasons why he should not make the move, or he would depreciate the idea as an experiment without a hypothesis or a control. Despite all this, there emerged evidence of his enormous fear of aloneness. The idea is abhorrent. He never quite relaxes when he is alone, except in his car or on the street. When he is alone he is always on the alert; and now it occurs to him that when he is alone, he is "depressed," can't study, kills time until someone comes home; then he can go to work. "If you were to go out of this room, I couldn't stand it unless I got up and read some of your books," he said. "It brings me a feeling of emptiness when I am alone." Maybe it is because he feels "unprotected" when he is alone. He doesn't like surprises. He can't stand suspense. He likes to get things done and over with. He can't wait for developments; that's what's wrong with analysis. It emerges that he thinks he lives "*among people and not with them.*" In the midst of such considerations as these he spoke for the first time of nocturnal attacks of panic during childhood after awakening from a nightmare, when he would stand outside his parents' bedroom, not daring to go in for fear of his father's anger. Finally, he revealed his mother as ridden by various phobias having to do with fear of attack by men when she was alone at home; and he asks if his own sadomasochistic fantasies might have something to do with this.

He reports a dream in which he appeared naked before me and I covered him with an afghan I have in my office. Spontaneously he bursts out that he is "baring [his] soul" in the analysis; but when I suggest that it seems he would like to feel sure of my friendliness and protection, he is no less vehement in his assertion: "You can talk about these feelings until you are blue in the face, but I still don't feel them."

I shall now briefly summarize the analysis as it evolved during the six months that followed. The patient "discovered" the restaurant in the basement of my office building. He saw me there once, en route to the doctors' dining room at its rear. He now established a pattern of seating himself where he could see me on the way to lunch. These encounters resulted in dreams and fantasies having to do with wishes for closeness and gratification, intertwined with destructive hate and attacks of anxiety. All this was verbally denied, and at times there were recurrences of episodes of acute withdrawal such as the one I have described. In contrast to this ambivalent transference, overt and positive warmth was directed during this time to the professor with whom he was working on his thesis. His thesis was approved, and the work went well. He gave up cigarettes in favor of a pipe and cigars—to which I am myself addicted.

Then, following an interruption by my winter vacation, he again began to talk of stopping the analysis. In this setting it became clear that his security depended on his "not needing" the person with whom he had a relationship. Thus, with his professor of whom he was consciously fond, he felt himself to be superior in several ways. But he could not trust himself to the relationship with me: what if he should really begin to feel that he needed me? There occurred a series of fantasies of being completely self-contained. Typical was one of being the commander of an atomic-powered battle cruiser. He felt that if he remained in the analysis it would mean getting really involved and, in the end, disappointed. Again it would be the "merry-go-round" of his love and hate for his mother. Still, the feeling remained with him that "something was going on." The analysis, he complained, was interfering with his intellectuality with which everything is predictable and controllable (Gitelson, 1944). Once, when I passed him in the restaurant, he was interrupted in a reverie about his research. That night he had a dream in which I was represented as cleaning out his perianal area with a spoon; and the associations revealed an anal symptom related to his intellectual control.

Now the denouement: Two months before the pending summer interruption his paternal grandmother died, leaving him a considerable fortune. His father then told him that beginning in the fall he would have to pay for the analysis himself. This he could comfortably do from income if I reduced my fee, and I therefore proposed it. He refused. A month later he announced his engagement to his girl friend. Despite his admitted apprehension, he maintained his decision to interrupt the analysis. There had been improvements, he admitted. And, indeed, there had been. But, he asserted, "they must have occurred by osmosis," for he certainly didn't know what, if anything, he had learned. For the present this is where we must leave him.

I have left to the discussants the many metapsychological problems presented by this case. My closing remarks are confined to a consideration of the clinical phenomena and some of the more general theoretical questions arising from them.

Scanning the picture, we find a rather strange, generally immature young man who presents a number of "neurotically determined eccentricities" and who, in addition to somewhat more subtle disturbances in his relationship to reality seems to have passed through periods in which specific psychotic symptoms have been present, but who has never been identified as having an overt psychosis; whose object relations are manifestly seriously impaired, yet who has been successful in evoking from others a response to anaclitic needs by virtue of a certain "boyish" warmth and clumsy affability, the vehicle for which has been his intellectual "talk and questions"; who since childhood has experienced chiefly somatic equivalents of affect and has no "feelings" or consciousness of love for any fellow creature, and almost no conscious anxiety; who spent nearly three years in analysis (with two analysts) before he manifested the first clear signs of libidinal transference; who lives affectively through imitation and in one aspect as a minor impostor; who is intelligent and has been able by and large to exercise his intelligence, while being at the same time compulsively rigid and hysterically disorderly in his intellectual operation; who harbours violent sadomasochistic fantasies without guilt, and whose ethical standards hover between "the golden rule" and the expedient necessity of states to inflict destruction in the interest of policy; who appears to be in danger of being overwhelmed by his instincts, which he holds at bay with paranoid, phobic, hysterical, and psychotic devices; yet, with all this, feels that he has only one symptom—and from this symptom he does not suffer.

We see, then, a successful even though pathological adaptation. But from the standpoint of the problem we are considering, there is more to be said.

The "miracled-up" world of the patient's childhood and the subsequent paranoid delusion of his adolescence would seem to have been signs of a potential total disaster in the adaptive function of the ego. *Nevertheless, from a functional standpoint, it would seem in the end that we behold, not "ego defect" or "ego weakness," but rather adaptive capacity which may be looked upon as strength. In the face of great internal stress this has insured survival by means of facultative accommodations in various ego functions.* The difference between this patient and the person with the hypothetically "normal" ego (in which the separate functions are not rigidly committed) is seen in the specialization (hyperfunction?) of certain of the ego's defenses, interests, and attitudes. In contrast to what we see in the "normal" personality as flux of energy[7] we find in the present case a psychic system which is characterized by "rigidity of the energy state" (Knight, 1953a). Is it possible to consider, then, that in so-called ego-distortions, we see in fact a *psychic system, which at a moment of crisis in its history has "jelled" to preserve a system of energy balance which otherwise was in danger of transition toward disintegration?* It appears that there was such a moment of crisis during our pa-

---

[7] ". . . i.e., the transitory changes in energy distribution and redistribution such as the temporary and shifting reinforcement of sexual, aggressive or neutral energy as it may occur in the course of any type of activity" (Kris, 1952, p. 27).

tient's puberty when the parents' marriage was finally dissolved, following which the hair-plucking and the imitational and "as-if" behavior appeared.

Turning now to particular aspects of the case, we are first impressed by the patient's denial of feeling, the absence of affectional bonds and of anxiety, and the somatization of affects. This is reminiscent of Zilboorg's (1933) case of "Anxiety Without Affect," which he felt was "probably" that of a potential catatonic. Of this patient, he said that it was "not unlikely that his way of handling his anxiety is most typical of catatonia. . . . the affect implied in the ideational content disappears, because this very ideation is no more perceived as one's own . . ." (pp. 61, 66). Relevant, also, is Jones's idea (1946) that there may be a hereditary physiological factor, comparable to "G" (Spearman's "General Intelligence"), which determines capacity to master the deepest infantile anxieties and to tolerate ego-dystonic impulses or affects. Which of these considerations apply to my patient?

In her discussion of the problem of the capacity to bear anxiety, Zetzel (1949) came to the conclusion that intermediate between the cases in which defensive anxiety and its symptoms appear transiently during developmental and adaptive crises and those in which primary anxiety proves overwhelming, there is an intermediate group in which "anxiety reaches a degree, or is dealt with by a type of defense, which must be regarded as pathological, but which must nevertheless be regarded as serving a useful purpose in that these manifestations of anxiety either phobic or psychosomatic are preferable to the disaster against which they are erected as a defence" (pp. 8–9).

Going on from this I would again raise the question which I have already brought up in the introduction to this presentation: May not the "borderline" case with its "ego distortions," such as the one I have described, belong to such an intermediate group? May not these patients possess a *strong* "innate factor" such as the one suggested by Jones? The important consideration is that the *anlage* of the autonomous ego has not been constitutionally injured, in contrast to what may be the case in schizophrenia.[8] It is thus by virtue of "strength" that these patients are able to accommodate to external and internal developmental stresses of unusual degree, this by means of adjustment rather than by "distortion" or "rupture." Looked upon in this way the imitational and "as-if" adaptations of my patient are a successful effort to instate himself in a *new learning situation, in relation to new objects,* toward which he reaches with his functionally useful anaclitic "boyishness" and his intellectual talk and questions. Echolalia and echopraxia may be the paradigms for this, but the difference is as between the ember and the ash.

[8] Here is what Katan (unpublished) says: ". . . denial does not lead to a breaking off of the ties with reality . . . denial is opposed to this. Denial is a mechanism by means of which the impoverished ego still tries to keep in contact with reality—the ego is [thus] trying to *diminish* the impact of the conflict; therefore, instead of denial leading to a breaking off of ties with reality, denial helps the ego to maintain contact with reality. We should not forget that denial does not change anything in the id."

And again: "Now take withdrawal as an ego defense, as we find it in childhood [and as we see it in the present case.—M.G.]. We know that the ego may withdraw, but the id does not withdraw too. Withdrawal as an ego defence, as a warding off of id-strivings, is completely different from the other kind of withdrawal . . . hebephrenia."

Another characteristic of this "intermediate group," which I think distinguishes it from the group in which ultimate disaster is unavoidable, is the survival of "object hunger." My patient strives to satisfy this, it is true, by means of "pathological" ego functioning. He makes a sort of "lifting-by-the-bootstraps" effort to make and maintain contact through his intellectual implementation of the ego's orientation to reality. Is this not a substitute, perhaps an intermediary, for massively inhibited object libido? May we not see in the patient's living "among people but not with them" the manifestation of a lifesaving activity of the ego (which, if you please, is "distorted" in this aspect)? After all, the ego has as one of its earliest functions the making available of objects for the libido. Clinically, it is clear that despite his "formal" isolation *my patient more or less successfully puts himself in the way of objects even as do young children, who to begin with play only in the presence of other children and only later play with them.*

My patient's conduct in the analytic situation has shown the same ego quality. For a long time he talked and asked questions, as he did with his father and with others. It was only later that he began, to a degree, to let himself be "with" the analyst. As we have seen, this involved exposure to libidinal and aggressive impulses that threatened to overwhelm him. I refer here to the instance in which he for the first time clearly recognized "feeling" as such and to the subsequent appearance of the transference. (Paradoxically, whereas "anger against injustice" had been known to him on occasion, as affection had not, it was "hate" that he feared to express.) In the transference we have observed the violent narcissistic rebound of object libido. Here, instead of an accretion for capacity of ego distance (through identification) and, with this, improved insight, there appeared increased though diffused body awareness, and his distance from me for the moment was increased. However, it would seem that this patient's isolation of himself from me is another instance of the functional utility of an apparent regression. Looked upon as a participant operation of the ego and not simply as a libido regression, this withdrawal from contact may be one of the ways in which the patient's ego exercises one of its "normal" functions: the control of stimuli (Katan). The clinical material has made it clear that *the patient can tolerate neither being with or without external objects. Too much of either is too much.* The problem seems to be concerned with the control of stimuli. Apparently the margin between satisfying object hunger and flooding by stimuli is not great. The basis for this would appear to be quite clear when we review the mother's overwhelming ministrations and seductions and the concomitant frustrations. The patient's "distorted" control of his relations with objects would thus seem to be a functional accommodation of the normal ego's capacity for regulating the stimulus threshold.

Another problem of this case and of others like it is concerned with the place of the psychosexual elements in the picture. There is no doubt that the "form" of the Oedipus complex is present and that there are "formal" signs of the tension that pertain to it (Gitelson, 1952b; Lampl-de Groot, 1952). It will be recalled that after the emergence of the transference, the patient produced a number of memories of the typical fantasies of the family romance. It would thus be likely that the patient's earlier reported fantasy of the unreality of everything and everyone except himself was a more extreme version of this defense against the Oedipus complex, determined by the extreme conduct of both mother and father. But even in the context of the scanty early history, it would seem that this was a much more radical alienation: on the one hand, a defense against unusually great internal tension generated by the excessive stimulation of both erotic and hostile impulses and their attendant anxiety; and on the other hand, the need to deny the effect of the external factors which threatened to evoke them. This was the basis for the potentially explosive rage which made him feel like a "booby-trap."

Alternatively to alienation, it would seem that the father's intermittent presence at home presented the patient with the actual though inadequately realized hope of establishing the protective reality of a "real" oedipal situation. It seems likely that the divorce impaired even this nominal protection. In the paranoid idea of his adolescence, in his choice of physics as a career, in the "as-if" behavior, in the development of a technique of "serious talk and questions" and, finally, in the setting up of a "doubled" family constellation after the remarriage of the parents, I think we see a new defensive adaptive effort, through identification, through delibidinized reaching toward father figures, and through a "formal" childlike return to the separated parents. And it would seem that this pattern repeated itself in the analysis. All of this is quite a different state of affairs from the earlier "alienation." It suggests to me, as have other similar cases, that the distorted Oedipus complex is a psychological foothold which these patients strive to maintain as a defense against the regressive plunge by which they feel threatened. As such, its vestiges are the signs of the ego's strength rather than of its defectiveness or weakness.[9]

From the adaptational point of view I have assumed, numerous other aspects of this case bear on the problems of "ego distortion." Some of these are suggested for which the data are inadequate.[10] Questions concerned with the patient's identifications, the formation of the superego and the ego ideal and their part in the production of the total picture, the bisexual problem and the problem of the body image, his psychosomatic illness, and the more recently reported neurotic symptoms—all these remain to be elucidated, not only in themselves but in their relation to the functioning

---

[9] Because the question has been raised in a previous discussion of this case, I want to say here that *I have no idea that the Oedipus complex exists for the purpose of providing a kind of ladder to maturity, or to protect against regression.* I do not take a teleological position. Rather, I have presented a *post hoc* description of the state of affairs in my patient and others like him (Greenacre, 1952) in whom the existence of the Oedipus complex, even in distorted or vestigial forms, is evidence of a capacity for a degree of development and maturation. Phenomenologically it is clear that those who advance, more or less, through the several stages of the Oedipus complex are those whose reactions of regression and fixation are not so deep or so immutable.

[10] It is unfortunate that the analysis came to an end when it did. It would seem that the patient was engaged in a decisive transference conflict at the time of his grandmother's death. I think if he had been able to maintain his father as a fee-paying "buffer" he might have dared to move more deeply into the analysis than he did in the end. As it was, the emotional commitment involved in the necessity of paying my fee personally was just too much. The patient was married about two months before this writing. He continues to "encounter" me in the dining room, is friendly and chatty. His work is going well. He has spoken to me about his marriage only in conventional terms.

of the ego. However, on the basis of the available information and the considerations which I have been able to bring to bear on it, I submit the following propositions:

(1) "Ego distortions" do not represent ego-specific pathology. This distinguishes them from the schizophrenic psychoses and from those disorders in which such functions as memory or intellection are injured prenatally or by intercurrent disease or trauma.

(2) Significantly, the patient I have described and other such patients (Beres, 1950), have encountered unusual stress in relation to their original objects, particularly the mother. The consequences are seen in pregenital disturbances in the economy of libido and aggression, in defective superego development, and in compensatory internal and external adjustive and adaptive accommodations of ego functions.

(3) These adjustments and accommodations in ego functions follow the "normal" patterns seen in transient cross-sections of the "normal" ego during developmental and adaptational crises.

(4) The fixed clinical picture presented by these patients is that of an adaptational balance or posture which occurs phasically during early development, in adolescence, and in certain menopausal cases.

(5) As Kanzer (1957) has suggested in another context, the ego aims are immature, that is, they have not moved their ultimate distance from the instincts, but they are intact manifestations of ego functioning. "Each phase of reality testing is successful in its own setting and is subsequently absorbed into the maturing ego if its integrative capacities develop normally" (p. 674). From the standpoint of the nosology of my case

the point is that we deal with arrests in ego development, not defects, not weakness, and not rupture. It is because of the "survival-adaptive" adequacy in the face of unusual pregenital traumatization that I suggest that in this type of case the ego really has "strength." Unlike the situation in schizophrenia there is in these cases no surrender of the object and no object loss (Katan).

(6) The functional balance of the ego in these patients is intimately correlated with the state of the other psychic processes, the balance of the libidinal and aggressive forces, and the external adaptive task. The ego state in these cases is thus one aspect of the total psychic state. In view of this fact and because of the pregenital roots (Greenacre, 1952) of the pathology, it would seem desirable that the syndromes we have been referring to in ego-specific terms be thought of as "narcissistic personality disorders."

# A Critique of Current Concepts in Psychosomatic Medicine

(1959)

THE TIME is past when we can think of psychosomatic phenomena in terms of the simple alternative, "conversion or anxiety equivalent." Recent literature[1] reveals the wide ramifications of the psychosomatic problem and of the researches into its various facets. While we are indebted to the imagination and enterprise of earlier workers and recognize their validity within limited sectors of the field, we must now consider psychosomatic phenomena as indices to a holistic problem in which the organism must be viewed simultaneously in all its dimensions: psychic and somatic; structural, dynamic, economic, and genetic; anatomical, neural, hormonal and enzymatic. In general medicine, we no longer speak of etiology, but rather ask: what are the necessary and sufficient condi-

---

*Editorial note:* The word "current" in the title of this paper could prove misleading: more than a dozen years later, consensus regarding this subject is still not in sight.

[1] Bandler, 1958; Benjamin, 1952; Bonaparte, 1950; Deutsch, 1953; Greene, 1956; Kubie, 1953a; Mendelson et al., 1956; Menninger, 1954b; Mirsky, 1953; Richmond & Lustman, 1955; Ross et al., 1950; Spitz, 1951; Whitehorn, 1947; Wikler, 1952.

tions, which taken together eventuate in a disease process? In the more complex field of psychosomatic medicine we are compelled to ask the same question.

The simplest of the psychosomatic phenomena, the conversion symptom, illustrates this complexity. The fantasies for which the hysteric uses the language of the body can be reconstructed psychoanalytically because "materialization" of a fantasy is only an exaggeration of a "bit of action" which is potential in even normal thought. Here is the forerunner of the "specificity theories." It has been considered that only the voluntary musculature and that which has gained psychic representation through conscious awareness, i.e., overt motor and sensory functions, can be involved in conversions (Alexander, 1943). Yet a hysterical seizure may involve the vegetative nervous system. Despite the centrality of the Oedipus complex in the genesis of classical hysteria, clinically the symptoms may take pregenital forms. Hunger, thirst, and excretory needs may replace sexual longings; anorexia may deny them; vomiting and diarrhea may express both pregnancy wishes and incorporation fantasies; hyperemia and swelling may represent erection; exudates may take the place of tears. While there may be no massive regression of the personality to pregenitality in conversion hysteria, there do appear to be partial regressions of the ego and the libido to the archaic modes of early childhood. Even in this "higher level" neurosis, we see manifestations of processes that extend far beyond the paradigmatic outline provided by the classical conversion formula (Alexander, 1943).

We are compelled to think similarly of what used to be called "organ neurosis," now known as psychosomatic disease. Present views of ego psychology and of character formation, newer conceptions of the relations and mutual influences of ego and id, no longer permit us to base prognosis on diagnosis, and diagnosis on notions of levels of psychosexual development. ". . . Psychogenic tic covers a continuous series of links from conversion hysteria to catatonia" (Fenichel, 1945, p. 317). Similarly, any given symptom may express conflicts arising at any level and contain elements from every level at once. Whereas there are hysterical conversion symptoms, the "specificity" of the fantasies attached to them—and that even "cause" them—can no longer be looked upon as demonstrating their etiology. We must renounce the hope, then, of seeing in psychosomatic phenomena either developmental or regressive manifestations in a uniform front.

Psychosomatic phenomena regarded as "anxiety equivalents" need to be viewed in the same light. The equivalence concerns not simply anxiety, but affects as a class. Anxiety is, in its ultimate development to panic, a primitive discharge syndrome that evolves when other, more appropriate, impulses to action are short-circuited by the various forces which support the repression of fantasies. Since subjectively perceived emotion is characterized as well by motor and secretory processes and sometimes, too, by sensation, if the conscious awareness of it is suppressed or repressed, the affect may still gain expression through the related organs and organ systems. Clinical experience confirms that each person has an idiosyncratic "somatic style" in experiencing and demonstrating affect or anxiety. One trembles and has cardiac palpitations, another is nauseated or develops polydipsia or hyperpnea, another faints, and still another has urinary frequency or diarrhea. All of these may occur with minimal or no conscious emotion.

Over 20 years ago, at two o'clock in the morning I was called to the home of a friend by his sophisticated wife. His father had died three days before. He had been unable to cry. He had wakened from sleep to find his heart racing, pain in the epigastrium, a profuse diarrheal stool and the contents of his bladder in his bed, his skin soaked with sweat, his face blanched, and his mouth parched and dry. He could not recall the content or affect of a dream which he had had. His subjective concern was with the idea that like his father he had had a coronary attack in his sleep. There was no aftermath to this incident other than great success in his business and the development of a gifted capacity in art. Here, certainly, was affect-equivalent but no psychosomatic disease.

Even pleasurable or erotic experiences and emotions may be associated with unpleasant somatic symptoms. Urinary frequency, strabismus, vomiting, respiratory disturbances and sinus tachycardia have been reported under such circumstances (Stevenson, 1950). Of course, guilt and anxiety may have been present behind the conscious elation or pleasure. Or the change in mood or relief of tension following depression or a sense of entrapment might have produced a sort of rebound phenomenon. But certainly a change in the homeostatic equilibrium was involved.

The previous examples are *ad hoc* reactions—critical responses to acute stimuli. Such crises may arise in life or in a therapeutic situation. In chronic or recurrent conditions seen in psychosomatic medicine, however, affect equivalents have a diminished discharge value as compared with emotions which are fully developed and experienced. After all, affects carry with them enteroceptive and proprioceptive awareness. This overtone contributes to, if it is not fully responsible for, their subjective quality, and indicates concomitant physiological activity. Tension—pleasurable or unpleasurable —is clinical evidence of this and is the side of affect which is susceptible to pharmaceutical and physical modification. The diminished discharge value of affect equivalents appears to be related to what Freud called strangulation of the affects. These affects consist of inadequately elaborated or unexpressed instinctual drives, themselves functions of neural and hormonal physiology.

Thus, in the presence of somatic affect equivalents, the mental content of emotions has been repressed and their physiological concomitants have been insufficiently discharged. But, more important, the primitive id content underlying the potentially conscious mental content remains in continuous association with chronically operating, infantile, physiological processes. As Hendrick (1948) suggests, ego regression which characterizes psychosomatic states may be associated with somatic regression to "physiological infantilism."

This level of functioning does not have the same quality as the physiological phase of normal emotions. Rather it is characterized by the unstable, undifferentiated, and unintegrated homeostasis of infancy and early childhood. Organic affect equivalents are not really equivalent, but are manifestations of disruption in the economy of the organ or organ-system itself. This consideration produces doubt about concepts of specificity that assume a repression of mental content, of impulse to action, and of affect, which in its chronicity has a one-to-one relationship with an effector organ. Such organs, while over- or underactive, are conceived of as preserving their adult quality of activity. In present genetic views, it seems even more likely than when Fenichel (1945) first said it that "the physical concomitants of unconscious affects are qualitatively different from those of the conscious ones." Thus an emotional "set" based on unconscious drives and conflicts can be associated with primitive or infantile somatic and hormonal "sets." The former is certainly psychogenic in the classical sense. The latter look like fixations or regressions along the line of physiological development.

The *problem of psychogenesis* in psychosomatic states is implicit here. The very term "psychosomatic" implies that somatic symptoms are "caused" by psychic contents or that somatic tensions are "caused" by affects. These are carry-overs from our rigid ideas about conversion and anxiety hysteria. But the issue is not "conversion or anxiety." I think it is neither one, as such, and much more than both.

No one frame of reference is more fundamental than another in the holistic approach to the psychosomatic problem. The organism functions as a complex system, aspects of which are understandable through study by a variety of techniques. Among these is psychoanalysis, which conceptualizes the organism's processes as conscious, preconscious, and unconscious (with the susceptibility of becoming conscious under given circumstances). Here we can certainly speak of psychogenesis, but as psychoanalysts, we can go no further. Beyond this is the preverbal and prestructural area of the personality into which we can project and extrapolate concepts based on the material we have. In such extrapolations, we psychoanalysts become dependent upon techniques and data which are foreign to us.

Nevertheless, as medical men, we must explore by other means other aspects of an organism that responds as a whole and try to find the common factors from which the unity of the psyche and soma arise. So we have observed and recorded infant behavior; we have joined forces with the pediatrician, the physiologist, the embryologist, and the neurologist. We have studied organs and organ systems, and physical and behavioral differentiation and integration. And we have found other sets of variables—somatic, physiologic, and behavioral—whose configurations impress us as corresponding to, even being one with, the psychological configurations with which we are most familiar.

We used to ask, "What are the *necessary* conditions which, taken together, are *sufficient* to eventuate in a disease process?" We must now ask in addition, "What are the common factors which are at once physiological and psychological; which do not 'cause' each other, yet are reflected in each other, are contingent and affect each other, and taken together, produce disease?" Put this way, we must forego a conception of cause that depends upon immediate, cross-sectional references, and are forced to take the long view, the genetic view. We gradually see the common *anlagen* of ego and id, of defensive mechanisms and biological adaptive mechanisms, of ego functions and their so-

matic instruments, of instincts and drives in their reciprocal dependence on the hormonal system, of psychophysiological homeostasis in relation to the mutually
balancing influences of the ego and the id. And we
begin to obtain data which promises to fulfill Freud's
vision that in the end the psychological would be seen
to be truly biological.

The crucial factors in the genesis of psychosomatic
disease seem to be found in the vicissitudes of earliest
infancy, when organ and instinct, and anxiety and
homesotatic needs are one and the same. I said in 1950
before the Chicago Psychoanalytic Society (in a discussion of a paper on thyrotoxicosis by Ham, Alexander
and Carmichael, 1951): "It would appear that the genetic problem resides in the somatopsychic events of
the period of transition from preverbal to early verbal
modes of mastery and defense. I do not think we can
really understand these patients until we understand
them in terms of the psychosomatic synthesis and
differentiation which occurs at that period." [2]

The literature presents increasing evidence that
the specificity theories which have dominated the
psychosomatic field are beginning to trouble even
former proponents. Armstrong (1958) states that no
conclusive evidence yet exists to say that a specific
psychodynamic pattern is either a sufficient or
necessary condition in the pathogenesis of any clinical
entity commonly called psychosomatic. Binger (1951)
says of cases of hypertension that they exhibit a certain
"more or less characteristic, though probably not exclusive, disorder of personality," but that there is no

[2] Greenacre (1958) has more recently spoken in a similar vein.

convincing evidence that this is more than a commonly occurring associated phenomenon. He says of his cases, that a "characteristic pattern of immaturity made its appearance early in life and persisted unchanged." But "What we need to know and we still do not know, is whether [the disorders] of personality observed . . . have any final, specific relationship to this disease . . ." (p. 273).

Saslow and his colleagues (1950) conclude, with regard to the specific emotional constellation ascribed to arterial hypertension, that the wide distribution of this dynamic syndrome in our culture and its striking appearance in cases of hypertension appears "to be only of partial etiological relevance, but neither necessary nor sufficient" (p. 300).

Kubie (1953b) retreats from his original enthusiastic acceptance of theories of specificity. He affirms the now general clinical experience that there are as many dissimilarities in the psychological data of psychosomatic disease as there are similarities, and he concludes with a question to which he has no answer: "What is there which is of a peculiar, or special or different, or specific nature about the regressive and dissociative processes which results in physiological disturbances?" (p. 80).

Grinker (1953) writes that "Most investigators are impressed by the stereotypical nature of the basic emotional constellations that are expressed only in the symptom," namely, dependency, frustration, and rage at primitive oral levels. When defenses break down and a pyschosomatic syndrome is replaced by a psychosis, the psychotic reaction is not specific to the particular psychosomatic disorder. "A particular psychosomatic expression is not constantly related to a specific emotional constellation" (pp. 42–43).

Engle (1958a) states:

Fifteen years of studying unselected patients on a medical service has made it clear to us that in a high proportion the development of the somatic illness is preceded by a period of psychological stress . . . [of] a rather distinctive type . . . a real, threatened, or fantasied object loss . . . responded to by affects defined (by Schmale) as "helplessness" and "hopelessness". . . . With this understanding we now have little difficulty in demonstrating such relationships among . . . not only patients with ulcerative colitis, peptic ulcer, rheumatoid arthritis and other traditional psychosomatic disorders, but also patient with bronchopneumonia, lupus erythematosus, autoimmune hemolytic anemia, lymphoma. . . . We propose that these affect states (helplessness and hopelessness) reflect a psychobiologic setting in which an organic process can develop . . . given the necessary somatic preconditions, helplessness and/or hopelessness may be followed by the organic change. Otherwise we may see only psychological consequences. In any event this does indicate to us that at the present time the identification of any particular diagnostic category as psychosomatic, as has been done in the past, is not justified.

Elsewhere Engel (1958b) wrote:

Most psychosomatic theories ascribe somatic changes to a deleterious influence of psychic process on the periphery. While there are situations where, because of lowered thresholds in tissue, this may be valid, I suggest that pathological changes in the tissues may also develop when certain influences of mind-brain are withdrawn, reduced, or altered. Such an idea develops logically from the empirical observations of separation and depression as a precondition for illness and from the significance of object loss for the maintenance of ego function. . . .

I want to emphasize that separation-depression may be a necessary but not sufficient condition for the development of organic disease. The other determinants are almost certainly biological. Separation-depression may influence *when* disease develops, but *not what* disease [p. 42].

Whatever the methodology on which the Rochester group bases its own psychosomatic theory, and whatever the weakness of the theory itself, there is no doubt that "specificity" as it has until now been understood has been discarded.

Having considered a few instances of changing attitudes toward theories of psychosomatic specificity let us now examine some examples of the alternatives.

Deutsch (1939) speaks of the choice of organ as being effected "antedating the full evolution of instinctual life. The instinctual response *at that time* created a psychosomatic unit" (p. 252). That is, a given organ and an infantile psychic conflict became coordinated. This applies not only to voluntary systems, but also to involuntary systems to the extent that they have been apprehended in awareness and have been installed as psychic representatives of organs and functions. In the end a rigid character defense and resulting affect stasis is the condition for the detonation of a neurotic organ reaction. The idea may be summarized by saying that a conflict and a diseased or transiently disturbed organ condition each other, the consequence being that later stimulation of any aspect of the psychosomatic complex thus established produces its total reaction as a unit.

Ruesch (1948) refers to "the infantile personality" as the "core problem of psychosomatic medicine." He believes that faulty or arrested maturation of the personality as a whole, associated with the persistence since childhood of infantile "self-expression" by means of recurrent somatic events, is a common denominator.

A widespread view of psychosomatic disease presents us, however, with persons who do not begin to exhibit the broad front of infantilism which Ruesch describes. We find this only in the severest type of hospitalized cases, such as Margolin (1953) has described. To say that the infantilism is concealed by various devices of defense, sublimation, and compensation is only to affirm that infantilism does not hold exclusive possession of the field. On the other hand, there are severely infantile personalities, in the terms implied by Ruesch, who ought to have the most serious "functional disease," but have relatively minor or no psychosomatic disorders.

Despite the growing conviction that infancy is the crucial period for the development of psychosomatic disease, psychoanalytic and physiological evidence no longer permit us to think of development as proceeding along a uniform and harmonious front with correspondingly uniform levels of fixation, to which uniform "broad front" regressions occur. Freud (1933) said, "Each earlier phase persists alongside and behind the later configurations and obtains a permanent representation in the libidinal economy and character of the subject" (p. 100). In connection with this, we find clinically that psychosomatic symptoms occur in all sorts of personalities. There appear to be no pure cases, and the regressions are partial in most cases.

An effort is beginning to develop the establishment of psychosomatic models or conceptions which are essentially monistic and organismic in their point of view. Substantially, these take their departure from the more recently evolving data and theories of early ego development and of their purported relationship to the physiology and ecology of infancy, and to the newer ideas about adaptation and stress.

Grinker (1953) finds in field theory a unifying principle for his pluralistic view of mechanism and etiology in psychosomatic medicine. He conceives of a continuum of soma, psyche, group, society, and culture as transacting systems within a universe, all in reciprocal relation to each other. Each system serves as the environment of the other. Boundaries are ill defined and variable, and depend upon transaction occurring at all other boundaries at any particular time and place. Such boundaries correspond to the living semipermeable membranes of a single cell. Integration between systems and the defenses against disintegration tend to maintain a steady state. Health and sickness are only variations in degree of the same processes. Activity in one system is transmitted to all others and stimulates in each of them processes which may be minimal but are definite, even though we cannot measure them. A system overloaded beyond its capacity for managing a given stress involves continuous systems in processes tending to support the first one. Because systems are in continuous transactions, Grinker assumes there is no threshold barrier between them, nevertheless; "A breakdown between boundaries and an intensification of activity in another system only occurs when stress becomes too severe" (p. 48). Continuous concomitance of psychological and somatic action patterns may exist (clinically and apart from acute reactions to stress) "only as the result of lasting traumatic impressions made upon a total system before differentiation" (p. 49). And, finally, Grinker suggests the hypothesis "that visceral activity is subject to learning or experiential processes [conditioning?], which, if impinged upon the undifferentiated organism, affects the process of differentiation, and all systems subsequently differentiated, including the psychological" (p. 52), and, "Regression under transactional stress produces revival of global functions with the recrudescence of primary affects expressed in primitive visceral fashion" (p. 60).

Margolin (1953) undertakes to deal with the metapsychology of psychosomatic symptom formation "in terms of ego psychology." He speaks, therefore, of "genetic and dynamic psychophysiological determinants of pathophysiological processes." Margolin sets aside the view that psychosomatic medicine is concerned with the diagnosis and treatment of particular clinical entities having a specific psychological structure. He, like Mirsky (1953), considers the valid approach to be the study of organs and tissues, rather than the signs and symptoms of disease. Mental events, he says, "are but links in the psychosomatic chain of events" (p. 4).

Here we have field theory and psychoanalysis combined. Like Grinker, Margolin speaks of a structural, functional continuum between the mind and the internal and the external environments. The continuum contains nodal points at which transformations of energy occur. He is critical of nosological schemes based on organ systems. As such, the systems do not have psychic representation, though there are central regulatory mechanisms which preside over the coordination of the adaptive response of the several systems. "Only those functions of an organ or of its constituent tissues which have been experienced have central [i.e., symbolic] representation" (p. 6).

Margolin therefore postulates a "fantasy" or an "illusion" of function, which is basically an extension of Schilder's classical concept of the "body image." Such illusions of function, Margolin says, are based on cognitions of organs and their operation. They undergo continuous modification under the influence of reality testing as part of the learning process. Regression, whether it occurs because of an acute conflict or for other reasons, may reinstate earlier illusions of function. Concordantly, a physiological regression occurs which leads to a breakdown of central regulation. Organs then act as though infantile homeostatic boundaries were present, whereas in fact the tissues have lost their tolerance for infantile functional fluctuations. The consequence is organ decompensation, this being more severe as the fantasy of function and its attendant mood-affect are more primitive.

I do not think Margolin has succeeded too well in dealing with the problem "in terms of ego psychology." Schur (1955) gives a clearer idea in psychological terms of how "physiological regression" conceivably comes about. Schur, too, assumes an undifferentiated somatopsychic phase of development. But the foundation of his thinking lies in the classical position that anxiety, as an ego function having a phylogenetic basis in the reflexes of animals and appearing innate and autonomous in the newborn, is subject to regression. He brings into focus a most important consideration in calling attention to the mutual interdependence and parallel development of the central nervous system and the motor apparatus, the stabilization of homeostatic processes, and the development of secondary thought processes. This sweep of developments is an integral part of ego formation. Together with, but especially in consequence of, the development of secondary thought processes, this leads to desomatization of the original somatopsychic unit. That is, as vegetative discharges decrease and are replaced by thought, anxiety loses its affective character and becomes "awareness of danger," that is, "signal anxiety." This is potentially unconscious and without discharge phenomena. With its development, problem-solving activities are instituted by the ego.

Schur's crucial idea is that "resomatization of responses is tied up with prevalence of primary process thinking and the use of deneutralized energy" (p. 124), whereas the intact ego's response to stress is "thought-like" and operates with neutralized energy. Schur suggests that the precursor of the function of neutralization is to be found in the somatopsychic phase of infancy, first in the form of the innate tendency toward maturation of central control, and second in the provision of need satisfaction by the maternal environment. The effective mother is the original neutralizer, the external precursor of central control. The model for neutralization is found in the homeostatic mechanism, and defects in either internal or external homeostasis produce defects in the neutralizing function and proneness to resomatization.

Defective neutralization does not always lead to psychophysiological regression. Part of the ego may remain uninvolved, and this reacts to the threat of regression. The result is controlled anxiety and a struggle to maintain or restore secondary thought processes. This is why the symptoms of psychosomatic illness may appear without the total disintegrations which are implied in concepts based on whole regression.

These principles also apply to the somatization of aggression. To the extent to which the secondary process is unimpaired, aggression mobilizes for action and is an expression of adaptive ego function. The more the primary process takes over, the more the whole range of connections with the person's past comes into play. The more violent the stimulus, or the more persistent, the more likely is resomatization to occur and to extend into the more primitive phases of the somatopsychic unit.

Space does not permit further elucidation of the many ways in which Schur's theory differs from the specificity theories which stem from Cannon's (1920) work. Nor is it possible to give a clear summary of the economic factors which he adduces to clarify the issue of psychosis and psychosomatic disease, the problem of chronicity and spontaneous remissions, and the paradox of the survival of high capacity for adaptation and even creativity in the psychosomatically ill person. It is possible only to affirm that in Schur's work, we are presented with a most explicit application of present-day psychoanalytic theory to the problems of neurotic organ disease.

I am a psychoanalyst. I do not seek out psychosomatic problems. When patients who have them come to me, I accept them for analysis, and occasionally, for psychotherapy, on the basis of criteria which have nothing to do with the presence or absence of neurotic organ symptoms. My questions have to do with the surviving integrative capacity of the ego of the patient. I hope, also, that what I see is not a mask for a brain tumor or other specifically organic disease. And then, if the patient does not require hospitalization, I treat him as I do any neurotic patient, i.e., according to his psychological state.

Only as a psychoanalyst can I speak with complete assurance about psychogenesis. Accepting this position, and having in mind that this means that the important considerations are the quality of the psychodynamic configuration and the economic distribution of libidinal and aggressive cathexes of guilt and restitution, and of anxiety and the capacity to bear it, I find it possible to take a psychosomatic symptom in stride, like any other symptom.

What I have done, then, is to lead you on an excursion through a never-never land of remembrance that I am a doctor as well as a psychoanalyst. I have reviewed vistas of days when it was still important to me to look into what goes on in the human body. In doing this I have incidentally presented you with a view of leading current concepts in psychosomatic medicine. And I have rediscovered for myself that these concepts are largely confrontations of psychoanalytic theory with various derivatives and modifications of it. In doing this I have tried to present illustrations which range from views most remote from psychoanalysis to those intrinsic to it.

I find overall psychoanalytic sense in Schur's concepts of ego regression and of desomatization of anxiety, aggression, and libido. Margolin's and Mirsky's views on the role played by hormones in the elaboration of instinct and drive impress me as singular instances of what Freud meant when he predicted the biological verification of his views about instincts. And Margolin's concept of the illusion of function seems to illuminate the problem of pregenital conversions. Finally, from a psychoanalytic standpoint, "choice of organ" described by Deutsch, impresses me as valid for psychogenesis as psychoanalysis has discovered it.

For the rest, the essential nature of psychosomatic illness remains an enigma. We still do not know why symptoms are neurotic in one person and somatic in another who does not appear to be substantially different. We are left with unsolved problems in constitution, heredity, embryology, physiology, and all those factors which some would place and define with apparent precision within the so-called "total field," and to which Schur more modestly refers as "the total condition of the person." Fate and experience make each human life. Conversion phenomena and anxiety are parts of the configurations of "multiple necessary variants" which together determine the process of disease. We know something about each psychologically, and largely it is this knowledge that continues to be our main guide in dealing psychoanalytically with neurotic disturbances no matter what their manifestations.

# On the Curative Factors in the First Phase of Analysis

## (1962)

---

## I

T HIS IS not a paper on technique. I am attempting to view theoretically the characteristics and qualities of the first phase of psychoanalysis, before its explicit method of treatment—systematic interpretation—can come into play. I am concerned with what I consider to be the largely nonverbal *givens* which operate at the initiation of the psychoanalytic process. These are necessary although not the sole precursor conditions for the establishment of an effective psychoanalytic situation. As such, they are basic to any psychotherapeutic effort, but in psychoanalysis they are contingent upon particular technical maneuvers and a structural orientation. It must not be assumed that I discount the importance of the experientially and intellectually determined diagnostic-perceptive function with which

---

*Editorial Note:* To the original published version of this paper, Dr. Gitelson appended a footnote explaining that it was "a revision and extension of [his] contribution to the symposium on 'Curative Factors in Psychoanalysis' presented before the 22nd Congress of the International Psychoanalytic Association at Edinburgh in 1961. In its present form it owes much to the discussion . . . evoked at the Congress, at a previous presentation before the Boston Psychoanalytic Society . . . and . . . before the Topeka Psychoanalytic Society."

we constantly screen every detail the patient offers to our attention. But this aspect of clinical psychoanalysis is richly documented in the literature. I have chosen, instead, to focus on that aspect of the problem about which, despite its ubiquity, the same cannot be said.

By and large, analysts have taken for granted that part of their therapeutic task which Freud spoke of in 1913:

> It remains the first aim of the treatment to attach [the patient] to it and to the person of the doctor. To ensure this, nothing need be done but to give him time. If one exhibits a serious interest in him, carefully clears away the resistances that crop up at the beginning and avoids making certain mistakes, he will of himself form such an attachment and link the doctor up with one of the imagos of the people by whom he was accustomed to be treated with affection. It is certainly possible to forfeit this first success if from the start one takes up any standpoint other than one of sympathetic *understanding* [italics added], such as a moralizing one, or if one behaves like a representative or advocate of some contending party—of the other member of a married couple for instance. . . . [The treatment] supplies the amounts of energy that are needed for overcoming the resistances by making mobile the energies which lie ready for the transference" [p. 140, 143].

The remarks to follow may perhaps best be viewed as a latter-day commentary on this simple statement.

## II

The "goal-directed," "active" point of view tends to characterize much of what passes for psychoanalysis today. The current emphasis on the "interpersonal," the "curative," and the "supportive" elements in the psychoanalytic situation is in large degree a caricature of the original meanings of the words "therapy," "treatment," and "cure"—that is, to take care of, to serve—and a far cry from the subtlety of the doctor's obligation or commitment. Paracelsus described this as consisting in "nothing but compassion . . . his virtue [being] that he truly understands his patient and is able to mobilize the patient's vital forces" (Jacobi, 1958).

For the most part, analysts have leaned over backward to avoid the formal appearance of being interested in "cure" as such. No doubt Freud, in "Analysis, Terminable and Interminable" (1937), dealt a serious blow to such therapeutic ambition as had persisted despite his earlier cautioning. Under this influence, some have been content to abide by the fact that in appropriate cases and with the application of correct technique the patient has got "well." Not that Freud objected to "cure"; he was only skeptical of what passed for it. And there is still room for such skepticism. Nevertheless, we find occasion today for concern with "curative factors" in terms of the contemporary meaning of the word "cure," in contrast to earlier interest in a "theory of therapeutic results." It would seem that a sense of guilt attaches itself to purely theoretical interest. The reason may be looked for in the social-psychological context in which psychoanalysis increasingly finds itself.

Perhaps we do not pay enough attention to the fact that psychoanalysts and psychotherapists are themselves unavoidably caught up in the anxieties of our time. They, like their patients, feel the swirl and react to social currents beyond their control. Science seems to have got out of hand, and those who are most sensitive to this fact respond with what seem to be the necessary alternatives—themselves somewhat paradoxical: activity is opposed to passive surrender; humanism is pitted against the cruel robot of the unconscious. We are familiar with some of the forms which these alternatives have taken; there is the emphasis on object-oriented procedures, on the meticulous sharing of the burden with the patient, on overrigorous scrutiny of countertransference, on passionately devoted therapeutic commitments—self-sacrificial and beyond the call of duty.

Psychoanalysis has produced a galaxy of therapeutic satellites which effect "cures." We cannot easily disown these results. In obvious and sometimes in deeper ways, the various psychotherapies derived from psychoanalysis, and some that claim an origin *sui generis*, seem quite as effective as the usual psychoanalytic procedure. All of us know people, mature without benefit of personal analysis, who have had a healing influence on others. We can sometimes trace certain "spontaneous cures" to the influence of fortuitous benign "human contacts" (Gitelson, 1948a).

Within the field of psychoanalysis itself the question of "cure" has been an important contributor to dissidence. Not only theory separates many analysts, but also disappointment in therapeutic results. The wish to assuage such narcissistic injury has been an important motive for modification and innovation as well as for outright repudiation of psychoanalysis and its technique. It may be that the present symposium is itself evidence of our therapeutic uncertainty. Pressing external factors may be reviving ancient conflicts, with the consequent arousal of anxious impatience with our work.

The upshot of these developments is that since the 1936 Symposium on the Theory of Therapeutic Results (Glover et al., 1937) there has been expanding concern with the nature of the *interpersonal* relationship of patient and analyst. Partly as a consequence of failure to understand the holistic implications of ego psychology, the influence of the environment is being given precedence over the biologically inherent factors which eventuate in intrapsychic structure, in fantasy, and in developmental conflict. Anna Freud (1959) has said that analysts expect therapeutic results to come about not from the widening of the ego as the result of interpretation but rather from the mechanisms of introjection-projection and from the corrective emotional experience. This point of view has led to criticism of the so-called "passivity" of psychoanalytic technique based on a "closed system" theory, and to proposals for one kind or another of therapeutic "activity" varying from the more subtle to the most overt and even grotesque. It is affirmed in one way or another that the necessary leaven for analysis is "humanization." And there is increasing effort to provide this.

I do not depreciate the so-called humanistic trends in psychoanalysis and its derivatives. Nor do I object to them per se. But I do wish to emphasize that they are represented as newly discovered "curative factors" and that their proponents distort or ignore the fact that the "dynamics" of their operation are not simply psychoanalytically explicable but are identifiable as such in the classical analytic situation and are intrinsic to it. I think that in the existing form of the analytic situation, without benefit of the corrections and additions which it has received in recent years, there reside all the "curative factors" which neo-analysis in its various forms presumes to have discovered.[1]

Anna Freud (1959), in the Los Angeles lectures which I have already cited, has also said that the infant and child do not present us with a "closed system," and that therefore, it is necessary to pay more regard to the environment and less to the biological reasonableness and synthetic functions of the ego. The aim with children is to lift them to a secondary level of development through the use of the analyst as a new object. Restated, we may say that this "secondary level of development" is intrapsychic structure, which in the end is in effect a "closed system." [2] The result is the very thing that characterizes the adult human—his relatively great autonomy vis-à-vis the environment. To the extent to which this autonomy (or inner-directedness) is infringed upon, anaclitic regression results. Anaclitic regression means a return to the open system (other-directed), the environmentally contingent state of infancy and early childhood. We must

[1] In *Psychoanalysis and Moral Values*, Hartmann (1960) has said that there are "those whom one might call 'hidden preachers.' They actually preach their own philosophies, their own old or new values [camouflaged with psychoanalytic terminology], while pretending to teach analysis, and present what are their own '*Weltanschauung*' as [being] logically derived from analysis" (pp. 23–24). Although Hartmann does not use these words with reference to the conduct of psychoanalytic treatment, I find it useful to apply them to the present context.

[2] I do not use this term in the strict sense of the philosophy of science, but metaphorically, in the sense of the "inner direction" of Riesman (1950).

therefore take cognizance of clinical phenomena in the psychoanalytic situation, particularly in the first phase, which are not fully accounted for on the basis of a "one-body" psychology.

We do not, in fact, ignore this in actual practice. Genetic aspects of ego psychology, however, make it unavoidable that we also consider it in our therapeutic theory. It is because theory has not been fully elaborated here that analysts and psychotherapists have felt justified in their impulsion toward the kind of overt conduct that has been called "interpersonal," "supportive," and "human." It is my position that in the case of the transference neuroses as well as in the narcissistic states, the patient who presents himself for consultation, and who we see in the first phase of analysis, is like the child we must "lift to a secondary level of development."

This thesis is not new. I shall only try to restate in new terms, based on newer knowledge of early human development, what Freud said about patients healing themselves through transference; that, in effect, psychoanalysis as a therapy is "healing through love." What happens "normally" in the psychoanalytic situation is, I believe, comparable to the course of events (under more or less normal circumstances) in the developmental situation of the child who is on the road to more or less non-neurotic autonomous adulthood. This course of events is especially typical of a satisfactory first phase of treatment; if this phase is seriously impaired for whatever reason, the analysis as a therapeutic procedure is likely to fail. As Glover (1955) put it, "there are occasions when an analysis may be hopelessly prejudiced in the first few weeks by [adopting] attitudes and policies which run counter to the patient's settled prejudices or affective codes" (p. 142).

## III

Because the "model" which will be used in the further discussion of curative factors in the first phase of psychoanalysis is the early "more or less good" mother-child situation—the as yet unrealized paradigm for Freud's "imagos of the persons from whom [the patient] was used to receive kindness"—the nature of the original anaclitic situation is of central importance.

The anaclitic position of the infant and young child is commonly looked upon in terms of the latter's "helplessness," of its inability to provide autonomously for its need satisfaction. But this is only a partial aspect of the situation; during the symbiotic phase of the diadic relationship, ego boundaries are not delineated, primary identification is dominant, and archaic fantasy prevails. As development proceeds, however, this centripetal state declines; reality testing begins; differentiation of self and non-self appears; awareness of personal identity crystallizes; skills, understanding, and communication evolve; the child is still "dependent," but "basic trust" is present, and the demand for gratification is no longer imperious and "total." These developments do not go on *in vacuo*. *Pari passu*, object-directed libido has emerged, and, with it, the need for an object. That need is not simply libidinal, but arises from the necessity for *support* and *guidance* for the development, integration, and maturation of the "partial functions" of the rudimentary ego. These begin to manifest themselves even while dependency is still great, and during this phase the mother figure is in the position of being the child's "auxiliary ego." As Winnicott (1960) has said, "One half of the theory of the parent-infant relationship concerns the infant, and is the theory of the infant's journey from absolute dependence, through relative dependence, to independence. . . . The other half of the theory . . . concerns maternal care, that is to say the qualities and changes in the mother that meet the specific and developing needs of the infant . . . " (p. 588). This includes the needs for libidinal satisfaction *and* ego support, and, at transition periods of newly emerging functions, protection against being overwhelmed by quantities or qualities of stimulation which the child cannot handle.

On the basis of this model, curative functions reside in both analyst and patient: in the former, his personal qualifications (as himself and as an analyst— more or less good) (Gitelson, 1952a) for the task he has undertaken; in the patient—his intrinsic potentialities for development and maturation. Let us first consider the latter.

## IV

In the 1936 Symposium (Glover et al., 1937), E. Bibring referred to these potentialities as the "natural tendencies" (that is, the biological or adaptational directedness) of the id toward normal modification of aims and objects. This is what we see in psychosexual evolution toward genitality. Stated differently, the impetus toward completion of development and maturation, that is, toward "health," stems from *anlagen* in the undifferentiated id, insofar as these are more or less free from external impediments and internal pathogenic defenses. This includes the impulse to mastery, which shows itself through the operations of the evolving ego, as do other qualities of the id which are "taken into the ego."

This "developmental drive" also appears as a "special instance of the repetition compulsion," acting against the more general regressive and fixational qualities of the repetition compulsion. Nunberg (Glover et al., 1937) has suggested that in the form of the conscious "will to be well" it "may prove to be the decisive factor in cure." We know that the infantile wishes imbedded here will enter into the resistance, which will also be true of other "curative factors" I shall discuss. But this does not detract from their importance as an indispensable source of energy for instituting the analytic situation and the analytic process.

In the first place, development is fostered through the existence of an environmental matrix provided by the more or less effective mother. In this early history I think we find the source of what Glover (1955) has called the "floating transference" that is palpably present at the beginning of an analysis in favorable cases. In other cases, it may be deeply defended, but its presence is discoverable, and in any event its existence is implied by the very fact that the patient has come for consultation and agreed to the treatment. In this "readyness for transference" (Glover, 1955) are implicit still other intrinsic potentialities for health. I do not refer here to the displacements which characterize the transference neurosis but to the cathectic tension intrinsic to the nature of libido as we conceive it. It is the spontaneous tendency of libido to move from its deepest narcissistic attachments toward the investment of external and internal objects that we see repeated in the "floating transference" of the first phase. "The first loving and hating is a transference of autoerotic pleasant and unpleasant feelings on to the objects that evoke those feelings" (Ferenczi, 1909, p. 49). Even as the first external objects receive the primitive narcissistic transference, so does the analyst in the first phase of analysis evoke toward himself the narcissistically regressed libido of the patient and initiate its transformation into "object cathexis." And in this context, even as we see in the course of development of psychic structure the evolution of primary process toward preconscious thinking, and from this the gradual appearance of secondary-process function, so do we see in the first phase of analysis the gradual transformation of rather chaotic derivatives of unconscious activity into the structured manifestations we ultimately identify as the transference neurosis. The point is that transference in its diffuse potential form is the "dynamism," as Loewald (1960) has called it, which remobilizes the instincts and drives and redeploys them for a new developmental beginning. In this sense it is really another aspect of Bibring's "developmental drive."

Considered from this point of view, we observe in the instinctual remobilization of the first phase what has otherwise been referred to as an "irruption of instinct." Sometimes this has been confused with and depreciated as an abreactive phenomenon. Its difference from the latter is that it is not simply an outburst or loosening of attached affect; its tempo is different; it is process rather than event; and even in its more primitive forms, it has reference to an external object—the analyst. In this context it is an aspect of transference in its comprehensive sense—the movement of libido toward objects, and, in particular, the cathecting of a fostering figure.[3] Thus, from the beginning, the opening phase provides an element of "structure" to narcissistic and primitive object libido (Loewald, 1960). Within its benign context, instinctual irruption is given the direction which ultimately leads to the transference neurosis, even as in infancy the conversion of narcissistic libido into object libido goes hand in hand with ego development and psychic structure (Loewald, 1960). The first phase under normal conditions provides the patient with an opportunity for ego change, just as in actual infancy relation to the mother provides the setting for original ego development. This beginning ego-change, based on developmental drive-transference and identification with the analyst, is the precursor of the therapeutic alliance and of the transference neurosis in which analysis proper comes to bear on the ego.

"Curative factors" are thus a second presentation in the analytic situation of influences that originally operate to favor more or less normal development. In the good analytic situation all of the influencing factors of the whole original development are represented. It is

---

[3] In the original developmental situation, it is a maternal figure who exists as a target for the primitive and unorganized drives in all their qualities, and who, teleologically speaking, lets the infant "be" what it is—accepts it with all of its qualities—including its development toward autonomy. In the analytic situation, it is the analyst and his "compassionate" healing orientation in the simple terms which Paracelsus used long ago, but also with his "expectations and anticipations" (Greenson, 1960) of what the patient might be.

for this reason that the correct management of the first phase of analysis is so important. In the beginning, "the humane relationship fosters a freer use of primitive mechanisms" of projection and introjection in both patient and analyst, introducing a factor of reassurance through rapport which may be decisive (Glover, 1955). The therapeutic significance of such a state of primitive rapport can be understood also from the standpoint of the so-called "free-floating attention" of the analyst. This is not simply a technical ego device for empathic "understanding" of the unconscious, but is also, and most important, a condition of the analyst's libidinal position vis-à-vis the patient—full attention devoted to the patient, and an "open-ended" acceptance of the patient *for himself.*

## V

This point of view acquires even greater cogency if we describe the analytic situation on the basis of a term recently introduced by Spitz (1956). He has spoken of the *diatrophic function of the analyst—his healing intention to "maintain and support"* the patient. Here we have countertransference in its affirmative sense. As Annie Reich (1951) has said, "Countertransference is a necessary prerequisite of analysis. If it does not exist, the necessary talent and interest is lacking" (p. 31).[4]

---

[4] A view in contrast to that of those who have overtly *"humanized"* the analytic situation because of their misunderstanding of "analytic passivity" and their consequent reaction against it. These analysts *act out an identification* with the patient in his anaclitic position while denying this in their "benign" activity. I think my following discussion will clarify this difference.

The diatrophic attitude arises as a response to the patient's need for help, even as the parent responds to the anaclitic situation of the child. According to Spitz it derives in the analyst from the stage of secondary identification in the second trimester of life when the passivity of the infant begins its movement toward the mimicry of the feeding activity of the mother. In its ego controlled form, that is, as a form of regression in the service of the ego, it is the basis for analytic empathy (Greenson, 1960). It converges with the patient's need for ego support,[5] and in this context the analyst, like the mother, has the function of an auxiliary ego. This is the basis of a good psychoanalytic situation. Just as the mother is the target for the child's drives and, in her capacity as auxiliary ego, guides their form and function—thus introducing the operation of the reality principle—so does the analyst draw the focus of the unconscious tendencies with which a patient enters analysis and, in his diatrophic function, provides the irrupting instincts and revived developmental drive with direction and purpose. The infant's ultimate capacity to connect coenaesthetic tension with its recognition and relief by the mother—that is, *to experience communication* (Rycroft, 1956) as "cause and effect"— is a manifestation of the synthetic function of the ego in its most primitive form. Correspondingly, the patient through his irrupting drives, encounters the analyst not only as a "presence," but, in the *"dosed" appropriateness* of the analyst's response, he discovers

---

[5] As against the views of Macalpine (1950) and Greenacre (1954), according to which the analytic situation is "asymmetrical" or "tilted." These views would appear to be true only when the analytic situation is considered from the standpoint of the transference alone.

the implicit limits and conditions of the analytic situation, as well as the possibility of movement toward an understanding and acceptance of its purpose. The mother's recognition and effective response to its coenaesthetic need—tension supports the infant's homeostasis, introduces it to communication, and thus initiates its capacity for adaptive synthesis. Comparably, the analyst's empathic imbrication with his patient's emotions provides a sustaining grid of "understanding" (or "resonance") which leads toward cooperation and identification, to the partial relinquishment of the anaclitic attitude, and in the end to a collaboration which Sterba (1934) has called "therepeutic alliance."

Sterba has emphasized correctly that to bring this about the analyst approaches and wins the autonomous ego in its function as an agency of perception and reality testing. Undoubtedly this ultimately happens. But *to begin with* we are dependent on the reoccurrence in the analytic situation of those "primitive mechanisms" of introjection-projection which phenomenologically we call "rapport," and which eventuate in transference.[6] In this connection it is worthwhile to consider whether the initiation of the first phase of analysis is really dependent on "suggestion" as this is commonly understood.

From the standpoint of the patient, "rapport" may be considered to be the *"optimistic"* feeling that the "hope" for, or "expectation" of the diatrophic response with which he comes to the analyst can be fulfilled. He comes, so to speak, with the wish that he and the

[6] Sterba, of course, recognized that the therapeutic alliance is based on emotional factors involving object cathexis and identification. My difference is with regard to emphasis on this aspect.

analyst will be "tuned in." Rapport is the first presentation of the "floating transference." In this state hypercathexis of the analyst-object pervades the attitude of the patient, no matter what the interfering state of his anxiety and defenses. Absorbed in this feeling-idea of the analyst, reality testing is reduced; the operation of the superego as a factor in this is diminished; the patient finds himself in a position comparable to the state of "object-finding," before primary narcissism is resolved. We see in this situation essentially a libidinal process which unifies the various forms and derivatives of narcissism and focuses them on the analyst. All this has been referred to as the "suggestive" influence of the analyst, and is thus degraded by comparison with hypnosis. But even if we remember Jones' (1923) statement: "If the patient is not treated by psychoanalysis he will treat himself by suggestion," we must consider that he actually is attempting to cure himself by libidinizing an object. In the light of what I have already said, the curative factor is found in the analyst's professional commitment with its diatrophic intent. He does not "offer" himself as an object, or, as has been suggested, as a replacement for the superego (Rado, 1925). The point is that the first analytic contact, if successful, sets up the anaclitic-diatrophic equation, resulting in the "rapport" which is the harbinger of transference.[7] The patient presents himself in the "floating transference" with the wish to be loved for himself alone. His "rapport" is in part a projection of the attitude: "the analyst loves me as I love myself."

[7] In the contrast, for example, with Bergler's idea (Glover et al., 1937) that the analyst offers to participate in sexual activity, thus proving himself to be an ally against the superego.

The analyst's participation is his diatrophic presence, wherein the patient discovers the availability of a "new beginning" and thus of a new development.

## VI

The instructive, advisory, and "persuasive" activities of the analyst, even in technically limited form, have also been stigmatized as forms of verbal "suggestion" in the nature of ideoplasty. E. Bibring (Glover et al., 1937) has cautioned us that "pedagogical influences" are "provisional" to analysis proper. Strachey (Ibid.) explicitly rules out "suggestion" in this sense as a nonessential ingredient of analysis. I do not, however, regard these activities as equivalents to "suggestion" and "persuasion" in the banal sense in which these terms are generally used. Rather do I see them to be *fostering influences* of the kind which emanate from the effective mother during the child's early development.[8] It is these which channel the libido. In this connection

[8] "The mother is the agent through whom many aspects of normal 'autonomous ego development' are supported, as well as the mediator of libidinal gratification. As ego development proceeds, ego functions serve libidinal demands, and while the mother supports each independently she also supports their interaction. *The mother's assistance to the child's autonomous efforts begins at birth,* in her ways of facilitating his first suckling, burping, even eliminating, then in holding him in a position to see; she soon offers a variety of stimuli to activity with rattles to touch, then bang, and other toys. The fact that the mother not only meets nutritional and other bodily needs and gives and evokes love, but also supports the development of the specific ego functions and the integrative functions of the ego, is important for understanding the seriousness of separation problems in the second year of life before the child has achieved stable autonomy. The mother's role in supporting the ego development of the child also includes helping the child to deal with anxiety and to modulate anger, frustration feelings, and the aggressive impulses aroused by these" (Murphy).

we may again refer to Strachey who explicitly viewed transference as a manifestation of the "power of suggestion," but who nevertheless looked upon it as a *"needed aid"* (italics added) in dealing with resistance, that is, analyzing it.

Our views of the institution of the analytic situation retain earlier opinions (Alexander, 1925; Rado, 1925) that it is the father principle and oedipal libido as structured in the superego that has central importance in the induction of both the hypnotic situation and the analytic transference. This assumption logically connotes regression to identification in the phase of omnipotence. And this leads to further assumptions about the danger of contaminating the rational psychoanalytic procedure with suggestion in the sense of magic. What I am trying to say on the other hand is—regardless of what may or may not be the case in hypnosis—that the *techniques which establish the psychoanalytic situation induce an infantile diadic condition having the qualities of transition from narcissism to object love.* When Strachey holds that neurotics have a greater transference potential and that this is increased in the analytic situation, I believe he is referring to the fact that the analytic attitude and its expression in technique is complementary to the anaclitically regressed state of the patient; appropriate analytic procedure creates an atmosphere of fosterage to which the patient responds. This might be looked upon as warranting the notion that suggestive influences are at work in the first phase of analysis. It is my view, however, that this is the case only if the analyst enters the analytic situation with his own narcissistic self-assertions and fantasies of omnipotence concealed behind a "humanistic" facade; in this guise he *is* a superego figure, and as such he exerts suggestive influence. But if his is the "essential" diatrophic attitude and *set,* he has no axes to grind; it is the reality of his qualification for his work that establishes the analytic atmosphere in which, as Strachey (1934) has expressed it, the patient's superego is "once more thrown into the melting pot" [9] and analysis can proceed.

## VII

This far my discussion has chiefly touched on the first factor in a roster of "Curative Principles" which E. Bibring surveyed in his 1954 paper. I have attempted to detoxicate our conception of "suggestion" by describing it in its operational context in the first phase of analysis. In passing I have also referred to abreaction as a curative factor, insofar as affective and instinctual mobilization frees libido for cathecting the analyst-object. An intrinsic aspect of the fact that this goes on in the presence of the analyst is that it is accepted, that it receives consensual validation in an object-oriented context. The consequence is increased self-awareness and self-esteem, with an accretion to narcissism from which accrues an impetus to the developmental drive. All this, I think, enters into identification with the analyst and fosters the development of the therapeutic alliance.

Bibring (1954) also stated that "manipulation" and "clarification" act concomitantly with abreaction in producing its effects. Unfortunately, the world "manipulation," like "suggestion," has been stigmatized by its common reference to various "activity" forms of

[9] "Perhaps it is another mark of the non-adult nature of the neurotic that his super-ego remains in a malleable state" (p. 136n).

psychotherapy and analysis. Looked at superficially, everything that happens *by first intention* to "produce rapport," that is, to evoke transference, can be stigmatized in this way insofar as it occurs outside of the transference system of the patient. But what must not be overlooked is that in analysis it is not an exploitation of the patient but an intrinsic part of the diatrophic attitude—the therapeutic countertransference whose convergence with the transference system produces the analytic situation. In this context "manipulation" is the commonly known and accepted "management of the transference" which has analytic legitimacy in the establishment and maintenance of the analytic situation and its climate.[10]

Similarly, clarification and confrontation, grossly viewed or ineptly used, may be depreciated as pedagogical suggestion. But sensitively imbricated with the manifestations of the synthesizing ego function in the patient, they foster self-awareness and self-observation and are a function of the diatrophic attitude in its support of reality testing. From this point of view they are curative factors directed towards increasing the pa-

---

[10] The word "manipulation" is understood by the lexicographers to mean (a) *to handle, manage, or use with skill; (b) to manage or influence by artful skill; (c) to adapt or change to suit one's purpose or advantage.* Only the last meaning has the stigmatic connotation usually attached to the world. Furthermore, the word "artful," in the second definition, while it means "cunning" and "tricky," also signifies "ingenious and characterized by art or skill." "Manipulation," therefore, according to E. Bibring (1954), refers to finding in the framework of the patient's psychological structure, the most helpful, constructive way to promote the therapeutic process. It plays a considerable role in the initial period, when it is essential in helping the patient to establish a good working relationship to the therapist. The patient will feel understood, and flight and freezing up are thus avoided. Herein lies the difference between therapists who always can hold their patients and those who rarely do.

tient's autonomy and preparing the way for analysis proper.[11]

If we now look at the clinical aspects of the first phase of analysis we are impressed by certain general characteristics.[12] We find, even under conditions of good rapport, an attitude of tentativeness, of "wait and see"; difficulties in following the fundamental rule cannot be fully accounted for by "resistance"; anxiety manifestations are tinged with a nonspecific quality; the content is kaleidoscopic; there is a "drag-net" reaching out for the analyst's response; a variety of action patterns and defensive maneuvers may be presented. All this and much more may consume hours, weeks, and even months of analytic work before the analysis "catches on." It is not unusual for this period (particularly in character-problem cases) to be specifically marked by situations created for the analyst— traps to try his mettle.

But a more general feature of the opening phase is seen in the patient's testing of the nature of the analytic situation. The analyst is "on trial" as much as the patient. The patient tries to "place" the analyst and to discover the nature of the relationship which is possible with him. The overall defenses are the same as those which have been typically employed in his extra-analytic relationships, but here and there extru-

[11] Ferenczi (1932) has said: ". . . when one suggests the truth, one only accelerates a process [of attaining it] which could be acquired by experience though much more slowly . . . not every child has to find out everything for itself . . ." (p. 260).

[12] There may be exceptions to what follows in those patients who come into treatment after a period of waiting, "preparation," and "looking forward." The analyses of candidates present special problems (Gitelson, 1954); as do those following previous psychotherapy or analysis.

sions of "test samples" of that which is defended against make their appearance. The patient is not simply mobilizing his courage; he is examining the quality of the analyst as an object; he is sampling the analytic situation for its stability, its predictability, and for the measure of confidence he can invest in it. To this end the patient starts out in an interpersonal situation, and the analyst cannot prevent it.

External objects offer too large a prospect of frustration and disappointment. Interruptions of analysis during the opening phase are thus not necessarily the consequence of too great rigidity, or narcissism, or "resistance," but may result from too much anxiety.[13] It is against this that the curative factors of the first phase must be effective. Not least important here is that aspect of the diatrophic capacity of the analyst which leaves him free of anxiety in the presence of the patient's anxiety. Here the analyst's task is equivalent to the "steadiness" of the effective mother. He manifests this quality in the equanimity, the grace, and the subtlety with which he manages the unavoidable "interpersonal encounter" of the opening phase. And on its success depends the possibility of establishing the classical analytic situation centering on the transference neurosis.

Finally, the "testing" which occurs in the first phase represents, in the patient, the operation of those "primitive introjective-projective mechanisms" to which Glover (1955) referred in speaking of the establishment of "rapport." Referring to the infantile situation,

[13] As Glover (1955) has suggested, never in the new patient's conscious experience has such a unique opportunity been offered him—to be accepted for himself is not easily believed.

Lampl-de Groot (1952) has said that "Even if the object is already recognized as something outside the self, the character of the attachment is still for a long time predominantly 'narcissistic' " (p. 339). Thus, love to begin with is anaclitic and "A certain amount of narcissistic gratification obtained from objects is indispensible for health and normal functioning" (p. 339). The clinical significance of all this is that the new patient presents himself to us in two aspects: as an "autonomous adult" who is requesting help with a specific problem or symptom, but who has shored up a more general developmental failure with various corrective-adaptive and defensive adjustments which have been more or less effective as a facade; and as a regressed neurotic with an infantile core of "narcissistic" immaturity, who needs the initial support of the auxiliary ego which he *hopes against hopelessness* that the analyst can provide. But this does not mean that we are called upon for the provision of "things" or other overt forms of gratification and support. The "symbolic" gratification which Sechehaye (1956) exhibits in her treatment of psychotics has only a "shadow" representation in the conduct of the preliminary consultations and the opening phase of analysis. For even with borderline cases the *implicitness of the diatrophic attitude in the person qualified to be an analyst is all that is required.* Of course, that "all" is quite a lot, as those who have studied the pathology of the countertransference can testify.

## IX

I have come full circle. I find myself agreeing with Balint's (1950) view that the "one body" theory which psychoanalysis developed on the basis of its study of the "internalizing" neuroses has produced a lag in our theory of the "two-body" situation that is the analytic treatment situation. I agree that the analyst's behavior in the psychoanalytic situation is his contribution to the creation and maintenance of that situation. I think it is valid to ask, as Balint does, how much of what kind of satisfaction is needed by the patient and analyst to maintain the optimal tension of the psychoanalytic situation. But, as I have tried to make clear throughout this presentation, the answer to the question is inherent in the very nature of the "good" psychoanalytic situation.

I would describe that situation as follows: one in which the patient experiences and manifests (i) his awareness of incompletion in development, his even marginal realization of defective reality testing and adaptive inadequacy—in our more common terminology, he has sickness insight; (ii) his hope that the possibility for change exists—he wants help and has what we refer to as the wish for health; and (iii) that there is evidence, if it be only in vestigial hopefulness, that a minimal original fostering experience has left its imprint and has been activated by the analyst out of the "readiness for transference." Concomitantly, the analyst has the capacity for tolerating the "stranger anxiety" which every encounter with a new human configuration involves, so that sooner or later he can recognize behind the variety of defensive distortions the ubiquitous anaclitic need which I have described and to which his own diatrophic impulse can respond,[14] while at the same time he accepts the implications of the developmental potential concealed behind regression and defense. I emphasize the last qualification because we see too frequently among those who plug "humanism" in one way or another that regression is taken at its face value and is indulged as such or depreciated and denied as such.

[14] My thesis has been most seriously questioned on this point, and it is here that I encounter the greatest difficulty in making myself clear. Perhaps the issue can best be presented by quoting Dr. Paul G. Myerson's remarks made at a discussion of this paper before the Boston Psychoanalytic Society:

The situation of the analyst has as its aim more than the establishment of rapport and the *releasing of an inherent tendency to master and to synthesize.* The analyst is trying to create a therapeutic alliance which is essential for a successful resolution of a transference neurosis. This fully flowered therapeutic alliance has indeed been nurtured by rapport—its flourishing depends upon the structuring of narcissistic and primitive object libido, but really upon a structuring which is coexistent with a very organized, integrated yet flexible type of object relationship and identification and *which, while based on closeness, permits autonomous functioning on the part of the patient of an extremely subtle sort.* The patient also has to be able—if you'll forgive this awkward way of expressing it—to counteract countercathexis, to allow unconscious derivatives to reach the preconscious, to observe those derivatives, to assimilate the significance of and to break down the isolation between various mental elements, etc.—all this in conjunction with and yet separate from the analyst. I think the analyst in all cases has this as his goal from the start; he aims not only to establish a rapport but simultaneously to create a working therapeutic alliance, and *in this respect he differs from the average good mother.* Not only in this respect, for the analyst's gratification of his patient *is symbolic,* which means that as he *gratifies* he *frustrates* much more than a mother. The analyst in his diatrophic situation if it is to be successful is at once more gratifying than a mother in that he accepts his patient as he is, more frustrating in obvious ways, and more insistent upon the maintenance and development of autonomy. Yet in fostering as well as in mothering, *there are wide variations in the extent and in the manner by which an analyst may gratify, frustrate, and mobilize independent autonomous activities.* There are repeated issues in every analysis, including the most

Neither can be the case. For the regressed position to which the patient retreats is the last position which he has more or less successfully mastered; and it is here that the analyst as auxiliary ego comes into play. At the same time, that aspect of the patient which speaks for his existing or desired autonomy as an adult requires recognition and respect. The "testing" which characterizes the patient's conduct during the first phase of analysis is thus a trial of the analyst's sensitiveness to the *whole* situation in the patient—his capacity for *understanding*—that sensory-affective-motor totality of understanding which we call "empathy." The posture, the gesture, the timbre, tone, and rhythm of the voice, the words to the exquisite point of the context—these constitute all and convey all that can be given. These are all we have with which to breech the regressive narcissism of the new patient and to evoke that which to begin with is "rapport," and in the end, "transference." This is the full extent of the "interpersonal" and the "supportive" which the abiding

---

classical ones, where *the analyst decides how far to gratify, how far to permit regression, how rapidly to encourage the autonomous capacities* of his patients. Some of these decisions will determine not only the extent of the rapport, but the depth and quality of transference neurosis, and efficiency of the therapeutic alliance. For example, early and extensive clarifications may gratify the patient and stimulate rapport, but at the same time may alter or minimize the negative aspects of the transference neurosis and not provide the right amount of frustration which may be necessary for separate, autonomous self-observation. At any rate, it is a debatable point and one worthy of study.

There is nothing in this excerpt from Dr. Myerson's discussion to which I take exception. And I do not believe that there is anything in this paper which is intended to imply a position which deviates from this view. The parts of the statement which I have taken the liberty to italicize emphasize my agreement. I would only add that I include here "therapeutic manipulation," i.e., "management of the transference" (see fn. 10) which encompasses the "diatrophic attitude."

developmental impulse requires for its revival. Freud has said that ". . . limitation of narcissism can . . . only be produced by one factor, a libidinal tie with other people. Love for oneself knows only one barrier— love for others, love for objects" (p. 102).

## X

I have been considering the implicit and explicit role of the analyst which is inherent, unavoidable, and even necessary in the introductory hours and the first phase of a psychoanalytic procedure. The classical view has considered this role an *unfortunate* contamination of analysis by "the power of suggestion." There is the added unfortunate possibility that the language available to me may imply that the analyst *plays* the "part of a good object" with the intention of "parasitizing" (Rado, 1925) the patient's archaic superego. In the hope of avoiding such misunderstanding, I shall try to restate my position in still other terms.

It is my notion that therapeutic contact between patient and analyst occurs at a level of complementary regression (Kris, 1952). The patient, behind a facade of symptom and defense (which Winnicott [1956] has called the "false self"), has preserved a quantity of developmental and maturational potential which E. Bibring has referred to as "developmental drive" (and which Winnicott locates in the "true self"). The patient's decision to enter treatment is a regressive maneuver which may be teleologically looked upon as a retreat to the anaclitic position in which ego development began. But over and above the revival of primitive libidinal impulses and wishes which this brings about, the need is reborn to resolve obstacles to development and maturation. The analyst on his part, as an aspect of his professional identity, makes a facultative regression (*in the service of the ego*) (Kris, 1952) to the diatrophic position.[15] This is responsive to the patient's anaclitic regression. But in addition to this, the analyst provides the cue and the differential pull which mobilizes narcissistic libido toward object cathexis and toward development and maturation (Loewald, 1960). The difference from "active therapy" is found in the fact that the latter, in its various interventions, provides direct libidinal gratification and, as in hypnosis, takes over the functions of the patient's superego. The "active" therapist, in fact, does "suggest" himself as a substitutive "good object." (Greenacre, 1959). In contrast to this, the analytic attitude, as manifested in the good analytic situation, provides "presence" to the libido and operates as an *auxiliary to the patient's ego with its own intrinsic potentialities* for reality testing, synthesis, and adaptation.[16]

[15] (a) See the second paragraph in Section V.

(b) "Empathy is . . . a two-way relationship. [It] can be influenced by the other person's resistance or readiness for empathic understanding . . . [It] requires capacity for controlled and reversible regressions in ego functions. The primitivization and progression of the ego in the building of the working model [of the patient] bears a resemblance to the creative experience of the artist as formulated by Kris. . . . By cathecting the working model as a supplement to the external patient one approaches the identificatory process. Empathy may be a forerunner, an early, tentative form of identification . . . [It] begins in [the] non-verbal . . . relationship of mother and child" (Greenson, 1960, pp. 422–423).

[16] I cannot pass by the opportunity presented at this point to quote a statement by a schizophrenic patient who is being treated by a respected colleague. It is an excerpt from a letter written to a good friend after many months of "testing": "I know now that basically understanding must come *before* [patient's italics] words are interchanged—that words are almost the result of understanding instead of the cause of them [sic]."

I certainly am not supporting the view that the essential nature of the analytic procedure is found in its provision of a "corrective emotional experience" aided by magical suggestion and representational gratification. My intention is to extend the classical view that *only the ego can be influenced therapeutically,* and that to this end accurate interpretation is the prime curative factor. But I have attempted to present evidence that this influence is exerted not simply on that aspect of the ego which is ultimately accessible to interpretation in its explicit meaning. I think that so-called "pedagogy," "clarification," "suggestion," and "manipulation" are verbal-nonverbal *preparatory incomplete interpretations* which foster in the patient's budding analytic ego (the therapeutic alliance) the ultimate capacity for the necessary deeper insights, even as the effective mother, as an "external function," brings to bear on the budding life ego of the infant that which in the end operates as its own reality principle. From this point of view we may see that the "developmental tension" of the id and the "tension of the synthetic function of the ego" collaborate, at the beginning of life, toward development, maturation, and adaptive defense, and in the analytic situation toward "cure."

Because of the limitation I have placed on the scope of this paper, I have referred only in passing to that great area of psychoanalytic work which is concerned with the transference neurosis and its resolution. I have assumed that we are agreed that without this as our technical focus nothing I have tried to say about the opening phase would make sense in an analytic discussion. However, there is this to add if I am to complete my thesis. In the transference neurosis we are confronted by projections and displacements of the "closed system" psychology which has eventuated from the development of psychic structure. As such it is inaccessible. But the "open system" of the infant and young child, recapitulated in the anaclitic regression of the patient in the first phase of analysis, provides channels of affective communication which make interpretation possible. The therapeutic alliance is the first result. But beyond this is the maintenance of flow of a homeostatic factor, the basic positive transference which permits analysis to go on despite its vicissitudes. I think that emotional insight, a synthesis of *understanding in context,* is in the end based in the affects which we subsume as "rapport" and "transference." These affects are the binding matrix of the transference neurosis, the ultimate effective interpretation and resolution of which require that the analysis as a whole be grounded in an understanding and effective management of the first phase.

In the 1936 Symposium, Glover (Glover et al., 1937) said,

Freud's original views, simple and schematic as they were, still constitute the most valuable and permanent contribution to the subject [of therapeutic results]. These were in effect (1) the existence of transferences, (2) the development of the analytic or transference neurosis and (3) the degree to which the existence of these two manifestations . . . was hidden by repression or obscured by projection, thus giving rise to resistances. Successful results depend on the extent to which these three factors were analysed [p. 125].

I have *considered only the nature of the first of these factors* in the context of the meaning of "cure." I take "that which tends to cure" to be the operation of "concern" and "care." In analysis this means concern and care for the strengthening and development of the ego, *pari passu* with the discovery of the unconscious and channeling of the forces of the id. In a way we are compelled to accept the existence of a built-in parameter in the very nature of the first phase and its management. But it is a parameter which moves toward resolution even while it is operating, if to begin with and throughout, we are committed to psychoanalysis as a therapeutic procedure.

# On the Present Scientific
# and Social Position
# of Psychoanalysis

## (1963)

---

As MEMBERS of society and of one of its healing professions, we once learned and more or less accepted the paradoxical necessity for controlling the impulse which expresses itself as therapeutic ambition. It seems to have been more difficult for us, however, to resist the temptation to extend ourselves beyond our expertise as psychoanalysts in areas of social commitment. Applications of psychoanalysis have become so numerous that it has been difficult to be certain where the boundaries of psychoanalysis lie. Under the pressure of the conditions of our times, we have engaged in various socially meliorative activities which have undoubted ethical appeal but are not psychoanalysis.

Another aspect of the current social situation in which we tend to reach beyond our scope is research. In the strictest view, research pertains to science. But science has become a part of the social fabric. Turn

---

*Editorial note:* This essay was Dr. Gitelson's Presidential address before the 23rd International Psycho-Analytic Congress in Stockholm. It aroused considerable controversy at the time and is still attacked by those against whom his arguments were directed.

where you will, and in the name of social need the plea for research is heard. No one will doubt the greatness of the need; but there are many other factors which enter into the wish to respond to this plea. I propose to discuss some of those which affect psychoanalysts and psychoanalysis.

The time may be appropriate to propose a counsel of modesty for psychoanalysis. I suggest that we have become to ambitious and expansive. The intrinsic potentiality of psychoanalysis as a science is no longer enough. Conscious and unconscious factors are converging to obscure our view of ourselves as scientists and as members of society.

As scientists we do not maintain the distinction which exists between our area of scientific focus and that of the cognate sciences. We speak of "applications" of psychoanalysis when often we are engaged in making *extrapolations* based on analogies and assumed continuities. We tend to forget that we have a specific area of competence in individual psychology and that this is based on the discovery of the peculiar psychological phenomena which come into view in the context of a peculiar dyadic relationship. It seems necessary to reaffirm that whatever we know with relative certainty about these phenomena, whatever we can predict about them with fair probability, whatever we can verify with reasonable confidence through the supporting observations of our psychoanalytic peers, stems from the peculiar experimental field which has become known as the psychoanalytic situation. I shall make a tautological assertion, but one whose cogency compels it: only in the psychoanalytic situation do psychoanalysts occupy their explicit scientific position for studying their proper material—the unconsciously emerging manifestations of instinct, primary process, affects, conflicts, defense mechanisms, and transferences.

One of the factors which has led psychoanalysts to extend themselves beyond their scope is the astonishing advance that has occurred in the physical sciences, and the consequent acceleration of the rate at which their data have been accumulating. This has stirred the earnest hopes of workers in other fields, but it has also generated attitudes of competitive inferiority. The prestigious results that have followed from the suitable and necessary methods of the physical sciences have made them the criteria of all scientific research. The wish for similar achievements has become intense, and the efforts directed toward attaining them sometimes verge on the frantic. And psychoanalysts, too, have caught the fever.

It is being overlooked that science is not simply a particular procedure and technology, that in essence science is not a point of view stemming from commitment to logical integrity in the search for truth, and that the position of a particular observer taken up for the study and understanding of particular phenomena is of secondary importance in a definition of science. It is a biologist to whom we can turn for a retrieval of this situation.

In an article in the American journal *Science*, George Simpson (1963), Professor of Vertebrate Paleontology at Harvard, says about the classical canons of the scientific method that important basic research has seldom really followed them exactly as they have been stated. Quoting James Conant (1947), he defines science as "an interconnected series of concepts and conceptual schemes that have developed as the result of experimentation and observation." This definition, Simpson says, is "freer and more impressionistic" than the classical formulation by Karl Pearson, and "to that extent it more nearly covers the varied gambits of research." Its main virtue is "its recognition of the role of speculation, intuition, or just plain hunch in finding a hypothesis (p. 82)."

In the light of the tendency of psychoanalysts to depreciate their technique, of great interest is Simpson's statement that "science . . . *is self-testing by the same kinds of observations from which it arises and to which it applies*" (italics added). This is its deductive aspect as stressed by modern writers on scientific method. And Simpson adds that "a fundamental, though not sufficient criterion of the self-testability of science is repeatability . . . *the data of science are observations that can be repeated by any normal person*" (p. 82; italics added). "Normal" in Simpson's context of course refers to the normality of the capacity for perception in a person of adequate intelligence. But it permits us to infer, in respect to the psychoanalytic situation as a valid area of scientific interest, that "normal" includes the special kind of capacity for perceiving which is the qualification of the psychoanalyst. Thus, the data of the psychoanalytic situation are also subject to "observations that can be repeated by any 'normal' person." And even if unique events occur, "evidence on them is acceptable if there is confidence that anyone in a position to observe them [i.e., 'anyone' who is 'normal' as defined] would have observed them" (p. 83).

I shall make one more point in this effort to clarify

the intrinsic scientific qualifications of psychoanalysis. In the observation of many phenomena, Simpson says, it is not their exact measurement or the determination of their occurrence that is the issue, but the establishment (to some degree of confidence) of probability within a certain range. For it is impossible to prove anything in the natural sciences with the finality of a mathematical proof. Instead we are dependent on the multiplication of relevant observations. The key word is "relevant." Relevant observations are such as could disprove a hypothesis. They must be made within a narrowing range of probability. Given these conditions, the more observations fail to disprove a hypothesis, the greater the confidence in it. This is the most common and conclusive process of self-testing among the natural sciences.

Predictability is a special case of such proof. When psychoanalytic hypotheses are applied in the psychoanalytic situation we may correctly deduce the appearance of certain consequences. Their nonappearance would disprove the theoretical assumptions on which the deduction was based. On the other hand their appearance would not be proof either, but it would certainly increase confidence. Predictability, however, is not the crux of a scientific theory. We see this, for example, in the theory of organic evolution: prediction has not entered into its establishment; it is based entirely on "relevant" observations. Similar criteria of "proof" obtain in other fields that have a temporal and historical quality, for instance, the time-linked process in geology. Here, also, operational observations have produced theories based on what one might call developmental reconstruction. These are *process theories,* and all of them have produced numbers and varieties of observations which are consonant only with them and with no other theories. Psychoanalytic theory meets these conditions.

The point of all this is that our view of the nature of science as a whole has been biased because of the historical primacy of the basic physical sciences. But now we are faced by the fact that modern physicists have found that at least some of their laws are not invariable; predictions are approximate; some observations cannot be made; and absolute proof of a hypothesis by testing it cannot always be obtained. Though it has been generally assumed, it is not necessarily true that uniform phenomena have absolute constants, measurable to any degree of accuracy. Biologists have long been aware of this state of affairs without seeing it as contradicting causality and orderliness in nature (Simpson, 1963). It is for this reason that I have outlined some of the evidence for the scientific position of psychoanalysis in the context of a definition of science that is not limited to "cut and dried methods [which] work in particular instances" (Simpson, 1963). When psychoanalysis is viewed in terms of the criteria I have presented (and I have not exhausted these!) it qualifies as a valid branch of science. Nevertheless, numbers of analysts tend to doubt this.

There has been wide discussion of the scientific problem presented by the "unobjective" quality of the psychoanalytic procedure. One of the more well-disposed and perceptive nonanalytic commentators on psychoanalysis, Alan Gregg (1953) has stated that "in psychoanalytic research the findings are more intimately affected by the researcher than is the case in any other medical field. That does not *ipso facto* make the findings less reliable, but it makes them less easily verifiable and more open to qualification or rejection" (p. 46). John Benjamin (1961) has spoken similarly: " . . . First order convictions based on private and semiprivate interpretations of evidence gained from experience may well be wrong," he says, "by virtue of the limitations of the human intellect in dealing with data without the help of painfully learned methods of avoiding erroneous conclusions" (p. 121). Nevertheless, Benjamin's "first order" experience with psychoanalysis has enabled him to say of such convictions that they have often proved to be significantly correct.

Analysts, of course, know something about the countertransference factors operating to impair the capacity for observation and to produce lapses and distortions of memory, and they have recognized the resulting damage to the basic data of psychoanalysis. Psychoanalytic theory and technique is suitable for making some corrective allowances for this. Indeed, various technological procedures have been proposed, and some indeed are being used with hope of *really* "objectifying" the psychoanalytic method and improving its "first-order" observations (Carmichael, 1956: Renneker, 1960; Shakow, 1960). But in so doing, a new psychological variable is introduced which changes the very nature of the psychoanalytic situation and thereby the field of observation. These objectifying techniques, in their employment of a monitor—human or gadget—subvert the basic principle of the psychoanalytic situation: the dependence of transference on the sustained privacy of the dyadic relationship. Furthermore, these technological methods are no more exempt than are psychoanalysts from what Kubie (1953c) has called the fallacy-proneness of man as an instrument. Films, sound tracks, and tapes do not interpret themselves. They, too, need to be "observed," and then the observations are at least once removed from the first-order data which are the proper business of the psychoanalyst.

The problem of objectivity is an old one and generally present. Claude Bernard (quoted by Kubie, 1953c) comparing the experimentalist, the scholastic, and the metaphysician, pointed out that "all [are] subject to the same internal human laws, plagued by the same emotions, prejudices, and biases, and that these operate equally in the philosopher and the scientist" (p. 140). Much later, Richard Tolman (ibid), the great physicist, speaking of "the effects of personal biases on results," referred to the fact that the scientist "selects his problem . . . not to obtain results . . . but to satisfy his own subjective needs . . ." Tolman affirmed that ". . . that which has objective validity is finally abstracted out from the welter of subjective experience in which scientists as well as other human beings are immersed."

It seems that we are caught in a vicious circle. For it is not only the psychoanalyst who ought to submit himself to correction for lack of complete objectivity in his work. If there is credibility in what Bernard and Tolman and other scientists have said about the fallibility of the human operators of scientific instruments, then even "objective" investigators of psychoanalysis are bound, at least in fairness, to be submitted to objectifying scrutiny. The paradox is that this can be done properly only by the use of the very method whose lack of objectivity it is wished to correct. How can we calibrate the subjectivity of the "objective" investigator of psychoanalysis without the instrumentality of the fallible psychoanalyst?

Let us now consider the interdisciplinary nexus of which psychoanalysis had considered itself a part long before the burgeoning of the idea among other scientists interested in the study of man. Whether it be biological impulses from whatever source, or environmental stimuli of whatever class, there is unconscious resonance in the id which tends toward action discharge under the regulation of the ego and superego. Thus it may be said that all behavior under whatever circumstances is the legitimate concern of the psychoanalyst (Glover, 1956). Psychoanalysts, therefore, could not deny the contingency of their field to academic psychology and education, to sociology and anthropology, to biology and the medical sciences. And they have not done so. On the other hand, the *success* of psychoanalysis in establishing its cogency to all of the sciences I have mentioned, as well as to psychiatry and the various humanistic fields, is an aspect of the problem I now wish to discuss.

Psychoanalysis finds itself in a period of history characterized by anxiety. The totalitarian trends of our time affect us from several sides (Bettelheim, 1963). We ourselves have become fearful of what I have called the "cruel robot" of the unconscious (Gitelson, 1962b) as we see it operating with apparently inexorable force in the world around us. Perhaps the clearest example of the reality which stimulates our free-floating anxiety is to be found in the calculating machines which the new applied science of cybernetics has produced. Norbert Wiener (1949) has said of these machines that their aura of uncanniness is related to the fact of the real danger we sense in them: For "such machines . . . may be used by human beings to increase their control over the rest of the human race; or political leaders may attempt to control their populations . . . through political techniques as narrow and indifferent to human potentiality" as the machines themselves. Associated with such social sources of anxiety is the intrapsychic anxiety of exposed isolation. The latter is reflected in the political aspects of the social situation in the form of a prevailing tendency to find protection through participation in mass movements and in popular associations. The consequences in the work of the psychoanalyst are the same, only more subtle.

I think that analysts are being tempted to back away from the uniqueness and isolation characteristic of their work. Besides this, the social situation to which I have just referred is intensifying the longing for contact and reassurance. Interdisciplinary participation seems to be in significant part a manifestation of this. Rationalized as a technique for the exploration of the organic place of psychoanalysis among the other sciences of man, it seems that the interdisciplinary idea has become a remedy sought for unconscious disturbance produced by social anxiety. As such, the idea is a fantasy of mergence.

Psychoanalysis, we have heard, is not sufficiently objective. And it is proposed that this be changed by corrective cooperation with the other human sciences. The idea is to collaborate, to check on psychoanalytic method, data, and theory by exposure to other meth-

· 351

ods, data, and theories; but the unconscious wish, I think, is to merge with a large whole. And at what cost to psychoanalysis? Rather higher than the idea is worth! Without wishing to turn away from the necessity and the ultimate possibility of refining our method and the logical structure of the theory derived from it, I think that interdisciplinary cooperation in its present form has too often meant the dilution if not the total disappearance of essential principles, and the loss of the explicit functional identity of psychoanalysis. That identity derives from the centrality of the concept of the *unconscious* in psychoanalysis; it is this which becomes fuzzy and indistinguishable from what in analysis is known as "preconscious;" in extreme instances it disappears altogether in some form of purposive reflexological theory.

The trend I have been describing is responsive to the anxious impulse to join the herd; but it is supported by the mobilization of defensive intellectuality (Gitelson, 1944). Analysts forget the incredible leap forward in our knowledge of the nature of man which followed up on the breakthrough into the unconscious. Many are troubled and puzzled by the fact that one great leap has not been followed by another, and another; that the last 25 years have not matched the discoveries of the first 25. Some seem to have reacted with an attitude of ennui—a sort of battle fatigue befogging the victory; while others find reasons to doubt what has been achieved and feel impelled to look for adjuvants. We need to consider the possibility that the same anxiety-provoking social factors which revive fantasies of naked destructiveness are making necessary a search for a means of shoring up what looks like a failure of repression. Not forgetting the logic of the view that psychoanalysis is, at least, one of the main roots of the cognate sciences, I think one must still consider that the forms taken by its excursions into the collaboration with these sciences can represent an intellectual flight from the unconscious.

The problems I have been discussing exist within the body of psychoanalysis. They are to be found among psychoanalysts who more or less still adhere to the general idea of psychoanalysis despite anxiety which produces reactive doubt and discontent (Gitelson, 1956). My thoughts would be incomplete, however, without considering some developments that are looked upon as belonging to psychoanalysis but differ from it in important respects. I refer to the cultural, the interpersonal, the biodynamic, and the adaptational theories. Allowing for the fact that these represent the views of some psychoanalysts, the group as a whole is known as "neoanalysis." These theories have one thing in common—the change they make in the concept of the unconscious. While certain recognitions of its phenomena survive in vestigial form, it is this central idea of psychoanalytic psychology that suffers the most.

It is clear enough how this has eventuated in the theories based on the several types of environmentalism. They ignore the fact that culture, both in its interpersonal and social aspects, passes through perception-consciousness into the unconscious and mobilizes its forces. But the effect is more subtle and sometimes less easy to recognize in theories, which, taking off from Freud's biological orientation, wind up psychologizing constitution, physiology, and reflexology, and turn to animal experimentation as a valid test of human psychology. In their context, that which is the dynamic unconscious of psychoanalysis becomes identical with the subliminal somatic states which are in fact a part of the internal environment of the id (Glover, 1956).

Something must now be said about "dynamic psychiatry" and "dynamic psychotherapy" (Benjamin, 1961; Gitelson, 1951). These had their beginnings in the United States. The historical and social factors that produced them have intrinsic validity and humanistic appeal. The problem is that their development has been a factor in the changes taking place in psychoanalysis.

Dynamic psychiatry is a mixture of Meyerian psychobiology, educational and social psychology, and American cultural values, to which psychoanalytic personality theory has been added. Unconscious motivation and the classical formulations of psychosexual development are taken for granted. Among the more sophisticated, the so-called "dynamisms" are also appreciated. These elements are eclectically combined in the treatment of mental illness. Dynamic psychotherapy, on the other hand, is less eclectic. It is in fact a highly modified derivative of psychoanalysis, directed toward limited therapeutic goals. At its best it can be very good; but not infrequently it is wild analysis.

In neither of these developments can we discern the possibility of disciplined scientific method. Both are heavily dependent on the artistry of the practitioner. In neither do we find a format for self-testing repeatability of first-order observations. Both lack an intrinsic scientific theory: the first is a pragmatic melange of clinical ideas; the second is a clinical application of the psychoanalytic theory which made it possible. In addition, even good "analytically oriented" psychotherapy must assume, as a matter of operational principle, that unconscious motivation is really preconscious. Furthermore it calls for a range of "flexible" accommodation to the so-called "needs"—more often wishes—of the patient which changes the field of observation from the externalized manifestations of the intrapsychic into a social-interpersonal field.

I do not make these statements as criticisms of valid and frequently quite successful psychological interventions. I mean to emphasize, however, that psychoanalysts involved extensively in this useful area of therapeutic activity tend to lose sight of its difference from their work in the psychoanalytic situation, of which the touchstone is the continuous operation of the dynamic unconscious and of resistance to it. The necessary and unavoidable "flexibility" and the limited goals of psychotherapy produce a shielding of the unconscious so that the relevant observations and first-order convictions of psychoanalysis are lost.

I must touch on one more aspect of the unconscious repercussions of the anxiety of our times which have resulted in alloplastic phenomena of still another kind among psychoanalysts. No one has forgotten the anxiety and guilt with which physicists reacted to the production of the first atomic bomb. We are aware of the sequel to that reaction—the magnificent mobilization of the social consciousness of scientists. We are also aware of two other consequences; the moral enlistment of some scientists in the service of the forces that have been let loose,[1] and the overshadowing of pure research by massive concentration on technological applications of its results. This is not the time to attempt an elaboration of the psychological ramifications of these consequences. For the present purpose it is enough to suggest that in this state of affairs we may recognize the basic need which drives man to substitute activity for passivity. No analyst will be unaware of the adaptive usefulness of this, or doubt the moral validity of its role in the altruistic aspect of man's nature. But neither may we overlook its aggressive-defensive aspects in the presence of anxiety. The impulse is to "do something!"

Once, when I was being excessively active with one of my early patients, Blitzsten, one of my teachers, said to me: "Doctor, when there are two people in the same room and one of them is anxious or in despair, it helps a great deal if the other is not." I think this is a counsel whose observance is useful not only in the psychoanalytic situation but also on the larger scene which analysts face today. As responsible members of society we have every reason for deep concern and for sophisticated participation in the events of our time. The problem is to distinguish between this and our identity as psychoanalysts. In think there is a tendency to move from competent function in our professional and specific scientific roles into active coping with our own anxiety by way of some of the active applications to which psychoanalysis is being diverted *in its own name.*

I hope I have made clear what I meant at the beginning when I proposed a "counsel of modesty." It is

[1] See the writings and public statements of Herman Kahn and Edward Teller as examples.

really a counsel of self-respect. This is gratuitous advice, as any advice is bound to be when the basic problems are unconscious in each of us. In the course of my discussion I have made various allusions to these deeper psychological factors. It is necessary, however, that I say something more about them.

Those who take psychoanalysis seriously obtain from it the satisfactions inherent in any creative work. But there are unique stresses involved in this work which have special effects on the psychoanalyst (Grinberg, 1963). The problem of the mental hygiene of psychoanalysts has not been, and perhaps cannot be, fully solved, despite the fact that the preparatory analysis is intended to be a foundation for it and often is. The practice of psychoanalysis is a lonely business. There is probably no endeavor which makes greater demands on the capacity to be alone. Drastic reduction in consensual communication is conducive to regression beyond what is technically useful in the service of the analyzing ego. Infantile sources of stimulus-hunger are revived; the need for "narcissistic supplies" is aroused; the compensatory wish for participation in, and active control of, the external world is intensified. The analyst's immersion in the unconscious produces a kind of agoraphobic separateness which makes it important for him to find somewhere some fenced-in common ground with others. Add to this the guilts and disappointments which attach to the difficulties of the therapeutic task and it would be surprising indeed if there were no disillusionment, no need for validation in the eyes of others, no hankering after conventional scientific fraternity, no wish to be safely bound by ordinary rules and methods.

Such elements in the analyst's emotional position are, of course, variable in their intensity and effect. In a given instance any one of them is only more or less important; the overall situation may be in relative balance by virtue of the nature of the analyst's original commitment to his career, his basic capacity for continued self-analysis, and his libidinal investments in his private life, his professional associations and activities, and his social and cultural interests. When this balance is threatened, a need to redress it arises. One of the manifestations of this need may be a change in the course of the psychoanalytic career.

A critique such as I have attempted is not intended to leave the impression that we should adhere to the *status quo.* The self-respect of which I have spoken is the security of knowing and accepting intrinsic potentialities and limitations. It means remaining open to surrounding possibilities, while not forgetting their discrepancies. It is a balance between flux and stability. It is historical identity and the capacity to tolerate developmental change. It is the ability to stand alone and to be with others. Finally, it is the capacity to tolerate uncertainty and to await the outcome rather than to wish for and search for omnipotent solutions. In short, self-respect is the maturity we strive for in ourselves and welcome in our patients. However, as we know, these attainments are relative. And the same may be said for our extended role in psychoanalysis as teachers, educators, and investigators. There are things that we need to look to in ourselves.

Beginnings have been made in recent years. In the scientific area we have begun to look at the logical gaps in our theory, at its need for better systematization, and at its semantic confusions (Rapaport, 1960); in the educational field we are beginning to think about the inconsistencies between our training procedures and our theory and the clinical principles we have derived from it (Lewin and Ross, 1960). These developments are evidence of a self-scrutiny which speaks for awareness of questions to be asked and of answers that need to be found. The questions are contained in our special field of interest, and their answers must be found within its context.

But other aspects of our situation do not match these developments. They arise from individual sources that coalesce into a general effect. When we venture into other fields, we tend to extrapolate beyond the limits of our own definite knowledge in these fields. As teachers we have a tendency to be authoritarian and paternalistic when we could afford modesty and tentativeness. As training analysts it is difficult to avoid the kind of investments in the careers of our analysands that produce defects in the resolution of the transference neurosis. Surviving ambivalence in the student may thus lead to passive acquiescence to psychoanalysis or, on the other hand, to rebellious and sometimes brilliant departures from our field.

On such matters there is much more that we could say to each other; and I think one day we should do this. But for the present I must end with a repetition of the closing comment in my published communication of last autumn (Gitelson, 1962a): "There is reason for interminable self-analysis for each of us, not merely as individuals, but also in our function as members of groups which are responsible for passing on the torch of self-knowledge which we received from Freud" (p. 375).

# Theoretical Considerations
## Bearing on the Problem
## of Character Neurosis

(1963)

---

W E CANNOT consider character neurosis without
first establishing a basis for this in a concept
of character.

The original psychoanalytic view of character took
form in the context of the theory of neuroses. According to this, a psychoneurosis in its overt symptomatic
manifestations is the outcome of a conflict arising and
unsolved in childhood. The conflict to begin with is
transiently external. It arises from the existence of biological drives, the so-called instincts whose aim is
gratification and self-assertion. In their original erotic
and aggressive-destructive forms, these clash with standards of the parental environment in which the child
is reared and on which it is dependent. Under the
influence of the regulating and controlling influences
of that environment, the pure form of the drive is first
suppressed and then repressed. Whereas the original
repression occurs under external pressure, it is subsequently maintained by self-regulating forces which derive from this. The drives in their original form thus
become unconscious.

Repression, however, is only more or less successful. When it is complete, we may for practical purposes assume that conflict, though not eliminated, has been stilled. But for the most part the drives survive, and consequently conflict with the regulating functions of the mind remains potential. Ordinarily this is manifested in clinically insignificant manners, habits, and sensory, affective, and motor characteristics. Dreams normally provide a buffering and regulating mechanism for this potential. And, as is well known, derivatives of drives, variously adjusted and elaborated, become socially suitable and ego-syntonic, and enter into the formation of the so-called "normal" personality. Instinctual drainage through diversion, neutralization, and sublimation thus reduces the strength of surviving conflictual tension. These factors support repression.

This does not mean that the drives become innocuous. To the extent to which their management has required the elaboration of more purely defensive psychic structuring and maneuver, the ego remains vulnerable to their irruption and penetration. The symptomatic neurosis is external evidence that the ego has failed defensively. The symptom itself represents an emergency defense which is effective because it both conceals the nature of the drive which has been released from repression and gives it, autoplastically, partial gratification. In the first function it prevents awareness of the primary conflict; and as gratification it reduces the tension of the unconscious impulse, thereby protecting the ego against more general distortion, as is seen in the asymptomatic character neurosis, or against rupture, as in the case of the psychotic breakdown (Freud, 1924).

We may now attempt a definition of character. I suggest the following:

Character is the final common pathway for the patterned manifestation of the drives and their specific defenses, as these are imbricated and interact with their refined, elaborated, and sublimated derivatives. The identifications that have occurred with significant persons provide a formative matrix for this pattern. The pattern is stable and predictable in social and temporal dimensions. Adaptively it operates according to the principle of multiple functions (Waelder, 1936a): at once to satisfy the drives, to spare the ego anxiety and guilt, to preserve harmony with the ego ideal, to provide narcissistic gratification and self-esteem, and, above all, to ensure reality orientation to the given environment. Character is thus an adaptive synthesis of forces stemming from the biological givens, the quality of the infantile environment, the psychic structure, the character of the identifications, and the mores of the social group in which later maturation and development occurs. It is an action and reaction pattern which has crystallized out of this flux of factors (Hartmann, 1939a). And at the heart of the hypothetically "normal" situation is the fact that the phallic position has been reached psychosexually, and the Oedipus complex had been resolved (Fenichel, 1931b).

Psychoneurosis may be looked upon as evidence of a partial disruption of this synthesis due to a failure of defense. The result is a disturbance in the economy of the character structure because conflict has been revived. The balance is restored through the formation of a symptom. The symptom is a compromise formation between an id impulse which has threatened to irrupt into consciousness or action, and a spastic and unconsciously determined reaction of the ego against this. The result is ego-alien and produces secondary reactions of lowered self-esteem and suffering. Nevertheless, the symptom serves to bind the irrupting impulse while giving it substitutive gratification, and thus it closes the breach in the defensive system. The conflict involved in such a situation pertains to an aspect of the Oedipus complex which has remained unsolved and has been repressed. Subsequent regression to an earlier form of instinct gratification and an internal or external revival of this produce emergency defense in the form of the symptom.

In the classical neurotic character, as it was first described by Alexander (1930), the problem also centers on the Oedipus complex. Repression and regression also occur although neither of these seems to be as effective as in the psychoneurotic. And the autoplastic modification of the ego involved in symptom formation is not conspicuous. Instead there is a plunge into external reality which is variously exploited to fit the unconscious wish and need. Why this is so—why symptoms appear in one instance and not in the other—we do not really know. It is possible that it is depends on the phase of ego development at which specific psychosexual vicissitudes occurred. It may be that the matter is determined by the constitutional capacity of the ego to oppose the drives, or, as Alexander suggested, that it is the unusual strength of the drives themselves which results in *relative* weakness in the ego. On the basis of clinical evidence it seems possible that in some cases specific circumstances surrounding the first appearance of an impulse or wish may produce a fixation to the conflict thus engendered, prior to repression and regression. This could be a determining factor in setting the person concerned on a career of repeated and unsuccessful efforts to find a solution in external reality (according to the Zegarnik principle) (English & English, 1958). However the case may be, it is the quality of compelled and patterned acting out which is the most striking aspect of the neurotic character. It is this characteristic which has given vivid cogency to its other designation, "the neurosis of fate" (Deutsch, 1930). Hamlet (Jones, 1947) and the well-known Don Juan characters (Freud, 1910a) are examples.

As a matter of fact, in many clinical situations we scarcely see the effects of repression and regression. More prominent are the rather easily identified displacements to mother, father, and sibling surrogates and the not too deeply concealed though often rather grotesque dramatizations of the Oedipus complex. Added to this is the prevalence of actual if disguised instinctual gratification, instead of the substitutive compromise of a symptom. The relationship of such phenomena to the condensation of gratification and defense, as we see this in psychoneurotic symptoms, is demonstrated in intimate and inevitable sequence of crime and invited punishment, and, in other cases, puzzling combinations of asceticism, self-sacrifice, debauchery, and failure of gratification.

But such instances are for books. More common, more subtle, and more fateful for the world, as well as for the persons concerned, are those character patterns which only careful study reveal to be indeed neurotic. The symptomatology is not only apparently ego syntonic but socially useful and even laudable, narcis-sistically gratifying, and even productive of prestige and tangible reward in the goods of this life. Of these "character neuroses" I shall now speak.

In life there are no pure types. In general usage the diagnosis "neurotic character" and "character neuro-sis" appear interchangeably. But sharp boundaries have heuristic convenience, and I have reversed the order of words in the diagnostic rubric to emphasize an impor-tant difference between this and the types previously mentioned. The so-called "character neurosis" (Fenichel, 1945), in contrast to the so-called "neurotic character," presents, outstandingly, the picture and structure of defense. If we look at this group in terms of its most commonly designated subclasses—obses-sional or compulsive character, hysterical character, or schizoid character—we are impressed by the fact that, as in the case of the psychoneuroses, the symp-tomatology is autoplastic. But it is the personality it-self that is shaped by the neurosis into a defensive pattern of socially adapted adjustment. I do not mean by this that these people do not live in the world. But their impact on it and their penetration of it stems, not primarily from libido or aggression, but from de-fense against these.

The phenomenology of the "character neurosis" ranges from a preponderance of self-centeredness, comparable to an encapsulated hysterical or compul-sive symptom, to an imbrication with other persons which is almost as deep though not so ostentatious as in the case of the "neurotic characters." However, where the latter are struggling with an unsolved prob-lem in which the conflict has been externalized and it would appear that for them other people have become libidinal and aggressive transference objects, the "character neurosis" remains largely internalized. What *is* externalized and transferred is the particular pattern of defense which has proven successful during earlier development and in later social accommodation. These are the people whom Wilhelm Reich (1931) so graphically described as presenting a "character armor" in analysis and who present a facade in life. Winnicott (1956) has referred to the latter as a "false self" because these persons experience themselves in the terms of their defense. Fenichel (1945) suggested that the formation of the typical "neurosis of character" and its several traits corresponds to a single massive act of repression which avoids the necessity for the *"ad hoc"* management of subsequent specific anxiety situations. In any case, characterological traits become fixed anchorages for defense against instinct irruption. As such, in various combinations they are "worked into the ego." This is what produces the relative constancy of the defensive attitude and establishes it as the "sign" of the personality, no matter how diverse may be the stimuli from the unconscious or from reality.

In consequence, the "symptom," whether it be the characterological style as a whole or its several explicit traits, is ego syntonic. As in the case of the psychoneuroses, the primary gain is preserved in various forms of concealed gratification. In contrast to the psychoneurotic symptom, however, secondary gain is greatly enhanced. This accrues from the approval of the world, whether it be by way of recognition of intellectual qualities, commendation for hard, faithful, and sometimes productive labor, the label of "good fellow," or applause for self-assertive achievement. In this way primitive oral, anal, and urethral impulses are sources of satisfaction.

Much of this passes as allegedly "normal" (Gitelson, 1954) and if taken at face value often gives the impression of really satisfying the instincts, even when transformed by passage through the ego. This is particularly the case when counterphobic activity (Fenichel, 1939a) is a part of the defensive structure, as it frequently is. But such activity does not in fact gratify the drives for which it stands. These are themselves inhibited. The expression of one instinct may substitute for the repression of another. In a character neurosis we may see how the ego, seeming to accept genital sexuality explicitly and presenting the impression of normality in this respect, is actually fobbing off on an unsuspecting public oral or anal impulses which are themselves repressed. On the other hand, oral and anal traits may substitute for sexual impulses. Furthermore, while character traits are deeply rooted in the instincts, their formal qualities and configurations are determined to a large extent by the nature of the culture in which they develop and operate. Thus, "normal" sexuality, even if libertine, is acceptable to the "modern" ego. The sad fact is, however, that it does not always serve the mature genital impulse, but is often a front for omnipotence fantasies, sadistic impulses, and oral greed. And saddest of all, it may be a reaction formation against affective emptiness and profound isolation.

Finally, we must consider that the distortions and disguises through which the various libidinal and aggressive impulses express themselves in the character defense are supported by the fact of the frequency with which they occur in a given group. The interpersonal usefulness of prevalent defenses not only serves to conceal them from the particular person concerned but from the eyes of the world at large. One might say that the mores of various social segments constitute an unconscious conspiracy of silence. There is a sort of tacit agreement not to acknowledge the forms in which the primitive nature of man continues to express itself.

Character, however, does not consist exclusively of fixation to an infantile trauma and its repeated re-enactment, as in the case of the first group I discussed, or of transformed instinctual drives, as in the case of the second group. I have already indicated in general terms that character—the resultant of a parallelogram of forces—depends also on the relationship and interaction of id, ego, and superego (Hartmann, 1952). And each of these contributes its particular hallmark.

The direct contribution of the ego derives from its several attributes. The qualities of intelligence, talent, perceptual capacities, body build, motor patterns, reactive rhythms—these, together with the organizing, adaptive, and defensive functions, provide modes and channels of expression for instincts and affects (Hartmann, 1939a). Directly and indirectly they outline both the external image of the person, and his self-image and self-experience. Oral incorporative, anal sadistic, and phallic aggressive impulses, for example, are determined in their expression by variations in the balance among these ego factors. It is not merely instinctual fixation points or psychosexual regression that determine the symptomatology of character. For this reason we see hysterical characters with an obsessional, or if you please, an intellectual facade; or obsessional characters with hysterical or paranoid "features"; or investment in truly creative work in the presence of idiosyncratic behavior. Furthermore, the ego's attributes are aspects of reality which confront the ego within its own context and reflexly call on it for adaptation or defense. From this point of view Adlerian theory has some cogency. Organ inferiority does have its real effect in modifying the quality of the ego and may determine a characterological response. But even so, it must be remembered that it is not simply a matter of organ inferiority and reactions to it. Inferiority feelings also arise from the castration complex, loss of love, humiliation, and the sense of guilt. Besides which, the instincts also exploit the ego's assets and liabilities, while the ego borrows the power of the instincts to implement its purposes. In any case the given attributes of the ego are of supreme importance in determining the shape of the person to the world at large and in his own eyes (Hartmann, 1939a).

The attributes of the ego are not exclusively inborn, however. The history of the nature of the relationship of the person to the formative people in his environment is of equal or greater significance in determining the ego's role as mediator between the instincts and the external world. It follows that the characters of the significant formative persons are of the essence in the effect they exert. Here we encounter and must consider the phenomenon of identification.

The crucial environmental objects, of course, are the parents, and to begin with, the mother. The relationship with her establishes the most deeply rooted patterns for the nature of the child's subsequent relationships with other people. It may be said that the climate of that first relationship established the fundamental and typical "mood" of the person. The intimacy of the symbiosis of mother and child is what makes it so extremely difficult to distinguish between what is constitutionally given and what is acquired through introjection and elaborated in an unconscious identity with the mother's "set." And, of course, this is further complicated by subsequent identifications with father and siblings, and later on with other significant persons. The latter, including the parents as they are and appear in later years, impose various modifications, for better or for worse, on the original identifications, which, nevertheless, are essentially indestructible and retain their effectiveness.

The earliest identifications enter into the formation of what have been referred to as "ego nuclei" (Glover, 1943). Much depends on the extent to which these are in the end miscible or, contrariwise, incompatible and in conflict. In the neuroses of character, this is one of the factors that enters into setting up the peculiar paradoxes they so often present—"splits" that reach their extreme in the multiple personality. But a more general complication in the normal establishment of identifications is the factor of bisexuality, the psychological determinants of which are more readily discerned clinically than are the determining factors which today we know are based on hormonal distributions. In any case, predisposing feminine tendencies in the male interfere with the normal tendency for the boy to identify finally with the father and other men. The reverse situation obtains in the female. The consequence, depending on still other factors, may be various degrees of psychosexual inversion, or reactive, overcompensatory, and pathologically deformed assertions of masculinity or femininity.

Identification is normally the basis for the withdrawal of primitive erotic and aggressive impulses from the objects toward which they are originally directed. This so-called "inhibition of aim" results in the "taming" of the relationship with the persons concerned, while the libidinal and aggressive energy which is thus made available enters into the promotion of psychic development. This released energy charges the ego's talents in the formation of sublimations, and it shares in the shaping of the ego-syntonic, adaptive, and defensive patterns. Failures in this aspect of the identification process account for the important role played by ambivalence in the personal relations of neurotic characters. Because of such failure they exhibit disturbances in the capacity for love and altruism, oscillations of mood, unsteadiness in thinking and working capacity, and, in grosser forms, overt primitive sensuality and destructiveness.

Most important of all is the part played by identification in the formation of the superego. The primary influence of the parents is thus internalized and made permanent. Aggressive and libidinal energy which is withdrawn from its original focus on the parents becomes available to the superego itself, providing it with powers which are exerted against the forces of the id and its derivatives in the ego. The superego originates in part from the conditionings which occur in the preverbal and pregenital relationship to the mother; it is transiently stabilized in the context of the

Oedipus complex in middle childhood; it appears in its ultimate form after puberty, and in this form it is crucial to the definitive molding of character. Its strength, however, is relative not only to the quality of identifications which have entered into its formation but also to the strength of the id.

The normal superego derives from stable relationships in which there is minimal ambivalence. Love has been preponderant over hate. The instincts have been of ordinary intensity, and the ego has had ordinary capacity for perception, organization, and adaptation to reality. The defective superego may be excessively severe, or it may be weak. The former may reflect the harshness of the formative figures, or it may be a spastic response to threat from excessively strong primitive destructive impulses, inborn or in response to the environment. A weak superego may reflect identification with weak or corrupt parental figures; or it may be only relatively so in the presence of unusually strong drives. The latter could be a consequence of constitutional factors or the outcome of cultivation through spoiling indulgence or even seduction. Thus the id, in its overall quality, as well as in terms of its specific elements, contributes explicitly to the characterological picture.

A specific example may be found in Freud's description of the "erotic" character type (Freud, 1931b). In these persons, libidinal development has advanced to the genital level; they have a strong orientation toward objects; and the wish for gratification is explicitly centered on love, especially in its anaclitic form. The life goal is pleasure, and this drive is strong enough to overcome or circumvent moral values and even good

372 ·

sense, so that these individuals are unreliable and irresponsible. In the aggressive form this type of impulse-ridden character has been referred to classically as "psychopathic personality," assumed to be without a sense of guilt. But we are no longer so sure this assumption is valid. The fact is that the prime effect of the operation of the superego, the sense of guilt, is still capable of exerting its influence. The ego, exploiting for this purpose the very impulses and drives that are being permitted gratification, is found to be inviting punishment and in other ways working toward securing external controls in lieu of the superego's failure to exercise them internally. The psychopathic recidivists who fill our prisons are evidence of this. More subtle types are ubiquitous. And in the erotic type we see also that despite the preponderant role played by the id, the ego and the superego are insignificant only by comparison. The evidence for this is found in the fact that even though the leading symptomatology takes the form of "acting out" without conscious guilt, the erotic types are nonetheless prone to conversion reactions, phobias, and anxiety.

In addition to the *erotic* type with which I have illustrated the more overt manifestations of the id in character neuroses, Freud also described two types in which the other psychic structures are dominant.

In the *compulsive* type, the fixations and regressions are found at the anal-sadistic level of psychosexual development. Persons with this character structure have intense sensitiveness to guilt. Their drives are strongly inhibited even in their "normal" context; they tend to be arid though sometimes kindly in their emotional qualities, lacking flexibility in their adaptive and adjustive capacities, faithful and self-sacrificing, but diffident and ambivalent in their personal relations. They are often dedicated in their social commitments and also productive, but at great cost in tension and effort. Their essential conservatism renders them vulnerable to new life situations which expose them to unaccustomed stimulation. They typically react to such stress with depression or psychosomatic disturbances. The "anal character" is a subtype, whose admixture produces the classical phenomena of reaction formations against sadistic and soiling impulses. The dynamic situation is, in general, one of domination by the superego and of rigidity in the adaptive and organizing functions of the ego (English & English, 1958).

The *narcissistic* types are, in common parlance, the egoists. They are oriented toward self-love, self-gratification, and self-interest. Insensitive to others, they are highly sensitive to anything suggestive of slight or indifference to themselves. They do not invest themselves deeply in their relations with others, excepting as it may serve their own ends. They are not open to influence or persuasion. Oral and phallic characteristics are intermixed and, if prevalent, creates sub-types. If the oral history has been ratifying, the resulting optimism and cheerfulness may provide an amelioration of the cold picture of the major type. If the phallic drive is strong, aggressive competitiveness becomes a characteristic. Because in these people there is commonly an underlying early injury to self-esteem, they tend to respond to traumatic frustration with depression and paranoid reactions.

But nearly always, what we see are mixtures of such so-called characterological "types." The typical ones described by Freud are the erotic-compulsive, the erotic-narcissistic, and the narcissistic-compulsive. Freud (1916) also spoke of three specifically psychological forms of character: "the exceptions," "those wrecked by success," and "criminals from a sense of guilt." Subsequently, various other types have been emphasized (Fenichel, 1945), for example: the masochistic, the passive-feminine, the urethral characters. On the basis of what I have already said, however, it will be clear enough that what we can expect to find in all these forms is a clinical demonstration of the fact that pathological character, like "normal" character, is a synthesis in function and a mosaic in form; a unification and systematization of patterns and traits which are to be traced to instinctual and adaptive elements in each, the id, the ego, and the superego in varying degrees of fusion and defusion.

No clinical forms demonstrate this more graphically than the so-called borderline cases (Gitelson, 1958). These patients seem to be peculiar to our times. It is only in the last 25 or 30 years that they have been studied analytically. The appellations applied to them are as various as the clinical pictures they present—"psychotic personality," "prepsychotic," "pseudoneurotic schizophrenia," "ego deficit," "ego distortion," and the most general designation of all "character disorder." Phenomenologically, they include among others, eccentrics, "as if" personalities, affectively inhibited people, impostors, fantastic liars, and persons with various manifestations of impaired reality perception and defective judgment. Like the clinical entities I have discussed previously, they are nonsymptomatic in the strictly autoplastic sense of psychoneuroses, but there

• 375

is this difference: the neurotic characters, and the character neuroses, as I have already stated, stem from the vicissitudes encountered in the Oedipus complex; in the present group the central conflict germinated in the preoedipal relationship to the mothering person or persons.

The Oedipus complex is characterized above all by the triangular situation involving the love of one parent and hostile rivalry with the other. In the pregenital situation the father is not yet a rival but simply another obscure figure of the environment who may be pleasing or displeasing; the mother is the central figure; other persons in the environment are not sexually differentiated and are only additional objects for passive and active polymorphous perverse aims. Freud (1931a) emphasized the great intensity of the preoedipal libidinal strivings, "greater than anything that comes later," and gave them neurosogenic status in their own right. Fenichel (1931a), who was less liberal than Freud himself in this regard, nevertheless modified his position to say: "Every single analysis provides fresh evidence of [the fact of the centrality of the Oedipus complex] if we *except* those cases of extreme malformation of character which resemble a lifelong psychosis and in which . . . the subject's object relations were destroyed root and branch at an early period . . ." (p. 181, italics added).

Fenichel goes overboard a bit. "Root and branch" is a little too much. However, it does emphasize the leading importance of the occurrence of severely disturbed relations with primary objects in the pathogenesis of these disorders. This hinges on parental indifference to some extent; but chiefly, it is the unpredictability, the unsteadiness of the milieu, beginning with the mother and recurring with auxiliary figures and in later life. From this follow serious impairments in that part of ego development which depends on the identification process, failure to integrate the phallic position with the Oedipus complex, defective formation of the super-ego and of the reality principle, and incompleteness of repression and reaction formation. These persons remain open to conscious awareness of primitive fantasies and impulses which they sometimes act upon. Their attitudes are frankly dependent, or this may be denied by omnipotence. Their relationships are preponderantly based on temporary identifications with those who happen to be around them; they live in the presence of others, not with them; they are affectively shallow. On the basis of primary identificatory learning—I refer here to mimicry—some of them conduct themselves with seeming adequacy, and, if they are intelligent and retain some ego autonomy, they may present a facade of seemingly normal ego operations.

With these persons the vicissitudes of development have not turned on the transient defensive anxieties attendant on the usual developmental and adaptive crises. The *actual frustration and precocious stimulation* we discover them to have lived through is often enormous—have, in fact, literally threatened to overwhelm them. But their developmental and maturational arrest is not merely due to weakness. It may be the manifestation of an inherent adaptive strength sufficient to have avoided actual destruction by psychosis or death. Each case represents an idiosyncratic way of life which has been compelled by gravely dis-

· 377

ordered early environmental conditions. Instinctual and ego development have been grossly out of phase. The ego is immature; that is, it has not moved to its potential distance from the drives, and it has not been sufficiently differentiated from them. But at its level of development it is intact. We might perhaps think of it as manifesting a capacity for defense in depth. It has survival value by way of facultative accommodation to the id and to external reality.

We recognize in this broad clinical sketch that these persons have on one hand the psychological character-istics of the infant, and on the other hand qualities of the schizophrenic. From the standpoint of psychoana-lytic ego psychology it is apparent why they have been referred to in terms of ego defect or weakness. But this is a debatable view. What we see is a broad front of incomplete development resulting from a lack of stable object relations and compatible identifications—central factors in the building of human personality and char-acter.

The borderline case may, strictly speaking, seem ir-relevant to our topic. However, you will have noted that throughout my discussion I have been moving back and forth from conceptions of character based on ideas about its "normal" structure and functions, to considerations referring to its pathology. Whichever way we turn we see overlapping. This is an inevitable consequence of the nature of our material. As soon as we look beneath the phenomenological surface we are confronted by the fact, as I have said before, that there are no pure types. Ideally, psychosexual development goes on in phase with the maturing powers of the ego to deal with vicissitudes of drives, and in the presence of environmental influences which are attuned to lend the support appropriate to progressively changing cross-sections of this process. But, in fact, this is only more or less the case. It is a question of economics. Given a range of operating formative factors, varying internal and external conditions produce various quantitative and configurational distributions of the derivatives of these factors. As Nunberg (1955) has said, "the difference between symptom neurosis and character neurosis (or neurotic character) is not as significant as it seems at first glance." And as for the relevance of the borderline case, we may recall Freud's observation (1937): "Every normal person is only normal on the average. His ego approximates to that of the psychotic in some part or other and to a greater or lesser extent; and the degree of its remoteness from one end of the series and of its proximity to the other will furnish us with a measure of what we have so indefinitely termed 'and alteration of the ego' " (p. 235). Hence, it may be necessary for us to define the "hypothetical normal ego," and with it the "normal character," largely in negative terms, that is, distinguished by the absence of particular defenses, attitudes, or properties.

My own preference is to look upon character development, normal or pathological, as being directed, in the overall, toward the establishment of some kind of systemic balance. The principle involved does not differ from that which operates in organismic structure and function as it has been observed at the biological level. Operationally, or from the standpoint of one or another value system, the upshot may be looked upon as "good" or "bad." The neurotic character may impress us as a hero, a fool, or a victim. The person with the character neurosis may be looked upon as a suitable member for our club, or an inconvenient or annoying presence. The person with the character disorder may just be "strange," or a sometimes charming or creative individualist. And, of course, there are the people with psychoneurotic symptoms. All of them have qualities of the others. And all of us who look upon ourselves as "normal" are only more or less so. Taste and circumstances alter cases.

This brings me to my final statement in this theoretical consideration of the problem of the "neuroses" and "disorders" of character: Why are they more prevalent today than the psychoneuroses; why do most of our nonpsychotic patients come to us with complaints of interpersonal unhappiness, feelings of inadequacy and incompleteness, vague tension and anxiety, psychosomatic symptoms, and emptiness in the presence of apparent surfeit? These questions present us with an enormous problem. It would be presumptuous to say more than that we are aware of its existence. I can make only a few generalizations. While I was thinking over what these could be, with complete fortuitousness, I ran into an article by Bruce Mazlish, of M.I.T., entitled "Our 'Heraclitean' Period." I think some citations from this article may advance our present purpose.

The title has reference to the philosophical views of Heraclites: that everything is in a flux and nothing remains fixed except the rational principle in the universe—the logos. Mazlish (1961) goes on to say:

> . . . ours is . . . a period in which forms and fixity have all but disappeared. We live in a kaleidoscopic world in which forms cannot be smashed because

they hardly exist . . . the true iconoclasts . . . have preceded us. For form-smashing in the Western World did occur . . . not in our time, but largely before World War I . . . from about 1830 on . . . [Marx, Darwin, Nietzsche, Freud, and other like them have produced the "Heraclitean" aspect of our time in the moral field.] The result . . . has been a widespread denial of faiths, abandonment of traditions, and repudiation of values . . . we no longer believe in forms at all. . . . Nor are there "fixed" views, whether of the self or of society. . . . Modern man is a little like the player in Gilbert and Sullivan, engaged in a game, "On cloth untrue, with a twisted cue, and elliptical billiard balls" [p. 336, 338].

Thus, in the absence of clear goals, we cannot say of ourselves that we are "on the march." But, with uncertain direction and shifting values we *are* "on the move." To use Matthew Arnold's lines, we have been

Wandering between two worlds, one dead
The other powerless to be born.

I think all this is reflected in the psychological climate of the families from which we and our patients come. The sexual status of the parents has become unclear, their hierarchal differentiation and function uncertain. The chief consequence is that repression is no longer the primary and central mechanism of defense and adaptation, inasmuch as it is dependent for its effective operation on definite structure in the personalities of the formative people and an established hierarchy of relationships among them in the operations of the family. In the absence of a model toward which to aspire, object relations become relative and conditional; identifications are impaired and conflictful. While the instincts and the mechanisms of defense retain their intrinsic qualities, whatever I have said about them in the context of the classical conceptions of character and neuroses becomes, operationally, a matter of "more or less," contingent on the new factors which now surround them. The secondary "adjustment" value of such defenses as identification with the aggressor, altruistic surrender, ego restriction, denial, isolation, and reaction formation make them more important than outright repression. In effect, what has become important is not repression of the content of the unconscious but the successful deployment of defenses, in the guise of adaptation but enlisted in the service of social accommodation. Personality, thus, to a large extent has returned to its original Latin meaning in the word "persona," a "mask." This is the essence of the "crisis of identity" to which Erikson (1950) has devoted his attention. It is also near the heart of the problem of the neurosis of character in our time.

# On the Identity Crisis in American Psychoanalysis

## (1964)

---

THE 30 YEARS of my commitment to psychoanalysis span nearly its entire modern period, most of which has been centered in the United States. The events that changed the world after Hitler came to power halted the development of psychoanalysis in Europe and moved it to the western hemisphere with a surviving foothold only in Britain. By far the larger number of European psychoanalysts found a haven and an opportunity for many scientifically productive years in this country. But these years have also seen the gradual appearance of social issues and problems similar to those which confronted Freud and his early collaborators. I have been in close touch with and to a considerable extent involved in these revived issues and problems, and I propose to review and discuss them.

Harold K. Schilling (1958) referred to science as having the qualities of a "social enterprise" which involved interaction, cooperation, and sharing. He

---

*Editorial Note:* In this, his final paper, originally presented to the Plenary Session of the Annual Meeting of the American Psychoanalytic Association in 1964, Dr. Gitelson continued to evidence his concern about the fate of psychoanalysis.

pointed out that "intersubjective testability" (Sullivan's "consensual validation") is a synonym for "objectivity" and that the word "empirical" refers primarily to social rather than solitary experience. "Science," he said, "is [of necessity] communal." The scientific community is characterized by having its typical way of life; its own ideals, standards, mores, conventions, signs and symbols, language, and jargon; its ethics, sanctions, authority and control, its institutions and organizations; "*its own creeds and beliefs, orthodoxies and heresies* [italics added]—and effective ways of dealing with the latter." This way of life is very hard to describe: "nearly ineffable—though nevertheless real. There is something intimate about it, something shared and deeply felt, though unspoken [and] it can be understood only from within the community" (pp. 1325–1326).

How easy it would be to conclude that the statement I have just cited was made by a devoutly orthodox analyst touting the "psychoanalytic movement." But this is a professor of physics speaking! If we turn to our own "language and jargon" for a moment, who will fail to note that Professor Schilling is paraphrasing the psychoanalytic view that reality testing is not simply a solipsistic ego function but is also a manifestation of social validations internalized in the superego? Does it not seem that "hard science" also has its credo and its "establishment"? And in view of this, is it so surprising that it was necessary for the pioneers of psychoanalysis to have to struggle for toleration if not acceptance by those whose orthodoxy was nineteenth-century science? Furthermore, the sciences which preceded psychoanalysis had faced a similar necessity and had been motivated by the same kind of extrascientific dedication. There is nothing inherent in the nature of science which would have insured without effort the continuity of the points of view, ideas, techniques, and findings of those who had become convinced of the validity of empiricism. It took "faith" in the substance of science to provide the energy for engineering the social conditions for its operation. The so-called "basic sciences" also had to struggle for a beachhead in their time, and to work for its consolidation into a viable social organization which could provide the stimulation, collaboration, and mutual criticism they needed for their survival and development.

In the seventeenth century the Royal Society began as a small group of men who met together to inform and animate each other, and to provide a publication and other means of communication for the spread of scientific knowledge. The French Academy had a similar beginning, as did the American Philosophical Society. Such organizations tend to grow. They are "social movements" out of which a scientific community develops. Their growth is a measure of their success in stimulating scientific creativity. "Scientists look upon social stimulation as a natural resource, and they join up" (Boring, 1965). In the same way, those who took up Freud's discoveries and organized the ways and means for their preservation and propagation began what has continued to be called the "psychoanalytic movement." Despite the stigmatic connotation of the word "movement," we see that it is applicable with equal appropriateness to the history of all the sciences.

But there is another way of looking at the problem of scientific movements. Recently, Thomas Kuhn's analysis of *The Structure of Scientific Revolutions* (1963) has provided evidence that what *we* refer to as a "movement" is the social reflection of an intellectual crisis in science. Such crises occur when existing basic assumptions in the understanding of natural phenomena no longer work—when new experiences produce paradoxes which do not fit into existing hypotheses. The consequence is an attempt at a new synthesis. In the naturalistic phase of science all phenomena have equal relevance, and attention ranges over the whole gamut of facts at hand. The practical crafts were a rich source of such facts, and the creative curiosity these evoked was of necessity attended by rationalization. But it is not such primordial beginnings of knowledge that concern us. For it was not until there were theories which attempted to introduce system and method into observations and their rationalization that we had science. Science is as dependent on a point of view as on its procedures and observations. Generalizations which are inclusive of these, Kuhn has called "paradigms."

According to Kuhn (1963), a scientific paradigm has the following characteristics: It is a generalization which is "sufficiently unprecedented [and intellectually challenging] to attract an enduring group of adherents away from competing modes of scientific activity." Simultaneously a paradigm "is sufficiently open-ended to leave all sorts of problems for the redefined group of [scientific] practitioners to resolve" (p. 10). A successful paradigm is one that has solved some of the problems which have been outstanding; but its chief importance rests on the fact that at the same time it has redefined the "legitimate problems and methods of a research field" and points to possible directions for its "future articulation and expansion." Thus a paradigm is largely a *promise of success* which must be actualized in the practice of what Kuhn calls "normal science." Normal science is the long course of follow-up work that succeeds on the appearance and acceptance of a paradigm which has revolutionized a previous outlook on nature; it is the "mopping-up operation" which engages most scientists throughout their careers. "Normal science" is what we see in the present state of psychoanalysis, as contrasted with the scientific revolution produced by its paradigms. Normal science may be defined as a point of view and a mode of research concerned with the solution of puzzles that have been generated by a paradigm. The consensus and commitment produced by a successful paradigm initiate and sustain "normal science."

Physics, astronomy, chemistry, and biology had already experienced a number of intellectual revolutions when psychoanalysis emerged from medicine. There is no necessity, here, for even an adumbration of the history of Freud's encounter with paradoxical phenomena which could not be understood in terms of existing biological and medical postulates and which required a new departure. However, it was not the discovery of previously unrecognized phenomena—transference, for example—or the puzzlement produced by old phenomena, such as hypnosis, that produced a scientific crisis. As Kuhn (op. cit.) states it: "the act of judgment that leads scientists to reject a previously accepted theory is always based upon more than a comparison of that theory with the world. The decision to reject [an existing paradigm] is always simultaneously a decision to accept another, and the judgment leading to that decision involves the comparison of both paradigms with nature and with each other" (p. 77).

It is just such a fundamental intellectual clash between old and new views that produces scientific revolution. It is the enlistment of followers in the cause of a new paradigm that generates the social mobilization which can be recognized as a "movement" in all the sciences, not only in psychoanalysis, to which the term has been applied pejoratively. Scientific revolutions lead to the restructuring of a given area of knowledge and research; scientific movements provide the necessary social organizations in support of the new idea. While these are at first quite informal and may in some instances remain so, more often formalization occurs in the organization of new societies, with their meetings, journals, conferences, and committees. These are necessary and useful in carrying on the normal work of a science during its quiet phase when elaboration of the factual details and the solution of new problems projected by a generally accepted paradigm are in process. The question is: what is the optimal degree of such social organization of science?

The scientist needs both privacy and communication. Descartes isolated himself in various hiding places in Holland to ensure the former. But through an intermediary he maintained contacts with selected colleagues with whom he found it possible to exchange both collaborative and controversial views. "It is almost impossible to imagine a scientist's contributing to knowledge without any stimulus at all." The minds of many creative individuals "work best with constant stimulation from small groups of others"—whether these be disciples or peers (Boring, 1965).

The continued growth of a scientific society, however, deprives it of original advantage. This growth results from the fertility of the original idea which it was established to promulgate. A scientific society provides a necessary clearing house for the relevance of the accumulating facts in its field, their fit with its theory, and the possible articulations of ambiguous facts with the theory. It is the latter function which encounters difficulties as the field enlarges and the number of its practitioners increases. For it is in this area that fractures of a paradigm tend to occur. And it is where this danger is present that intimacy, informality, and friendship among small groups of workers in the field make possible the kind of rigorous and collaborative scrutiny that can lead to the identification of articulation or the birth of a new paradigm.

As matters stand, while the social activation of creativity continues to be the professed purpose of scientific societies, professional advantage increases in importance; recognition begins to loom larger as a goal than does scientific achievement; "new little societies [with special interests] are formed in an attempt to recapture the advantages of the lost [social] stimulation" (Boring, 1965). These develop either as splits from the parent body or by the introduction of organizational structure into small, originally informal groups which feel "starved for social activation." This is what Boring has called the "paradoxical growth" by which a healthy scientific society loses its original usefulness and is followed by the appearance of new generations of smaller groups which in turn become too large. "[This] has been the pattern of the proliferation of the sciences." It has occurred along lines of cleavage provided by the evolution of established theory and in the gaps left by the appearance of insoluble anomalies. As the findings in each field of investigation increase, and as these begin to include paradoxical new findings, the effort to articulate new facts with old theory and new theory with new and old facts produces branchings, divagations, and new departures. In each instance a new supporting "movement" may appear. Movements are an intrinsic aspect of the social nature of the scientific community and of scientific history. Psychoanalysis is of that history and community.

Such "movements" have often been subliminal. The transition from Newtonian physics to relativity theory —not yet fully complete—and the theory of quantum mechanics, which in its turn produced doubts and qualms in Einstein, are examples of the emergence of new paradigms that have attracted followers—both incidentally and as specialists—whose quiet work of application and validation has remained within the parent science. Comparably there have been several quietly accepted revisions of theory in psychoanalysis. I refer to such changes as have occurred in the theory of anxiety, in the model of psychic structure, and in the place of ego psychology in genetics and psychic functioning. Such developments in psychoanalysis are of the same order as the theoretical revisions Kuhn has described for the other sciences. Some of them have been revolutionary. Certainly there have been and there are those who have not gone along with them. But no more than in the case of physics has this sundered the scientific body of psychoanalysis.

Nonetheless, there are certain peculiar aspects of the process of scientific revolution in psychoanalysis. Some of these stem from intrinsic factors and others from surrounding historical conditions. I refer to the fact that in psychoanalysis there have been numbers of divergences which have taken schismatic forms. Sometimes these have been lethal theoretical mutuations of the parent stock, such as Jungian and Adlerian psychology, in which the theory simply did not fit the body of relevant facts. I do not intend to dwell on these splits and others like them in the earlier history of psychoanalysis. But there are more recent viable adaptations to new conditions which stem from the psychoanalytic corpus—for example, the so-called "basic science" of psychodynamics and its offspring, dynamic psychiatry and psychotherapy (Gitelson, 1942b, 1951, 1956, 1962c). Though currently there has appeared an inclination to invalidate even these (see Grinker, 1964, final paragraph of section 1, p. 230), they nevertheless require our attention since they are the basis for the view—though not stated in these terms—that a scientific revolution is in process in psychoanalysis (Rado et al., 1963). There is an inclination to declare the existing psychoanalytic paradigm defunct or rapidly expiring (see Grinker, 1964, paragraph beginning at the end of the first column, p. 228); psychoanalysis, though actually operating as "normal science" (Kuhn, 1963), has been declared bankrupt; a new synthesis which will clarify everything is thought to be already here or visible on the horizon (see Grinker, 1964, first paragraph beginning in the first column, p. 234).

It is questionable whether this is indeed the case. It takes more than the fact that there is something less than a perfect fit between a prevailing theory and its data to vitiate such a theory. For it is one of the functions of a hypothesis to define the existence and nature of unsolved problems for which the hypothesis provides a principle of solution; the normal work of the sciences consists of the application of such principles to the solution of such puzzles; until such puzzles become anomalies which current theory and method can no longer resolve, there is no stimulus to new paradigm formation; when such a stimulus is generated by the actual state of affairs in a given science, then a new paradigm may be born; and when that happens and it seems to be more fruitful in application to the relevant data when compared with the existing paradigm, then we may speak of the resulting debate on the substantive issues as a state of scientific revolution. Such a debate will inevitably be characterized by the human qualities of the scientifically qualified participants in it, but it will in the end be resolved by the logic of the relevant facts. *However, without a clearly defined alternative paradigm for explicit comparison with an existing paradigm,* and with the facts which are relevant to the problems and anomalies projected by the existing paradigm, *we do not have the conditions for a scientific revolution* (Kuhn, 1963). This I believe to be the situation in psychoanalysis today. Nevertheless, the conditions do obtain for rebellion without a cause. I will now attempt to discuss these conditions.

By the time the forced emigration of psychoanalysis was at its height it had become more or less stabilized in Europe as a valid branch of knowledge. The criteria for this statement rest on the fact that its basic theories had been formulated and were being examined and extended; that psychoanalytic practitioners and investigators were to be found in most of the countries of Europe and in America; that there was an established literature of journals and books with a relatively wide circulation, and that standards of training and education had been worked out and were being applied. These developments are all concordant with the establishment of "normal science," as Kuhn has described it, after a scientific revolution has been successful. The "psychoanalytic movement," as the inevitable supporting and propagandistic arm of a new development in science, had thus served its purpose and was on the wane.

The paradoxical fact is that in the United States, at the same time, a "movement" was being born. But it was a two-pronged development: one broadly social—the mental hygiene movement; the other, comparable to the movements we see in underdeveloped areas seeking to eke out their deficits—the efforts of psychiatry to escape from its neurological sterility and institutional thralldom, and to establish for itself a scientific foundation as effective therapeutic specialty. Thus, even before the political situation in Europe forced the massive transfer of psychoanalysis to the United States, the social situation in the United States had stimulated its importation from Europe. These factors operating together resulted in what has been called a "psychoanalytic movement" in the United States. But, as I have indicated, psychoanalysis was already a "normal science" by the time it became established here. It was the hope drawn from it by social idealists and idealistic neurologists and psychiatrists that generated what was really an extra-analytic movement in support of Freud's already accomplished scientific revolution.

As you will remember, until the twenties it was customary for American doctors to complete their educations in the medical centers of Europe. American neuropsychiatrists interested in the new science of psychoanalysis followed this course. Returning, they sought out their like-minded fellows and gathered into small psychoanalytic parlor groups, "to inform and animate each other." Like the European pioneers of whom we have recently been reminded by the publication of the *Minutes of the Vienna Psychoanalytic Society* (Nunberg & Federn, 1962), they, too, made their experiments in the psychoanalytic method; they, too, debated and discussed its data and concepts. But there was this difference in the early phase of American psychoanalysis: it was welcomed to a landing on the shores of the American scientific community by a significant group of its respected members; it received a serious intellectual hearing—was even warmly embraced. For the scientific beach-head had been gained in Europe; in the United States it was carried far inland on an indigenous "wave of the future." Its cogency made psychoanalysis a basic element of human sciences in America—an element which may be denied or disowned but of which there can be no riddance.

Thus, while we can see that the "psychoanalytic movement" was a sociohistorical necessity which had its day in Europe, we must also recognize that such a need never really existed here. The overoptimistic burgeoning of the mental hygiene movement in the twenties, and the subsequent expansion of psychiatry as a profession in the thirties were more than enough to foster the social acceptance and scientific prestige of psychoanalysis. In the end this fact has received a curious but not unfamiliar twist. For it was the wishful humanism of the mental hygiene movement and the need for a scientific foundation on the part of a psychiatry whose barrenness diminished its professional stature that, together, projected on psychoanalysis their own extravagant social hopes and ambitions; and both groups fell in love with the image.

The American penchant for getting things done, in so many ways an admirable quality with great social usefulness, provided the conditions for this phenomenon. There were so many mentally ill people; so many pleas and demands for help. Those of us who came to psychoanalysis from psychiatry were drawn to it intellectually, certainly, but we were also driven by social guilt, or something that passed for it. At any rate, dynamic psychiatry and dynamic psychotherapy, the American offspring of psychoanalysis and psychiatry, were generated by this drive (Gitelson, 1951). In different terms such a development was long ago envisioned and welcomed by Freud (1919); it is without question a rational and valid social application of psychoanalysis—one in which analysts may take some pride. Unhappily, however, this had not been the sole outcome.

I began my career in psychiatry and psychoanalysis near the beginning of this unhappy affair. I was, in fact, one of those who was a partner to it (Gitelson, 1942b). Under the influence, as I then thought, of the brave campaign to empty the mental hospitals into the child guidance clinics, and the pious hope that ultimately even the need for these would disappear through the instrumentality of psychoanalysis, I participated in these wishes and ambitions. I recognize some here, and there are others in this audience and elsewhere who were my companions in this venture into a brave new world. None of us can say that we were not disillusioned. Unfortunately many have also been bitterly disappointed. The difference is as between insight and transference reaction. The consequences have been several.

It was Freud and his more sophisticated collaborators and successors who first became aware of the existential boundaries of the therapeutic efficacy of the new technique; it was Freud who stated that only neurotic unhappiness and its manifestations could be affected by psychoanalysis, that there were certain limitations even here, and that the most important function of psychoanalysis belonged to its potentialities as an investigative method. The original repudiation of psychoanalysis in Europe which gave the psychoanalytic "movement" its extraordinary intensity was putatively directed against its theory. In the United States the theory not only found a place in the cognate sciences and among intellectuals generally, but from the beginning and until this day it has had its central place in psychiatry, no matter how misunderstood, disguised, or denied. Nevertheless the stronger appeal of psychoanalysis for American medicine derived from its psychotherapeutic and social hygienic promise. Too much was read into that promise. It is understandable, therefore, that it was the *presumed* universal and exclusive therapeutic efficacy of psychoanalysis that first drew criticism. Only secondary to this has psychoanalytic theory also come into question.

Paradoxically, but not incomprehensible to psychoanalysts, the child has turned against the father while accepting its birthright. Some of the more obvious and prevailing manifestations of this are seen in the terminology. The most well-established is the word "psychodynamic" as a replacement for psychoanalytic." Another word used similarly though far less extensively is "biodynamics." The phrase "psychoanalytically oriented" is tending to disappear. Increasingly present in current discourse are such terms as "interpersonal" and "transactional"; these sometimes appear in the context of the term "psychoanalysis" or stand by themselves and represent a more exclusive and inclusive generalization. In recent years we have also been hearing the term "adaptational psychodynamics" spoken of as the "introspectional branch of human biology" and said to be derived from Freud's "introduction of the tool of introspection" (sic!).[1] The curious fact is that insofar as such terms and propositions have substance, it is to be found in the survival in them of the pale shadow of existing psychoanalytic concepts. Zetzel's critique (1963) of the adaptive hypothesis shows this clearly.

Moving beyond such ambivalent attachment to psychoanalysis, and thus altogether beyond its horizon, are such developments as research that assumes the

[1] See "International Psychoanalytic Forum Meets in Amsterdam," N.Y. State District Branch (A.P.A.), *Bulletin*, December 1962, p. 11.

parity of animal and human psychology and of the psychoanalytic situation, and the psychotherapies derived from psychoanalysis. One is a degradation of the problem presented by the configuration which is the human mind; and the other represents insufficient sensitiveness to the meaning of unconscious processes, of resistance, and of transference, all of which are affected by the artifacts that are introduced in psychotherapy.

Lustman (1963), in a recent discussion of current issues in psychoanalytic research, comments on the regressive revival of a "nineteenth-century [antitheoretical] criterion of science which is [being] brought to bear on psychoanalytic theory" (p. 57). This is leading "some research analysts to abandon the analytic method for the comparative methodological safety of laboratory research . . . and others to not-so-creative borrowing" (p. 59). He says further, and I agree with him, that "The hue and cry for fastidious methods and meticulous theory seem not to recognize that method and theory cannot be superimposed, regardless of fit, but must be precisely geared to the phenomenon under study, that is, if it is to be meaningful even though not neat" (p. 56). Hence, while "lack of experimental sophistication" is one of the "sophisticated" criticisms of psychoanalysis, this attitude overlooks the fact that "*Experimental* sophistication and *scientific* sophistication "which prevents [or should prevent] analysts from distorting and diluting their area of study through the use of *available* experimental techniques developed by neighboring disciplines" (p. 61). Nevertheless, we are in the midst of increasing amounts of this sort of thing. The rationalization for it is that psychoanalysis has reached a dead end and is in need of a revolution.

There is in the psychiatric literature evidence that psychiatry is once again on the march in search of a scientific foundation (Grinker, 1964). It is held, for example, that psychoanalysis, together with hypnosis, the introspection of the phenomenologists, and the psychotherapy of Janet "swung the emphasis in psychiatry away from description toward deeper phenomena whose 'meanings were interpreted as causes and whose metaphors were considered as reality' "; it is said (regretfully) that the " 'dynamic' approaches within a dyad have superseded and even resulted in a depreciation of the basic psychiatric techniques through which so much progress was made in the 19th century"; it is said that "Observation of behavior rather than inference about feelings [sic!] is the keystone of psychiatric research"; it is said that "the acquisition and validity-testing of behavioral data are the core operations of psychiatry as a science," and that "careful clinical observations and descriptions *as contrasted with inferences based on stereotypes* [italics added] yield information which can be handled statistically and reported in form suitable for replication and for correlation with other measurable systems" (pp. 229–231). Such expressions in the community of "big science" are significant for psychoanalysis because they represent a return of the repressed in the form of the wish to reverse history by expunging the effects that psychoanalysis has exerted and still exerts on psychiatry— even if this be only in the form of "psychodynamics."

I think these statements represent repudiations of psychoanalysis.

This is the sort of thing which I have referred to previously as rebellion without a cause. This is a return to a naturalistic preparadigmatic state of science in which human phenomenology is dehydrated into existence in "a total field of multiple transactions *without connotations of significance, hierarchical importance or conceptual devices called levels*" (Grinker, 1964, p. 234, italics added). In effect, we are being advised to go fishing with whatever bait we have and see what we come up with. There is nothing wrong with this except for its scientific atavism. It is rather late in the day for us to disregard the fact that we know the differential ecology of trout and shark, and that to catch one or the other we have to know where we are and what we are looking for. It is too late for us to expunge the experience which 60 years of psychoanalysis has brought to us. Nevertheless, scientism in the accoutrements of science seems to have larger attractions.

Paul Weiss (1962) has discussed a comparable problem in biology, "Experience prompts and guides experiment," he says, and "experiments in turn confirm or amplify or modify the content of experience. . . . Experience, experiment and logic play back and forth upon each other in mutual enhancement; it takes this triple interplay to promote knowledge" (p. 468). But (in biology) experiment is a "junior partner in this partnership." Its targets must be the products of experience which should shape expectation, and expectation should dictate experiment. "The historic successes of our predecessors still argue for the virtue of taking off for the exploration of the unknown from clearcut questions born from expectations, not from vague expectancy . . ." (p. 469), and expectations arise from experience.

We can see the cogency of this to our own field if we are reminded of the fact that it was Freud's preliminary experience with hypnosis and with forced verbalization which produced the "expectations" which resulted in that most long-sustained and most often repeated of all experiments—the use of free association in the analytic situation. In the years that have passed it has become clear that the very knowledge we have gained from that experiment has, within the context of psychoanalysis, precluded its modification. For it happens to have shown itself to be exquisitely suited for both confronting nature "with conditions unprecedented in her standard repertory" (Weiss, 1962) *and at the same time* preserving full respect for the human prerogatives of the subject. An alternative experiment capable of demonstrating endopsychic and interpsychic processes without violating our human responsibility has not yet been devised. Thus we are confronted by a paradox for scientific method; the psychoanalytic experiment has itself become an extended life experience, which, as such, provides a foundation for possible conventional experiments based on expectations logically derived from that experience.

What I am trying to demonstrate is that psychoanalysis, an aspect of biology, occupies a middle ground between the extreme scientific positions of physics and historical learning. The one concentrates on general principles expressible in a minimal number of formulae. The other is concerned with "the particular specific and often unique shape of events." The life sciences have moved along this axis from the descriptive-normative toward the analytical-formulative (Weiss, 1962). But psychoanalysis, like biology, will never attain, as such, the putatively complete reductionism of physics. Like biology, it is destined to retain its autonomy—its mechanisms will have to be studied in their own right and in their full diversity; its generalizations, which are bound to stop short of the inclusiveness of the laws of physics, may each be subject to experimentation. But no such studies of the human personality will have their necessary scientific sophistication, no matter how refined their "design," unless they are governed by the psychoanalytic experience.

As a matter of fact, a number of psychoanalytic generalizations have been examined by nonanalytic methods, but, so far as I am aware, no such study has been other than confirmative. Nothing has been found that did not fit psychoanalytic theory when it was psychoanalytic theory that was being tested. Hartmann (1959) has said of such efforts that on the whole they have "not so far decisively contributed toward a clarification or systematization of psychoanalytic theory" (p. 349). Despite all claims to the contrary, the prime requirements for a scientific revolution are lacking: apparent counterinstances which do not articulate with existing theory, and new theory which bears more heavily on known facts. When these considerations are kept in mind, assertions such as "psychoanalysis . . . has not become the therapeutic answer" and psychoanalysis "seems to be mired in a theoretical rut vigilantly guarded by the orthodox and, except for relatively few examples, prevented from commingling with science" (Grinker, 1964, p. 228)—such assertions, I repeat, remain simply that. The one is irrelevant; the other is incorrect.

This is only a sampling of the situation out of which there has developed a new "movement"—though none of its protagonists would like to consider it that. It is a movement without scientific grounds: it has not invalidated any of the data of psychoanalysis; it ignores the articulations which psychoanalysis has effected between its data and its theory; it has not exposed new data which cannot be articulated with psychoanalytic theory: it appears to be unaware of the developments in psychoanalytic ego psychology, which in fact meet the criticisms that have been directed against the putative solipsism of psychoanalytic theory; and most important, it has not produced the shadow of a comprehensive theory that can be weighed against psychoanalytic theory and the data on which it is based. We are presented with a point of view which has no thesis—only an antithesis in the form of a shibboleth: "dogmatic orthodoxy."

Let me refer again to Kuhn's (1963) monograph. I shall quote from it while making running insertions to clarify points specifically relevant to psychoanalysis:

"Let us then assume," Kuhn says,

That crises [in science] are a necessary precondition for the emergence of novel theories and ask how scientists respond to their existence. Part of the answer, as obvious as it is important, can be discovered *by noting first what scientists never do* when confronted by even prolonged and severe anomalies . . . *they do not renounce the paradigm that has led them into crisis.* They do not, that is, treat anomalies as counterinstances. . . . this generalization is simply a statement from historic fact. . . . Once it has achieved the status of a paradigm, *a scientific theory is declared invalid only if an alternative candidate is available to take its place* [p. 77; all italics added].

It is not enough to dream wishfully for the coming into being of an alternative candidate for paradigm status. Nor, as I have said before, does an apparently new fact without an adequate theory to account for it upset a previous theory; it simply becomes one of the puzzles which the existing theory may not be able to solve, though it may indeed one day be solved by the actual birth of a new paradigm.

This is the state of affairs in psychoanalysis. No more than other scientists, can psychoanalysts reject their paradigms when faced with anomalies or counterinstances.

They could not do so and still remain scientists.

Though history is unlikely to record their names, some men have undoubtedly been driven to desert science because of their inability to tolerate crisis. Like artists, creative scientists [and psychoanalysts] must occasionally be able to live in a world out of joint . . . [and to endure] the "essential tension" implicit in scientific research. . . . Once a paradigm through which to view nature has been found, there is no such thing as research in the absence of the paradigm. To reject one paradigm without simultaneously substituting another is to reject science itself. That act reflects not on the paradigm but on the man. Inevitably he will be seen by his colleagues as "the carpenter who blames his tools."

. . . [For] there is no such thing as research without counterinstances . . . the puzzles that constitute normal science exist only because no paradigm that provides a basis for scientific research [in any field] ever completely resolves all its problems. . . . Every problem that normal science sees as a puzzle can be seen, from another viewpoint, as a counterinstance and thus as a source of crisis [pp. 77-79].

Restating the issue in my own terms, it is not enough to declare that there are seeming divergences from theory, as is the case with those who turn away from psychoanalysis. Such divergences must in fact be proven to be unassimilable into the existing theory, whose validity, as I have shown, must in the meanwhile be assumed. If this cannot be accomplished, then indeed a new theory must be attempted. But the evidence for its cogency must be convincing if it is to generate a scientific revolution. We do not have such evidence.

This brings me again to the history of American psychoanalysis. We have seen that, like the other sciences, psychoanalysis has had its paradoxical social growth: its arduous and small beginnings, its heyday of enthusiastic and rapid development, and, in the United States, its attainment of at least relatively large organizational stature with its inevitable offshoots. What is interesting and important for us today is the particular nature of the paradox which has characterized the growth of psychoanalysis here.

It can be said that in the United States psychoanalysis and psychiatry grew up together. At the same time that the Nazi storm was scattering psychoanalysis in Europe, psychiatry was at last becoming a profession in the United States. The American Board of Psychiatry and Neurology was organized in 1934; its examinations paid more than a little attention to "psychodynamics." As early as 1932 psychiatrists were receiving foundation support for higher level training in psychiatry—that is, in psychoanalysis.[2] In my own psychiatric beginnings, case conferences were already "psychoanalytically oriented"; out of a group of 10 interns (there were no "residents"), I knew three who were being formally analyzed, while the rest of us were, of course, "analyzing" each other. When I was being examined for the Board by one of the great psychiatrists of the day I did not find it surprising or unfair or offensive that he asked me to account psychoanalytically for the disappearance of a lifelong stammer in the acutely ill schizophrenic patient who had been assigned to me. The point is that psychoanalysis in the United States grew simultaneously from two directions. Its pioneers and its students arrived on the scene together.

These circumstances did not stem from a psychoanalytic movement. As we have seen, that had had its necessary day in Europe. In the United States the psychoanalytic idea no longer needed such fosterage. Psychiatrists were not turning to the new psychoanalytic institutes because these were conducting a campaign for converts. The students of the institutes were the progeny of the mental hygiene movement and of the reborn psychiatry of the thirties. They were turning toward what seemed a promise for the future to many

[2] At the Chicago Institute for Psychoanalysis, for example.

of their leaders as well as to themselves. The Second World War affirmed this (Gitelson, 1956). Psychoanalysis, deployed as dynamic psychiatry, was able to meet the demands of a brutal reality. Psychiatry discovered that even with only the rudiments of psychoanalytic theory it was possible for medical officers to qualify for the kind of psychotherapeutic improvisation that Freud (1919) had looked forward to. The military experience confirmed for psychiatry its own hopes of the thirties that psychoanalysis could indeed provide it with a psychotherapeutic rationale. The postwar consequence was a tremendous surge toward psychiatry and psychoanalysis as a *profession*. I state this in the singular because the choice was unitary; psychiatry without psychoanalysis had become unthinkable (Brosin, 1952; Gitelson, 1951, 1956, 1962c).

It seems necessary to repeat, *for this is the crux of the matter:* the rapid growth of American psychoanalysis in the last 20 years has been the consequence of its being caught in the current of a new social movement—now the mental *health* movement. Psychiatry carried psychoanalysis along for its own purposes in this movement and is disappointed to discover that the real thing is rather more of a burden than the idea of it.[3] On the other hand, *psychoanalysis has become involved in a crisis which is not its own.* The nature of its beginnings in America, and the perpetuation of this in its statutory requirements for affiliation with psychiatry, have placed psychoanalysis in an impossible position for the untrammeled development of its

---

[3] The "Associated Psychiatric Faculties" of Chicago (Brosin, 1952), which attempted for some years to operate a unified training program in collaboration with the Chicago Institute for Psychoanalysis, in the end suspended the effort.

intrinsic scientific possibilities. Psychoanalysts, having had social responsibility thrust upon them by the exigencies of the World War crisis, have found themselves committed to it in peace.

Reacting to this pressure, the American Psychoanalytic Association at one point considered the possibility of drastically modifying basic principles of training (Gitelson, 1948b). A number of institutes for a time actually experimented with modifications. While all this proved fruitless, there *was* a considerable postwar expansion of existing institutes, an increase in their number, and a corresponding increase in admissions to training. The impelling motives were, first, the feeling that it was necessary to match the expansion of a psychiatry in which "dynamic psychology" had become an established fact of life; and, second, the wish to take advantage of government money which had become available for that purpose. Not only was there a great increase in the number of candidates, but in the opposite direction there was an unprecedented demand, to which analysts responded, to undertake the teaching of the "dynamic psychiatry" which the best residencies required. This was not a bad idea. Psychiatry and psychoanalysis can supplement each other. But neither has been content with that, and each has suffered consequences (Gitelson, 1962c).

On the one hand, those engaged in the training of psychiatrists have attempted an outright transplantation of psychoanalysis into the wards and clinics (ibid). Alternatively, those trained in these wards and clinics have tended to bring with them into analysis often ineradicable eclectic attitudes which are incompatible with the postulates and methods of a special field (Gitelson, 1954). I am in agreement with Rado's position (as quoted by Grinker, 1964) that "psychiatry is a heterogeneous collection of basic sciences without unified structure" (p. 229). In this respect it is like medicine whose therapeutic eclecticism is necessarily dictated by the variety of the fields of knowledge which are concerned with the phenomenon in which it is interested. It need be no derogation to speak of psychiatry as riding "in all directions" (Grinker, 1964). Psychiatry as such is not a science; it would indèed be derelict if it did not search out everything the natural and social sciences can offer to support its great and necessary labor. But psychoanalysis *is* a basic science; despite the fact of its unavoidable embedment in a special therapeutic procedure, it is first and foremost human individual psychology. Out of the necessity of its subject matter *it cannot be otherwise* than that its postulates, theories, and methods must be special and separate. Psychoanalysis is not psychiatry; it is only selectively applicable in psychiatry, even as mechanics or chemistry or molecular biology are applicable in medicine. Psychiatry can enrich the life experience of the psychoanalyst. It cannot determine the scientific course of psychoanalysis. Thus, only in the light of the history of psychoanalysis in the United States can one accept as reasonable a recent editorial in the *Journal of the American Medical Association* (1964) which begins with the statement: "Psychiatry *and* [italics added] psychoanalysis today have not lived up to their well-advertised and hoped-for promise" (p. 946). I would consider this a fitting obituary for a marriage of convenience.

I have been discussing the historical basis of the

crisis which psychoanalysis has borrowed from psychiatry. However, this is not its only problem. In another place (1964) I have referred at some length to other factors that need to be considered, and in the present context I shall again mention one of them. I refer to our own discontent with the apparent stasis in the scientific development of psychoanalysis. Many are puzzled and troubled that there seems to be no sign of impending "break-throughs"—even though some of the pessimists have themselves been brilliant participants in the achievements of the past. We tend to overlook or to discount the continuing and able spadework which goes on and which is, as I have noted, the task of any science during its "normal" period of testing and working through (Kuhn, 1963). More than we like to contemplate, we are reacting to the conditions of which I have been speaking, and to the existential anxiety of our times (Gitelson, 1964). There may be among ourselves a return of the repressed. Such factors, I think, may be having their reflected as well as direct effects on younger colleagues particularly. Add to this the social conditions created by the present inflation of scientific currency (Gitelson, 1964; Lustman, 1963), and we receive some hint of the motives for the excessive ardor attached to the hope for and the pursuit of a revolution in psychoanalysis. In some instances the latter has burst through the boundaries of our field (Lustman, 1963).

This is not to say that there is not a quiet ferment going on within the body of psychoanalysis today. There have always been the individuals, the unique ones among us—some of them so-called controversial figures—who have been continually stirring the brew we have elected to cook.[4] There are also informal and more or less formal small groups pursuing the solution of puzzles generated by and relevant to the psychoanalytic paradigm.[5] All this is characteristic of a living science during its longer or shorter "normal" state after one paradigmatic revolution and before the *bona fide* appearance of another one. Revolutions arise from such internal ferment. They do not, like tumorous growths "unrestrained by differentiation and functional adjustment" (Weiss, 1962), burst through their organismal boundaries. Revolutions in science are born, not made. Unfortunately, in American psychoanalysis this is obscured by the fact that schism has had the putative direction of "liberalization." Whatever implications it may have for the therapeutic applications of psychoanalysis, this appealing political term applied to the work of a science serves to obscure the definition of that science rather than to report a revolutionary development in it.

It may be that this view will seem oriented toward a policy of isolation. On the contrary, I am proposing a policy of "differentiation and functional adjustment" within the context of the human sciences as a whole. This is not a new proposal. It is the position arrived at nearly 40 years ago by Freud (1926, 1927). I myself have moved through most of my career to come to it.

To sustain this position it is necessary to define clearly the differences between psychoanalysis as a profession and psychoanalysis as a scientific activity. With regard to the first, we have gone a great way in

[4] Erikson's and Rapaport's work may be considered examples of this.

[5] The collaboration of Hartmann, Kris and Loewenstein, and of the Yale group are examples.

the United States. Much of what I have said is concerned with the history of that course and its consequences. These consequences include much that is good. I think it is correct that the therapeutic application of psychoanalysis and its derivatives have found a wider scope here than anywhere else in the Western world; nor is this to be decried. But the problems of psychoanalysis in the United States have arisen because the course of this achievement has obscured the boundaries of psychoanalysis as an investigative science. Therapeutic versatility and scientific rigor are incompatible. Those who impugn psychoanalysis as "rigid" overlook this. They do not recognize, or they refuse to accept, the necessity for the integrity of the classical model of the psychoanalytic situation as the only available condition for the controlled study of human individual psychology in its deepest sense.

Perhaps this is too much to ask of doctors of medicine whose calling stems from the healing impulse. Perhaps it is necessary to revise the exclusive operational relationship between psychoanalysis and psychiatry. Perhaps we must realize that we need to redefine our place in the family of sciences and to redesign our format accordingly.

Freud's view (1927) was that psychoanalysis "is not a specialized branch of medicine" and that "A scheme of training for psychoanalysts . . . must include elements from the mental sciences, from psychology, the history of civilization and sociology, as well as from anatomy, biology and the study of evolution" (p. 252). Kubie (1954, 1957) not so long ago gave considerable thought to these problems and proposed a specialized modern curriculum and a distinctive degree for students primarily interested in psychotherapy (and psychoanalysis?). More recently Shakow (1962) proposed that if psychoanalytic institutes are to be attached to universities, then they ought to have independent academic status and be available to all relevant departments, including the medical school. I do not discount such ideas. They may perhaps one day materialize. But I think it is necessary to start from where we are today.

Therapeutic emphasis in psychoanalytic training is eventuating in psychoanalytic careers which are increasingly eclectic, increasingly indistinguishable from the skilled practice of intensive psychotherapy, increasingly validating the position of those who a few years back favored the establishment of a psychoanalytic subspecialty board of the American Board of Psychiatry and Neurology. No one can object to this insofar as it provides a higher grade of professional care for those who can benefit from it. For I think the primary function of psychiatry is *mental healing.* Therapeutic psychoanalysis and its modifications and derivatives—whether they carry the name or not—are therefore here to stay. But the danger foreseen by Freud (1927), and now materializing, is that therapeutic investment may submerge scientific development. None more than psychoanalysts understand and value the importance of the ramifications of *affect, feeling,* and *emotion;* and none are more subject to the essentially anti-intellectual trends which, in recent years, have been expressing themselves "intellectually" toward the psychoanalytic method of scientific investigation. The problems for psychoanalytic training today arise from these facts.

In the same context as that from which I previously quoted him, Freud (1927) said: "I am bound to admit that, so long as schools such as we desire for the training of analysts are not yet in existence, people who have had a preliminary education in medicine are the best material for future analysts" (p. 257). This situation has not changed. The history of psychoanalysis in this country commits it to training medically qualified therapeutic specialists. Does this mean that we may not consider the qualifications which are important for those who can be psychoanalysts?

Perhaps it is necessary to cast a wider net for students of psychoanalysis. The emotional qualities that insure the fulfillment of the human obligation to patients are basic to the practice of medicine. But in the psychoanalytic field the practitioner must also have the intellectual qualities and scope which will bring to it the necessary scientific sophistication. The present timorous and tentative approach to the training of specialists from other disciplines, *for research in their own fields,* conceivably might be bolder and broadened into a program of unhedged training which would fully qualify them for a research career in psychoanalysis itself. The prevailing tendency to place exclusive value on antecedent psychiatric training as such may need to be revised in respect to the barrier it erects against scientists with other qualifications who might advance the conceptual horizon of psychoanalysis (Shakow, 1962). While there may have been valid reasons in the late thirties for American psychoanalysis to declare its exclusive adhesion to medicine as its parent discipline, the question must be raised whether these reasons retain their cogency today. In respect to this it may be comforting to recall that psychiatry itself has gone a long way since then and is looking with favor on the practice of psychotherapy by psychologists, the clergy, and other persons of good will.

It is clear that I have returned to the "question of lay analysis" (Freud, 1926). I have been turned in this direction by my consideration of the history of psychoanalysis in America. *I think the time has come for psychoanalysis to accept its identity as a separate scientific discipline,* whose practitioners can be various kinds of intellectually qualified persons who are humanly qualified for the human experiment that is the psychoanalytic situation.

It could be argued that the debate in which I have been engaged is itself evidence of a scientific crisis *in* psychoanalysis and of a pending scientific revolution in the field. This debate, however, is not concerned with the scientific substance of psychoanalysis but with the social and psychological issues surrounding that substance. It is a debate peculiar to our field, in which matrix cannot with ease be separated from substance. It is a debate which is compelled by what is clearly a "countermovement" to psychoanalysis, which itself had long ago ceased to be a "movement" and had become concerned only with its substance.

I suppose I should feel apologetic to this audience for belaboring it with such argumentation as I have. I feel no such need. I think it is necessary for all of us to be reminded of what we know. The point is that analysis does not end all conflict; it merely provides us with a tool for dealing with it under future unforeseen conditions of life which may evoke old conflicts and stimulate new ones. As it happens, Freud predicted such future conditions in the United States, and we are now in their midst. The repressed has returned. In a new social situation which attaches rich secondary gains compliance with conventional science the effort at rerepression is taking the form of dilution or denial of what we know. We suffer not only from confusion about what psychoanalysis is, but also from irresolution about what its position should be. We are caught in an identity conflict between psychiatry, which is a therapeutic specialty of medicine, and psychoanalysis, which is a basic science. In such a situation, confrontation, I hope, may free us to analyze rather than to "act," and to behave in accordance with our understanding.

# References

Alexander, F. (1925), Metapsychological description of the process of cure. *Internat. J. Psycho-Anal.*, 6:13-34.

———— (1930), The neurotic character. *Internat. J. Psycho-Anal.*, 11:292-311.

———— (1943), Fundamental concepts of psychosomatic research. *Psychosom. Med.*, 5:205-210.

Armstrong, S., Jr. (1958), Editorial. *Amer. J. Med.*, 24:323-333.

Axelrod, P. I. (1944), An experiment in group therapy with shy adolescent girls. *Amer. J. Orthopsychiat.*, 14:616.

Balint, A. & Balint, M. (1939), On transference and countertransference. *Internat. J. Psycho-Anal.*, 20:223-230.

Balint, M. (1950), Changing therapeutic aims and techniques in psychoanalysis. *Internat. J. Psycho-Anal.*, 31:117-124.

Bandler, B. (1958), Some conceptual tendencies in the psychosomatic movement. *Amer. J. Psychiat.*, 115:36-43.

Benedek, T. (1953), Dynamics of the countertransference. *Bull. Menninger Clinic*, 17:201-208.

Benjamin, J. D. (1952), Directions and problems in psychiatric research. *Psychosom. Med.*, 14:1-9.

———— (1961), Knowledge, conviction and ignorance. *J. Med. Educ.*, 36:117-132.

Beres, D. (1950), Effects of extreme deprivation in infancy on psychic structure in adolescence. *The Psychoanalytic Study of the Child*, 5:212-235. New York: International Universities Press.

# References

———— (1956), Ego deviations and the concept of schizophrenia. *The Psychoanalytic Study of the Child*, 11:164–235. New York: International Universities Press.

———— Schaeffer, V., & Goldman, J. (1946), Psychiatric program in an agency serving youth. *Amer. J. Orthopsychiat.*, 16:84–99.

Berkman, M., Rappaport, E., & Sulzberger, B. (1939), The therapeutic effects of an authoritative situation in children's courts. *Amer. J. Orthopsychiat.*, 9:347.

Berman, L. (1949), Countertransference and attitudes of the analyst in the therapeutic process. *Psychiat.*,12:159–166.

Bettelheim, B. (1963), Eichmann, the system, the victims. *New Republic*, 148:23–33.

Bibring, E. (1947), The so-called English school of psychoanalysis. *Psychoanal. Quart.*, 16:69–93.

———— (1954), Psychoanalysis and the dynamic psychotherapies. *J. Amer. Psychoanal. Assn.*, 2:745–770.

Binger, C. (1951), On so-called psychogenic influences in essential hypertension. *Psychosom. Med.*, 13:273–276.

Blos, P. (1946), Psychological counseling of college students. *Amer. J. Orthopsychiat.*, 16:571.

Bonaparte, M. (1950), Psyche in nature or the limits of psychogenesis. *Internat. J. Psycho-Anal.*, 31:48–52.

Boring, E. G. (1965), The social stimulus to creativity. *Science*, 142:622–623.

Bowlby, J. (1942), *Personality and Mental Illness.* New York: Emerson Books.

Brenman, M. (1952), On teasing and being teased; and the problem of "moral masochism." *The Psychoanalytic Study of the Child*, 7:264–285. New York: International Universities Press.

Bromberg, W. & Rogers, C. (1946), Authority in the treatment of delinquents. *Amer. J. Orthopsychiat.*, 16:672.

Brosin, H. W. (1952), Psychoanalytic training for psychiatric residents and others. *Amer. J. Psychiat.*, 109:188–195.

Brunswick, R. M. (1940), The preoedipal phase of the libido development. In: *The Psychoanalytic Reader*, Ed. R. Fliess. New York: International Universities Press, 1948, pp. 261–284.

Cannon, W. B. (1920), *Bodily Changes in Pain, Hunger, Fear, and Rage.* New York: Harper, 1936.

Carmichael, H. T. (1956), Sound film recording of psychoanalytic therapy. *J. Iowa State Med. Soc.*, 46:590–595.

Church, A. S. (1946), Adolescence and juvenile delinquency. *Nervous Child*, 4:142–146.

Conant, J. B. (1947), *On Understanding Science.* New Haven: Yale University Press.

Curran, F. J. (1939), The drama as a therapeutic measure in adolescence. *Amer. J. Orthopsychiat.*, 9:215–231.

———— (1940), Psychotherapeutic problems of puberty. *Amer. J. Orthopsychiat.*, 10:510–521.

Deutsch, F. (1939), The choice of organ in organ neurosis. *Internat. J. Psycho-Anal.*, 20:252–262.

———— (1953), *The Psychosomatic Concept in Psychoanalysis.* New York: International Universities Press.

Deutsch, H. (1930), Hysterical fate neurosis. In: *Neuroses and Character Types.* New York: International Universities Press, 1965, pp. 14–28.

———— (1942), Some forms of emotional disturbance and their relationship to schizophrenia. *Psychoanal. Quart.*, 11:301–321.

Drewry, H. H. (1939), Treatment possibilities in an institution for delinquents. *Amer. J. Orthopsychiat.*, 9:379–386.

Eisner, E. A. (1945), Relationship formed by a sexually delinquent adolescent girl. *Amer. J. Orthopsychiat.*, 15:301–308.

Eissler, K. (1953), The effect of the structure of the ego on psychoanalytic technique. *J. Amer. Psychoanal. Assn.*, 1:104–143.

Engle, G. (1958a), Discussion of "Psychosomatic phenomena: conversion of anxiety equivalent? Theoretical and therapeutic implications," by M. Gitelson. Presented to the Chicago Psychoanalytic Society.

———— (1958b), Discussion of "Some conceptual tendencies in the psychosomatic movement," by B. Bandler. *Amer. J. Psychiat.*, 115:42–43.

English, H. B. & English, A. C. (1958), *Comprehensive Dictionary of Psychological and Psychoanalytical Terms.* New York: McKay.

Erikson, E. H. (1950), *Childhood and Society.* New York: Norton.

Fenichel, O. (1931a), The pregenital antecedents of the oedipus complex. In: *Collected Papers*, I. New York: Norton, 1953, pp. 181–203.

# References

———— (1931b), Specific forms of the oedipus complex. In: *Collected Papers*, I. New York: Norton, 1953, pp. 204–220.

———— (1938), Ego disturbances and their treatment. In: *Collected Papers*, II. New York: Norton, 1954, pp. 109–128.

———— (1939a), The counterphobic attitude. In: *Collected Papers*, II. New York: Norton, 1954, pp. 163–173.

———— (1939b), *Problems of Psychoanalytic Technique*. New York: Psychoanalytic Quarterly, 1941.

———— (1945), *Psychoanalytic Theory of Neuroses*. New York: Norton.

Ferenczi, S. (1909), Introjection and transference. In: *Sex and Psychoanalysis*. New York: Brunner, 1950, pp. 35–93.

———— (1932), The therapeutic argument. In: *Final Contributions to the Problems and Methods of Psychoanalysis*. New York: Basic Books, 1955, p. 260.

Fliess, R. (1942), The metapsychology of the analyst. *Psychoanal. Quart.*, 11:211–227.

Flugel, J. C. (1945), *Man, Morals and Society*. New York: International Universities Press.

Foxe, A. N. (1944), Psychopathic behavior. *Amer. J. Orthopsychiat.*, 14:308–313.

Freud, A. (1936), *The Ego and the Mechanisms of Defense*. New York: International Universities Press, 1966.

———— (1950), Problems of training analysis. In: *Indications for Child Analysis: The Writings of Anna Freud*, Vol. 4. New York: International Universities Press, 1968, pp. 407–421.

———— (1959), Lectures to the Los Angeles Psychoanalytic Society. Abstracted by H. Tausend, reporter. *Bull. Phila. Assn. Psychoanal.*, 9:111–112.

Freud, S. (1905), Fragment of an analysis of a case of hysteria. *Standard Edition*, 7:3–122. London: Hogarth Press, 1953.

———— (1910a), A special type of object choice made by men. *Standard Edition*, 11:164–175. London: Hogarth Press, 1957.

———— (1910b), The future prospects of psycho-analytic therapy. *Standard Edition*, 11:140–151. London: Hogarth Press, 1957.

———— (1913), On beginning the treatment. *Standard Edition*, 12:122–144. London: Hogarth Press, 1958.

———— (1916), Some character types met with in psycho-analytic work. *Standard Edition,* 14:311-333. London: Hogarth Press, 1957.

———— (1917), A metapsychological supplement to the theory of dreams. *Standard Edition,* 14:219-235. London: Hogarth Press, 1957.

———— (1919), Lines of advance in psychoanalytic therapy. *Standard Edition,* 17:158-168. London: Hogarth Press, 1955.

———— (1921), Group psychology and the analysis of the ego. *Standard Edition,* 18:67-143. London: Hogarth Press, 1955.

———— (1924), Neurosis and psychosis. *Standard Edition,* 19:148-153. London: Hogarth Press, 1961.

———— (1926), The question of lay analysis. *Standard Edition,* 20:179-250. London: Hogarth Press, 1959.

———— (1927), Postscript to the question of lay analysis. *Standard Edition,* 20:251-258. London: Hogarth Press, 1959.

———— (1931a), Female sexuality. *Standard Edition,* 21:223-243. London: Hogarth Press, 1961.

———— (1931b), Libidinal types. *Standard Edition,* 21:215-220. London: Hogarth Press, 1961.

———— (1933), New introductory lectures on psycho-analysis. *Standard Edition,* 22:3-182. London: Hogarth Press, 1964.

———— (1937), Analysis terminable and interminable. *Standard Edition,* 23:211-253. London: Hogarth Press, 1964.

Fromm-Reichmann, F. (1948), Notes on the development of treatment of schizophrenics by psychoanalytic psychotherapy. *Psychiat.,* 11:263-273.

Gabriel, B. (1944), Group treatment for adolescent girls. *Amer. J. Orthopsychiat.,* 14:593-602.

Gardner, G. E. & Wollan, K. I. (1941), Activity interview in the study of delinquency. *Amer. J. Orthopsychiat.,* 11:143-149.

Gesell, A. (1940), *The First Five Years of Life.* New York: Harper.

Gitelson, M. (1942a), Direct psychotherapy in adolescence. *Amer. J. Orthopsychiat.,* 12:1-23. *This Volume,* pp. 35-61.

———— (1942b), Evaluation of therapeutic results in psychotherapy. In: *Proceedings of the Brief Psychotherapy Council.* Chicago: Institute for Psychoanalysis.

———— (1944), Intellectuality in the defense transference. *Psychiat.,* 7:73-86. *This Volume,* pp. 62-98.

# References

———— (1948a), Character synthesis. *Amer. J. Orthopsychiat.*, 18:422–431. *This Volume*, pp. 99–114.

———— (1948b), Problems of psychoanalytic training. *Psychoanal. Quart.*, 17:198–211. *This Volume*, pp. 142–155.

———— (1951), Psychoanalysis and dynamic psychiatry. *AMA Arch. Neurol. & Psychiat.*, 66:280–288.

———— (1952a), Emotional position of the analyst in the psychoanalytic situation. *Internat. J. Psycho-Anal.*, 33:1–10. *This Volume*, pp. 173–200.

———— (1952b), Re-evaluation of the role of the Oedipus complex. *Internat. J. Psycho-Anal.*, 33:351–354. *This Volume*, pp. 201–210.

———— (1954), Therapeutic problems in the analysis of the "normal" candidate. *Internat. J. Psycho-Anal.*, 35:174–183. *This Volume*, pp. 211–238.

———— (1956), Psychoanalyst, U.S.A. *Amer. J. Psychiat.*, 112:700–705. *This Volume*, pp. 239–253.

———— (1958), On ego distortion. *Internat. J. Psycho-Anal.*, 39:245–257. *This Volume*, pp. 254–290.

———— (1962a), Communication from the president about the neoanalytic movement. *Internat. J. Psycho-Anal.*, 43:362–375.

———— (1962b), On the curative factors in the first phase of psychoanalysis. *Internat. J. Psycho-Anal.*, 43:194–205. *This Volume*, pp.

———— (1962c), The place of psychoanalysis in psychiatric training. *Bull. Menninger Clinic*, 26:57–72.

———— (1964), On the present scientific and social position of psychoanalysis. *Internat. J. Psycho-Anal.*, 44:521–524. *This Volume*, pp. 342–359.

Glover, E. (1931), The therapeutic effects of inexact interpretation. In: *The Technique of Psychoanalysis*. New York: International Universities Press, 1955, pp. 353–366.

———— (1943), The concept of dissociation. In: *On the Early Development of Mind*. New York: International Universities Press, 1956, pp. 307–323.

———— (1945), Examination of the Klein system of child psychology. *The Psychoanalytic Study of the Child*, 1:75–118. New York: International Universities Press.

———— (1955), *The Technique of Psychoanalysis*. New York: International Universities Press.

_____ (1956), The frontiers of psycho-analysis. In: *On the Early Development of Mind.* New York: International Universities Press, pp. 421–440.

_____ Fenichel, O., Strachey, J., Bergler, E., Nunberg, H., & Bibring, E. (1937), Symposium on the theory of the therapeutic results of psychoanalysis. *Internat. J. Psycho-Anal.,* 18:125–189.

Greenacre, P. (1945), Conscience in the psychopath. In: *Trauma, Growth, and Personality.* New York, International Universities Press, 1952, pp. 165–187.

_____ (1952), Pregenital patterning. In: *Trauma, Growth, and Personality.* New York: International Universities Press, pp. 293–302.

_____ (1954), The role of transference: practical considerations in relation to psychoanalytic therapy. In: *Emotional Growth.* New York: International Universities Press, 1971, pp. 627–640.

_____ (1958), Toward an understanding of the physical nucleus of some defense reactions. In: *Emotional Growth.* New York: International Universities Press, 1971 pp. 128–144.

_____ (1959), Certain technical problems in the transference relationship. In: *Emotional Growth.* New York: International Universities Press, pp. 651–669.

Greene, W. A., Jr. (1956), Process in psychosomatic disorders. *Psychosom. Med.,* 18:150–158.

Greenson, R. R. (1960), Empathy and its vicissitudes. *Internat. J. Psycho-Anal.,* 41:418–424.

Gregg, A. (1953), The place of psychoanalysis in medicine. In: Alexander, F. & Ross, H., *Twenty Years of Psychoanalysis.* New York: Norton, pp. 28–49.

Grinberg, L. (1963), Relations between psycho-analysts. *Internat. J. Psycho-Anal.,* 44:362–367.

Grinker, R. R. (1953), Some current trends and hypotheses of psychosomatic research. In: *The Psychosomatic Concept in Psychoanalysis,* Ed. F. Deutsch. New York: International Universities Press, pp. 37–62.

_____ (1964), Psychiatry rides madly in all directions. *AMA Arch. Gen. Psychiat.,* 10:228–237.

Grossman, G. (1938), The role of the institution in the treatment of delinquency. *Amer. J. Orthopsychiat.,* 8:148–157.

# References

Grotjahn, M. (1953), Panel presentation on: recent trends in psychoanalytic training. Unpublished.

Hacker, F. J. & Geleerd, E. R. (1945), Freedom and authority in adolescence. *Amer. J. Orthopsychiat.*, 15:621-630.

Ham, G. C., Alexander, F., & Carmichael, H. T. (1951), A psychosomatic theory of thyrotoxicosis. *Psychosom. Med.*, 13:18-35.

Harris, I. D. (1962), Dreams about the analyst. *Internat. J. Psycho-Anal.*, 43:151-158.

Hartmann, H. (1939a), *Ego Psychology and the Problem of Adaptation*. New York: International Universities Press, 1958.

_____ (1939b), Psycho-analysis and the concept of health. In: *Essays on Ego Psychology*. New York: International Universities Press, 1964, pp. 1-18.

_____ (1952), Mutual influences in the development of the ego and the id. In: *Essays on Ego Psychology*. New York: International Universities Press, 1964, pp. 155-181.

_____ (1959), Psychoanalysis as a scientific theory. In: *Essays on Ego Psychology*. New York: International Universities Press, 1964, pp. 318-350.

_____ (1960), *Psychoanalysis and Moral Values*. New York: International Universities Press.

Heimann, P. (1950), On counter-transference. *Internat. J. Psycho-Anal.*, 31:81-84.

_____ (1952), A contribution to the re-evaluation of the oedipus complex—the early stages. *Internat. J. Psycho-Anal.*, 33:84-92.

Hendrick, I. (1948), Homeostasis. In: *Synopsis of Psychosomatic Diagnosis and Treatment*, Ed. F. Dunbar. St. Louis: C. V. Mosby, pp. 55-56.

Jacobi, J., Ed. (1958), *Paracelsus—Selected Writings*. Princeton: Princeton University Press, 1958.

Jacobson, E. (1954), The self and the object world—vicissitudes of infantile catheses. *The Psychoanalytic Study of the Child*, 9:75-127. New York: International Universities Press.

Janvier, C. (1943), Adolescents in action. *Amer. J. Orthopsychiat.*, 13:82-88.

Jenkins, R. L. (1941), Treatment in an institution. *Amer. J. Orthopsychiat.*, 11:85-91.

Jennings, H. H. (1943), *Leadership and Isolation, A Study of Personality in Interpersonal Relations*. New York: Longman Green.

Johnson, A. M. & Fishback, D. (1944), Analysis of a disturbed adolescent girl and collaborative psychiatric treatment of the mother. *Amer. J. Orthopsychiat.*, 14:195-203.

Jones, E. (1923), The nature of auto-suggestion. In: *Papers on Psychoanalysis*. Baltimore: Williams & Wilkins, 1961, pp. 273-293.

———— (1931), The concept of a normal mind. In: *Papers on Psychoanalysis*. Baltimore: Williams & Wilkins, 1961, pp. 201-216.

———— (1946), Valedictory address. *Internat. J. Psycho-Anal.*, 27:7-12.

———— (1947), *Hamlet and Oedipus*. New York: Norton.

Journal of the American Medical Association (1964), And madly rides. Vol. 187#12, p. 946.

Kanzer, M. (1957), Acting out, sublimation, and reality testing. *J. Amer. Psychoanal. Assn.*, 5:663-684.

Katan, M., Is the diagnosis of schizophrenia in early childhood justifiable? Unpublished paper provided by the author.

Kilpatrick, E. (1945), Children against the world. *Nervous Child*, 4:115-128.

Knight, R. P. (1953a), "Borderline states." In: *Drives, Affects, Behavior*, Ed. R. M. Loewenstein. New York: International Universities Press, pp. 203-215.

———— (1953b), The present state of organized psychoanalysis in the United States. *J. Amer. Psychoanal. Assn.*, 1:197-221.

Kris, E. (1952), *Psychoanalytic Explorations in Art*. New York: International Universities Press.

Kubie, L. S. (1948), Special problems on the preparatory analyses. Unpublished panel presentation.

———— (1953a), The central representation of the symbolic process in psychosomatic disorder. *Psychosom. Med.*, 15:1-7.

———— (1953b), The problem of specificity in the psychosomatic process. In: *The Psychosomatic Concept in Psychoanalysis*, Ed. F. Deutsch. New York: International Universities Press, pp. 63-81.

———— (1953c), Psychoanalysis as a basic science. In: *Twenty Years of Psychoanalysis*, Ed. F. Alexander & H. Ross. New York: Norton, pp. 120-150.

———— (1954), The pros and cons of a new profession: a doctorate in medical psychology. *Texas Report on Biol. & Med.*, 12:125-170.

———— (1957), Need for a new subdiscipline in the medical profession. *AMA Arch. Neurol. & Psychiat.*, 78:283-293.

Kuhn, T. S. (1963), *The Structure of Scientific Revolutions.* Chicago: University of Chicago Press.

Lampl-de Groot, J. (1946), The pre-oedipal phase in the development of the male child. *The Psychoanalytic Study of the Child,* 2:75-83. New York: International Universities Press.

———— (1952), Re-evaluation of the role of the oedipus complex. *Internat. J. Psycho-Anal.*, 33:335-342.

Lewin, B. D. (1950), *The Psychoanalysis of Elation.* New York: Norton.

———— & Ross, H. (1960), *Psychoanalytic Education in the United States.* New York: Norton.

Little, M. (1951), Counter-transference and the patient's response to it. *Internat. J. Psycho-Anal.*, 32:32-40.

Loewald, H. W. (1960), On the therapeutic action of psychoanalysis. *Internat. J. Psycho-Anal.*, 41:16-33.

Lustman, S. L. (1963), Some issues in contemporary psychoanalytic research. *The Psychoanalytic Study of the Child,* 18:51-74. New York: International Universities Press.

Macalpine, I. (1950), The development of transference. *Psychoanal. Quart.*, 19:501-539.

Margolin, S. G. (1953), Genetic and dynamic psychophysiological determinants of pathophysiological processes. In: *The Psychosomatic Concept in Psychoanalysis,* Ed. F. Deutsch. New York: International Universities Press, pp. 3-36.

Marmor, J. & Zander, A. F. (1945), Psychological problems in training sixteen- and seventeen-year-old youths in the U.S. maritime service. *Amer. J. Orthopsychiat.*, 15:571.

Martin, A. R. (1939), Psychiatry in a boys' club. *Amer. J. Orthopsychiat.*, 9:123-135.

Mazlish, B. (1961), Our "Heraclitean" period. *The Nation,* 192:336-338.

McDonald, M. W. (1938), Criminally aggressive behavior in passive feminine boys. *Amer. J. Orthopsychiat.*, 8:70-78.

Mendelson, M., Hirsch, S. & Webber, C. S. (1956), A critical examination of some recent theoretical models in psychosomatic medicine. *Psychosom. Med.,* 18:363–373.

Menninger, K. A. (1954a), Psychological aspects of the organism under stress. *J. Amer. Psychoanal. Assn.,* 2:67–106; 280–310.

———— (1954b), Regulatory devices of the ego under major stress. *Internat. J. Psycho-Anal.,* 35:412–420.

Michaels, J. J. (1946), Strength through character. *Amer. J. Orthopsychiat.,* 16:350–355.

Minutes (1941), Forty-third meeting of the American Psychoanalytic Association. Unpublished.

Minutes (1942), Forty-fourth meeting of the American Psychoanalytic Association. Unpublished.

Minutes (1945), Joint committee of executive council, council on professional training and special commission on educational policy of the American Psychoanalytic Association, Chicago. Unpublished.

Minutes (1947), Forty-eighth meeting of the American Psychoanalytic Association. Unpublished.

Mirsky, I. (1953), Psychoanalysis and the biological sciences. In: *Twenty Years of Psychoanalysis,* Eds. F. Alexander & H. Ross. New York: Norton, pp. 155–176.

Mitchell, M. (1944), Development and use of relationship with a delinquent adolescent girl. *Nervous Child,* 4:95–99.

Murphy, L., Some aspects of the first relationship. Unpublished.

National Conference on Postwar Problems of Psychoanalytic Training (1946). Unpublished.

Nunberg, H. (1955), *Principles of Psychoanalysis.* New York: International Universities Press.

———— & Federn, E., Eds. (1962), *Minutes of the Vienna Psychoanalytic Society,* Vol. 1. New York: International Universities Press.

Orgel, S. Z. (1941), Identification as a socializing and therapeutic force. *Amer. J. Orthopsychiat.,* 11:118–126.

Powdermaker, F., Levis, H., & Touraine, G. (1937), Psychopathology and treatment of delinquent girls. *Amer. J. Orthopsychiat.,* 7:58–71.

Rado, S. (1925), The economic principle in psycho-analytic technique. *Internat. J. Psycho-Anal.,* 6:35–44.

# References

———Grinker, R. R., Sr., & Alexander, F. (1963), Editorial. *AMA Arch. Gen. Psychiat.*, 8:527–529.

Rangell, L. (1955), Panel reporter: the borderline case. *J. Amer. Psychoanal. Assn.*, 3:285–298.

Rapaport, D. (1960), *The Structure of Psychoanalytic Theory—A Systematizing Attempt* [*Psychological Issues*, Monogr. 6]. New York: International Universities Press.

Rappaport, E. (1959), The first dream in an erotized transference. *Internat. J. Psycho-Anal.*, 40:240–245.

Reich, A. (1951), On countertransference. In: *Psychoanalytic Contributions.* New York: International Universities Press, 1973, pp. 136–154.

———(1954), Early identification as archaic elements in the superego. In: *Psychoanalytic Contributions.* New York: International Universities Press, 1973.

Reich, W. (1931), The characterological mastery of the oedipus complex. *Internat. J. Psycho-Anal.*, 12:452–467.

Reider, N. (1950), The concept of normality. *Psychoanal. Quart.*, 19:43–51.

Renneker, R. E. (1960), Microscopic analysis of sound tape. *Psychiat.*, 23:347–355.

Richmond, J. B. & Lustman, S. L. (1955), Autonomic functions in the neonate: I. implications for psychosomatic theory. *Psychosom. Med.*, 17:269–275.

Riesman, D. (1950), *The Lonely Crowd.* New Haven: Yale University Press.

Rosenbaum, M. (1959), Panel reporter on: experimental study of psychophysiological correlations. Unpublished.

———(1965), Dreams in which the analyst appears undisguised—a clinical and statistical study. *Internat. J. Psycho-Anal.*, 46:429–437.

Ross, W. D., Hay, J., & McDowall, M. F. (1950), I. The association of certain vegetative disturbances with various psychoses: II. the incidence of certain vegetative disturbances in relation to psychoses. *Psychosom. Med.*, 12:17–183.

Ruesch, J. (1948), The infantile personality: the core problem of psychosomatic medicine. *Psychosom. Med.*, 10:134–144.

Rycroft, C. (1956), The nature and function of the analyst's communication to the patient. *Internat. J. Psycho-Anal.*, 37:469-472.

Sachs, H. (1947), Observations of a training analyst. *Psychoanal. Quart.*, 16:157-168.

Saslow, G. et al. (1950), Possible etiologic relevance of personality factors in arterial hypertension. *Psychosom. Med.*, 12:292-302.

Schilling, H. K. (1958), A human enterprise. *Science*, 127:1324-1327.

Schur, M. (1955), Comments on the metapsychology of somatization. *The Psychoanalytic Study of the Child*, 10:119-164. New York: International Universities Press.

Sechehaye, M. D. (1956), The transference in symbolic realization. *Internat. J. Psycho-Anal.*, 37:270-277.

Shakow, D. (1960), The recorded psychoanalytic interview as an objective approach to research in psychoanalysis. *Psychoanal. Quart.*, 29:82-97.

_____ (1962), Psychoanalytic education of behavioral and social scientists for research. *Science and Psychoanalysis*, 5:146-161. New York: Grune & Stratton.

Silverberg, W. V. (1947), The schizoid maneuver. *Psychiat.*, 10:383-393.

Simpson, C. G. (1963), Biology and the nature of science. *Science*, 139:81-88.

Slawson, J. (1938), The use of the authoritative approach in social case work in the field of delinquency. *Amer. J. Orthopsychiat.*, 8:673-678.

Spitz, R. (1951), The psychogenic diseases in infancy. *The Psychoanalytic Study of the Child*, 6:255-275. New York: International Universities Press.

_____ (1956), Countertransference. *J. Amer. Psychoanal. Assn.*, 4:256-265.

Sterba, R. (1934), The fate of the ego in analytic therapy. *Internat. J. Psycho-Anal.*, 15:117-126.

Stern, A. (1945), Psychoanalytic therapy in borderline neuroses. *Psychoanal. Quart.*, 14:190-198.

Stevenson, I. (1950), Physical symptoms during pleasurable emotional states. *Psychosom. Med.*, 12:98-102.

Stone, L. (1954), The widening scope of indications for psycho-

# References

analysis. *J. Amer. Psychoanal. Assn.*, 2:567–594.

Strachey, J. (1934), The nature of the therapeutic action of psychoanalysis. *Internat. J. Psycho-Anal.*, 15:127–159.

Thompson, C. (1938), Notes on the psychoanalytic significance of the choice of the analyst. *Psychiat.*, 2:205–216.

Topping, R. (1943), Treatment of the pseudo-social boy. *Amer. J. Orthopsychiat.*, 13:353–360.

Tryon, C. M. (1944), The adolescent peer culture. *43rd Yearbook, National Society for Study of Education:* I, Adolescence. Chicago: University of Chicago Press.

Valentine, C. W. (1943), Adolescence and some problems of youth training. *Nature*, 152:122.

Van der Sterren, H. A. (1952), The "king oedipus" of Sophocles. *Internat. J. Psycho-Anal.*, 33:343–350.

Waelder, R. (1936a), The principle of multiple function: observations on overdetermination. *Psychoanal. Quart.*, 5:45–62.

———— (1936b), The problem of freedom in psychoanalysis and the problem of reality testing. *Internat. J. Psycho-Anal.*, 17:89–108.

———— (1937), The problem of the genesis of psychical conflict. *Internat. J. Psycho-Anal.*, 18:406–473.

———— (1945), Present trends in psychoanalytic theory and practice. *Yearbook of Psychoanalysis*, 1:84–89. New York: International Universities Press.

Webster's New International Dictionary (1947). Second edition. Springfield, Mass.: G. & C. Merriam Co.

Weiss, E. (1949), Some considerations of the concept of countertransference and the therapeutic implications involved. Unpublished.

Weiss, P. (1962), Experience and experiment in biology. *Science*, 136:468–471.

Whitehorn, J. C. (1947), The concepts of "meaning" and "cause" in psychodynamics. *Amer. J. Psychiat.*, 104:289–292.

Wiener, N. (1949), *Cybernetics, or Control and Communication in the Animal and the Machine.* New York: Wiley, 1961.

Wikler, A. (1952), A critical analysis of some current concepts in psychiatry. *Psychosom. Med.*, 14:10–17.

Winnicott, D. W. (1949), Hate in the countertransference. *Internat. J. Psycho-Anal.*, 30:69–74.

———— (1956), On transference. *Internat. J. Psycho-Anal.*, 37:386–388.

———— (1960), The theory of the parent-infant relationship. *Internat. J. Psycho-Anal.*, 41:585–595.

Yellowlees, H. (1940), The problem of adolescence. *Lancet*, 238.

Zetzel, E. (1949), Anxiety and the capacity to bear it. In: *The Capacity for Emotional Growth*. New York: International Universities Press, 1970, pp. 33–52.

———— (1963), The significance of the adaptive hypothesis for psychoanalytic theory and practice. *J. Amer. Psychoanal. Assn.*, 11:652–660.

Zilboorg, G. (1933), Anxiety without affect. *Psychoanal. Quart.*, 2:48–67.

———— (1944), Present trends in psychoanalytic theory and practice. *Yearbook of Psychoanalysis*, 1:79–94. New York: International Universities Press, 1945.

# Name Index

# Name Index

# Name Index

# Subject Index

# Subject Index